Hispanic Voices

Hispanic Voices

Hispanic Health Educators Speak Out

Edited by

Sara Torres, RN, PhD, FAAN

Chair, Department of Community Nursing
College of Nursing and Health Professions
University of North Carolina
Charlotte, North Carolina

NLN Press • *New York*

Pub. No. 14-2693

The views expressed in this book reflect those of the authors and do not necessarily reflect the official views of the National League for Nursing.

Library of Congress Cataloging-in-Publication Data

Hispanic voices : Hispanic health educators speak out / edited by Sara Torres.
p. cm.
Includes bibliographical references.
ISBN 0-88737-653-3
1. Hispanic Americans—Health and hygiene. 2. Hispanic Americans—Diseases. 3. Hispanic Americans—Medical care. I. Torres, Sara.
RA448.5.H57H574 1996
362.1'089'68073--dc20 95-50265
CIP

This book was set in Garamond by Publications Development Company, Crockett, Texas. The editor was Maryan Malone. The designer was Allan Graubard. The printer was Clarkwood Corp. The cover was designed by Lauren Stevens.

Printed in the United States of America.

Foreword

Our knowledge of health took a giant step forward in 1989 when the federal government recommended that states record on their death certificates whether someone was of Hispanic origin. With the new data that were generated came startling new findings which have forced a rethinking of the conceptual frameworks used to explain health.

For too long what was believed about the health of Hispanics was based on incomplete information and speculation. Many healthcare professionals assumed that the health of Hispanics would fall at some point along a simple continuum of health that placed non-Hispanic whites at one end and non-Hispanic blacks at the other end. Today we know that this linear viewpoint was wrong and a disservice to all.

Hispanic Voices: Hispanic American Health Educators Speak Out is another important step in building the knowledge base on Hispanic health. Collaborative efforts like this book ensure that we will be able to improve the health and well being of all the members of our Hispanic community.

As you read through the chapters, certain themes will be apparent: Hispanics are consistently underserved; Hispanics suffer disproportionately from chronic illnesses; and the key to improved health is health education which is meaningful within the cultural and linguistic context of peoples lives. Most important of all, remember that although there are differences among the diverse Hispanic groups, we are more alike to each other than we are to non-Hispanic whites. Recognizing this, it is in our combined efforts that we demonstrate our greatest strengths.

Jane L. Delgado, PhD
President and CEO
National Coalition of Hispanic
Health and Human Services Organizations

Preface

Hispanic Voices: Hispanic Health Educators Speak Out! is the second in the NLN Press series dedicated to exploring the health care concerns of minorities. With Hispanics now the fastest growing minority in the United States, and expected to be the largest minority by the year 2000, the uniqueness of this book, especially in the nursing literature, is matched only by its timeliness.

With this book, too, the current dearth of literature on the state of health and health care for Hispanics need not seem so formidable. Indeed, this book was written to partially fill the existing lack of educational materials on the health care of Hispanics in the United States and to help health care professionals to recognize the diverse cultural dimensions involved in such care. Thus, rationales for the need to develop culture-specific intervention strategies for working with Hispanics and proposals for improving the delivery of such care, along with other issues of importance to the health of Hispanic populations, are prominent features throughout.

THE "VOICES"

As you read this book, you will hear the voices of Hispanic nurses as they share their knowledge, experiences, research, pain, and frustrations related to the state of Hispanic health and health care in the United States.

Certainly, too, the development and conceptualization of this book involved many decisions regarding the selection of content and which authors to include. Hispanic nurses with various experiences and from all levels of education and educational programs were invited. The result is before you in a medley of voices: Hispanic nurses who, in addition to being educators, are clinicians, nurse practitioners, researchers, and administrators in many specialties—psychiatry, neonatal, pediatrics, medical-surgical, maternal/child, gerontology, administration, and community nursing.

You will hear voices of Hispanic nurses with baccalaureate, masters, and doctoral degrees. You will also hear voices of Hispanic nurses who teach in all levels of the educational strata: diploma, associate, baccalaureate, and graduate levels. You will hear voices from Hispanic nurses who teach at small private colleges and at large, nationally prominent private universities; at small state universities and at large, nationally prominent state universities.

An attempt was also made to include voices geographically distributed from and about the major Hispanic subgroups in the United States—Mexicans, Cubans, and Central and South Americans—including the island of Puerto Rico. As a result, the book features four Hispanic subgroups residing in ten different states and Puerto Rico. There are also several chapters on the health care issues of Puerto Ricans living in Puerto Rico. Where available, data on Hispanic subgroups are provided to present variances in demographic profiles and health status among groups.

To allow each author the freedom to express his or her opinions on the state of health and health care of Hispanics, very little structure and guidance was provided in terms of focus or outcome. The need to explore and to reveal was primary. What emerged were pertinent discussions of some of the major issues facing health care educators and providers who work with Hispanics. Congruent themes emerged regarding the health and health care of Hispanics in the United States: lack of access to health care, lack of data and research on Hispanics, lack of health promotion and disease prevention services and programs, and the underrepresentation of Hispanics in nursing. These were the same themes that were voiced throughout the United States several years ago when the U.S. Surgeon General held the National Hispanic/Latino Health Initiative.

Hispanic health care is an incomplete picture. Any discussion of health and health behavior related to Hispanics needs to be considered within the context of existing data. In addition to the dearth of research on Hispanic populations, however, most of the research conducted to date has focused primarily on the Mexican population. The need for research on the other Hispanic subgroups is *clear* and *pressing*. In some cases, data are limited, in others nonexistent. Additional research to identify the unique characteristics, norms, health behaviors, problems, and strengths of Hispanics, especially Hispanic children as they grow and develop, must take place and become the custom, not the exception.

Although we have endeavored to include content on the major health problems and issues facing Hispanic populations, any area not covered is due more to the lack of information and research, particularly nursing research, in the Hispanic population, than anything else. This is also true for other health care problems related to family violence, alcohol and drug use, maternal/perinatal health, and so on.

There are many terms that are used to identify the Spanish-speaking people in the United States. Common, recent terms include Hispanic and Latino. The word *Hispanic* was chosen in this book to describe those descendants from Latin America, such as Mexico, Puerto Rico, Cuba, and Central and South America. However, because some now prefer the word *Latino,* Latino is used interchangeably with Hispanic.

ORGANIZATION AND CONTENT OVERVIEW

This book is organized by topic into fifteen chapters. The topical organization seemed more suitable for making points related to specific health care issues. Two of the chapters are brief but were included to provide a "slice of life" of some health care problems in the Hispanic population. The brevity of the "slice-of-life" chapters also reflect the limitations of the existing body of literature and the lack of information and research previously mentioned.

The first chapter introduces basic, relevant cultural issues and implications for the delivery of health care to the Hispanic population. Readers are advised to be vigilant in several ways, especially with there being neither a single meaning nor homogeneity to what is embraced by the term *Hispanic.*

Chapters Two, Three, and Four focus on Hispanic children and adolescents. Chapters Two and Four present a profile of Hispanic children and adolescents' health status in the United States, including educational, economic, and health risks that exist among Hispanic children and adolescents, particularly of Mexican-American and Puerto Rican descent. Emphasis is placed on how poverty continues to widen the socioeconomic gap that exists among Hispanic children and adolescents and how this affects access to health care for this population. Both chapters concluded that the disparity in Hispanic children and adolescent health is likely to widen unless steps are taken to develop a national agenda that addresses their health care. Chapter Three presents a "slice-of-life" on attitudes toward the birth of premature infants in Puerto Rican families.

Chapter Five proposes that the health problems of Puerto Ricans in the continental United States are intimately related to the health problems and general circumstances on their island of origin and presents an analysis of the health status of Puerto Ricans in the United States and in Puerto

Rico. Interventions for selected diagnoses identified in Puerto Ricans are postulated. Chapter Six discusses Puerto Rico's aging population characteristics, present health status, and results of a study on the self-care of the elderly in Puerto Rico.

Chapters Seven, Eight, and Nine discuss specific chronic diseases that are the major causes of death for Hispanics: cardiovascular disease, diabetes, and HIV/AIDS. All authors emphasize the need to develop culturally appropriate models for intervention and treatment. Chapter Ten, which focuses on acculturative stress and depression in the Hispanic population, emphasizes the importance of sociocultural context when dealing with such issues.

Chapters Eleven and Twelve focus on special populations. Chapter Eleven presents a "slice-of-life" on the homeless in Puerto Rico and describes a model with four levels of intervention currently in use on the island. Chapter Twelve communicates an especially sensitive portrayal of the plight and health care needs of Hispanic migrant farmworkers.

Chapters Thirteen and Fourteen discuss the shortage of Hispanic nurses to meet the health care needs of the Hispanic population. Chapter Thirteen focuses on the issues regarding the recruitment of Hispanic faculty. Chapter Fourteen introduces a community-based model for the recruitment, retention, and graduation of Hispanic registered nurses.

Finally, Chapter Fifteen discusses how spiritual well-being influences health and presents a study on this topic conducted in the Hispanic population.

IN CLOSING

Although this book is by no means all-inclusive, the characteristics, experiences, needs, and recommendations of the content presented are representative of the major issues and obstacles confronted by health care professionals in the delivery of health care to Hispanics.

It is expected that knowledge and awareness of the factors that influence the health and behavior of Hispanics will assist health care professionals to be more effective in their work. The fundamental assumption is that helpers can improve their effectiveness in the delivery of health care to Hispanics if appropriate attitudes, information, and self-understanding exist.

We hope that this book will be well received. Health care consumer demographics in the United States are changing systemwide. Professional activities of health care, such as prevention, case finding, case management, treatment, care, and cure, will mandate a new level of knowledge, sophistication, and intensity related to working with culturally diverse groups.

The delivery of culturally appropriate health care is an exciting and challenging field, and we must all take the initiative in reaching out to learn, advance, and grow. Cultural diversity is a fact of life, and how we deal with it will have major implications for the quality of health care and life for Hispanics in the United States.

Sara Torres, PhD, RN, FAAN
Department of Community Nursing
College of Nursing and Health Professions
University of North Carolina

Acknowledgments

It would be difficult to acknowledge by name the many individuals whose support, encouragement, and dedicated work made this book a reality. All the contributing authors played significant roles in the creation of this book. They donated their time, energy, and experience to further the healthcare of Hispanics. Their commitment and encouragement were remarkable.

Gracias to NLN Press for initiating this series of books by health educators devoted to the healthcare of diverse ethnic/racial groups in the United States. Their enthusiastic support of this project is commendable. A special thanks to Allan Graubard, from NLN Press, who read and reviewed this document at every stage to insure a standard of excellence. His invaluable input, interest, and guidance are appreciated.

SARA TORRES, RN, PHD, FAAN

Editor

Sara Torres, RN, PhD, FAAN
Chair, Department of Community Nursing
College of Nursing and Health Professions
University of North Carolina
Charlotte, North Carolina

Contributing Authors

Melinda L. Alba, MS Candidate
University of Illinois
School of Public Health
Chicago, Illinois

Evelyn Ruiz Calvillo, RN, DNSc
Associate Professor
California State University
Los Angeles, California

Helen M. Castillo, PhD, RN, CNA
Associate Professor and Chair, Nursing Department
College of Nursing and Health Sciences
El Paso, Texas

Evelyn Crouch-Ruiz, PhD, RN
Associate Professor
School of Nursing
Pontifico Catholic University of Puerto Rico
Ponce, Puerto Rico

Myrtha I. Díaz de Torres, MSN, RN
Professor and Acting Dean, School of Nursing
Medical Sciences Campus
University of Puerto Rico

Blanca Rosa Garcia, PhD, RN, FNP
Chairperson/Professor
Department of Registered Nurse Education
Del Mar College
Corpus Christi, Texas

Josephine A. (Ulibarri) Hibbeln, RN, MSN
Assistant Professor
The University of Toledo Community and Technical College
Toledo, Ohio

Teresa C. Juarbe, RN, PhD
Assistant Professor, School of Nursing
San José State University
San José, California

Elsie Méndez, MSN, RN
Faculty, Mental Health and Psychiatric Nursing
School of Nursing
Inter American University of Puerto Rico
San Juan, Puerto Rico

Gloria E. Ortiz, MSN, EdD, RN
Director
School of Nursing
Inter American University of Puerto Rico
San Juan, Puerto Rico

Nilda P. Peragallo, PhD, RN
Associate Professor
University of Illinois at Chicago
College of Nursing
Chicago, Illinois

Eugenia V. Pérez-Montijo, BSN, RN
Coordinator, Nursing Center
School of Nursing
Inter American University of Puerto Rico
San Juan, Puerto Rico

Catalina Quesada, PhD, RN
Professor
School of Nursing
Pontifico University of Puerto Rico
Ponce, Puerto Rico

Ester Ruiz Rodriguez, PhD, RN, CS
Assistant Professor
Arizona State University

Dahlia Zuñiga Rojas, PhD, CFNP, RN
Assistant Professor
Division of Nursing, Mathematics & the Sciences
Incarnate Word College
San Antonio, Texas

Sally E. Ruybal, PhD, RN
Professor
College of Nursing
University of New Mexico
Albuquerque, New Mexico

Alice Santiago, MSN, RN
Director, Department of Nursing Fundamentals
School of Nursing
Inter American University of Puerto Rico
San Juan, Puerto Rico

Mary Lou de Leon Siantz, PhD, RN, FAAN
Associate Professor
Department of Psychiatric/Mental Health Nursing
Indiana University School of Nursing
Indianapolis, Indiana

Antonia M. Villarruel, PhD, RN
Assistant Professor
University of Pennsylvania
Philadelphia, Pennsylvania

Maryann Yzaguirre, MSN, MS, RN
Instructor
Department of Registered Nurse Education
Del Mar College
Corpus Christi, Texas

Contents

CHAPTER ONE

Cultural Diversity: Implications for Nursing

Helen M. Castillo, PhD, RN, CNA

A major need exists for health care professionals to openly and honestly dialogue about cultural issues related to the health care of Hispanics. Hispanic culture, "Hispanismo," is related to health care, and the need for sound, practical knowledge about the culture is clear. As the largest growing minority group, Hispanics need to become actively involved in making the critical decisions that affect the health of Hispanics and society as a whole. In view of the health care crisis and reforms proposed, decisions made today will impact the future health care of this country, and Hispanics must take part in that process. In this chapter, selected research studies are cited to initiate further interest and discussion of Hispanic health care. Ideas posed will hopefully initiate constructive dialogue between colleagues and serve as a catalyst for the development of culture-specific models for future quality health care.

CULTURE: A Personal Perspective

As an only child from an Hispanic family of Mexican heritage, my primary language was Spanish, although I spoke English well. Entering the kindergarten classroom filled with five-year-old strangers who spoke only English was not a happy prospect. I recall the traumatic, enlightening, and eventually positive experience of discovering that I needed to make new, creative, and emergent choices. To leave, to never return to school, was my first choice. I partly succeeded and did not return until the following academic year. Reluctantly returning to the first grade, I was transferred into the second grade instead because I had gained accelerated knowledge at home. Based on these early school experiences, my perceptions were altered. Had it not been for the family support I received, and the gentle reprimand for not liking school, this "kindergarten dropout" might never have returned to school. Children with similar experiences may be lost from the educational system without having their potential for future contributions recognized.

Perspectives are colored by our past. Childhood experiences together with social and religious upbringing strongly influence our cultural values and beliefs. Physical characteristics also affect how others view us and how we view the world. Our place in society is often based on our abilities or disabilities. For example, handicapped persons point out physical barriers that deter them from achieving many of their personal goals. Once the barriers are identified and removed, accessibility is possible. So it is with Hispanic cultural issues, barriers to achievement must be removed.

Cultural perceptions are influenced by inaccurate or limited information that tends to build cultural chasms and communication walls between groups. Such barriers need to be identified early, then openly discussed to eliminate them when possible. We must initiate creative, productive exchanges about cultural issues to eliminate barriers that cause conflict.

The Latin phrase *Non schola sed vita discimus* reminds us that "We don't learn for school but for life." Similarly, Plutarch, who focused on the strengths and talents of learners in the first century, encouraged students to excel in whatever they did well. Conversely, schools and universities have historically focused on learners' weaknesses, rather than building performance on their strengths (Drucker, 1989). While teaching strategies are changing toward Plutarch's thinking, remnants of negative approaches still remain, especially as they affect students from Hispanic and other cultures. Major changes are needed.

My early experiences were grounded in a bicultural Hispanic background that influenced my perceptions about education. They provided a personal frame of reference for application to students in similar circumstances, and raised my level of awareness about Hispanics' bilingual needs. These experiences serve as the basis for comments that follow. Additionally, selected comments reflect other Hispanic nurses' experiences as individuals in providing health care to Hispanic children and adults. As society struggles with its growing multiculturalism, Hispanic cultural diversity needs will emerge.

CULTURAL DIVERSITY

The Importance of Cultural Diversity

The workforce in America is becoming increasingly more diverse, especially with regard to gender, race, and nationality (Fullerton, 1987;

Johnston, 1991). According to Cox (1993), in the 1990s about 45% of new additions to the workforce will be non-White. Trends indicate that these will be first-generation immigrants mostly from Asian and Latin countries, almost two-thirds female, immigrating beyond this country into France, Italy, and Germany (Horwitz & Forman, 1990; Johnston, 1991). The World Bank (1995) reports that Mexico and other Latin countries will continue to be major players in the world investments market. The importance of Hispanic culture in the economic, educational, and health care markets is clearly evident as binational corporations and multinational business operations proliferate. IBM, Exxon, Coca-Cola, Dow-Chemical, and Digital Equipment, for example, derive more than half their revenue from overseas markets. This trend extends to service operations like Citicorp, which obtained 52% of its revenues from foreign markets in 1991 (U.S. Corporations, 1992).

Understanding cultural diversity and its influences on national health care is critical. In nursing, these organizational changes are drastically affecting hiring practices and position requirements for key posts. Bilingual, biculturally knowledgeable nurses are sought to plan and provide care to Hispanic patients throughout the country. Universities are also courting qualified bilingual nursing faculty for positions where large Hispanic student populations are served. Faculty who can develop new course content to meet the educational needs of Hispanic students at all grade levels are in demand.

The North American Free Trade Agreement (NAFTA) and Diversity on the United States-Mexico Border

The enactment of the North American Free Trade Agreement (NAFTA, January 1, 1994) raised expectations that Mexico will become an even greater player in binational efforts. In spite of the peso devaluation, Mexico is expected to be instrumental in effecting major change along the United States-Mexico border, with the anticipated change to be mutually beneficial to both countries.

Economically, Mexico and the United States have been binational business partners for more than a decade. This relationship continues to grow. The long history of U.S. corporations in international partnering with Mexico has peaked the interest of hospital corporations to establish collaborative business partnerships with Mexico, Panama, and other countries. For-profit hospitals along the U.S.-Mexico border are actively targeting wealthy Mexican clientele as potential recipients of their health care services. Assessments and ongoing feasibility studies have been conducted by U.S. groups to identify health care services for Mexican citizens who can afford these services.

Influential Mexican groups are also requesting health education programs as provided by for-profit health care agencies to encourage Mexican participation in the education and care offered. Health care recipients targeted in these efforts are expected to refer other future paying clients by word-of-mouth. Entrepreneurial U.S. hospitals and health care organizations are creating access to selected services and providing needed care in Mexico at a lower cost. On the Mexican side, persons needing further care are referred to the parent U.S.-based hospitals across the border. A binational approach to nursing and health care is now a requirement in Mexico and is reflective of the Hispanic focus effectively being marketed by Spanish-speaking, bilingual providers. Hispanic providers who know the culture and customs, and who are trusted by their Mexican colleagues for their knowledge and understanding of Mexican cultural needs, are critical to the success of these efforts.

Customer satisfaction is of highest priority in these enterprising, innovative organizations in the development of health care services on the U.S.-Mexico border. Thus, the importance of cultural awareness and sensitivity toward Mexican culture cannot be overly emphasized, and nurses are the key players. Indepth knowledge about the Mexican culture and management styles in Mexico are required of employees in these organizations in order to succeed. Long-term success will also be measured by the volume of Mexican paying clients using the health care services provided.

NAFTA and the United States-Mexico Border

The 1994 enactment of NAFTA focused quick attention on U.S.-Mexico border communities. Less than two-years-old, NAFTA continues to elicit conflicting opinions about its benefit to the United States.

Renegotiating the NAFTA pact rather than expanding it is an option posed to offset workers displaced by free trade (Wallach, 1995). Although claims exist that jobs have been lost because of Mexico's currency crisis, free-trade proponents including the U.S. Commerce Department counter that NAFTA created 100,000 U.S. jobs in 1995. Free trade was not responsible for the peso crisis of December 1994, or the capital flight that sent shock waves into Mexico's economy (Miramontes, 1995). In addition, and as supporters claim, the full effects of NAFTA are not expected for another ten to fifteen years.

Twin Plant (*Maquiladoras*) manufacturing is a major positive effect of NAFTA on the border. Maquiladoras are also changing the health care system in Mexico by providing health care to their employees. This directly affects U.S. border communities by providing a higher level of care to Mexican employees who previously sought care on the U.S. side. Still other major collaborative efforts have resulted between universities in the United States and Mexico, such as education in health care and the environment, higher education, and binational research. Scientific, technological, and educational solutions have been proposed to solve key problems in health care along the U.S.-Mexico border. Health care planning priorities continue to focus on binational border problems that cannot be separated or resolved by either country alone. Nursing needs a cadre of leaders to serve as active participants in these key binational efforts.

MOVING TOWARD CULTURAL DIVERSITY: VALUES REVISITED

As restructuring continues, organizations need to reexamine their values and priorities to complement Hispanic consumers, especially in health care. It is time, as well, to refocus on the recipient rather than on the provider of health care services. Diversity must be institutionalized so that organizations and institutions become multicultural reflections of the larger society (Bruhn et al., 1995).

Culturally Sensitive Models of Care

Developing culturally sensitive models of care relevant to the diverse populations we serve will help us to identify cultural aspects of care in nursing practice, education, and research. Especially needed are sound theoretical models based on accurate data about Hispanics. Culturally sensitive models of care should be developed by health care providers who know the practices and preferences of the Hispanic consumers they serve. Often, health care policies are not culture-specific or sensitive to Hispanic health care needs. Language and age considerations in care systems are lacking and need to be included as a part of the continuum of care.

Accurate data about Hispanics—baselines for appropriate care, interventions, and evaluation of care provided—are lacking and critically needed by nursing and other health care providers. At hospitalized patients' bedsides, such data would aid in assessing clients appropriately, planning their care, and guiding behavioral change to improve the level and quality of nursing and primary care. These are minimal requirements for health care providers to give culturally sensitive care, and to evaluate the effectiveness of the care they provide. This is especially true in communities where high numbers of Hispanics live and where access to care is limited or nonexistent. In this country, excellence and quality care are touted as major health care goals, yet the state of health care is unsatisfactory for many minorities. To determine Hispanic health care needs, the first step is the establishment of accurate data banks at regional, national, and international levels.

Major health care decisions in America are influenced by a multitude of variables that we must recognize and respond to: an increasingly diverse population, skyrocketing costs of new technology and health care services, and financial constraints placed on the health care system.

WHO ARE HISPANICS: QUIENES SON LOS HISPANOS?

Hispanics are expected to be the largest segment of the U.S. minority population by the year 2000. As active participants in decision-making roles, they should also be well-informed and knowledgeable about the issues at hand. More importantly perhaps, Hispanics need to propose workable solutions and alternatives to health care problems in a system struggling unsuccessfully to meet present health care demands.

Hispanic Americans have long been categorized generically, and incorrectly, as one and the same ethnic or cultural group. Agencies use *Hispanic* as a broad identifier primarily for data collection purposes. Available demographic and research data need redefinition of designated cultural subgroups within the Hispanic category.

Hispanics originate from the countries of Argentina, Bolivia, Brazil, Chile, Colombia, Costa Rica, Cuba, Dominican Republic, Ecuador, El Salvador, Guatemala, Honduras, Mexico, Nicaragua, Panama, Paraguay, Peru, Puerto Rico, Spain, Uruguay, and Venezuela. Of surprise to many is the extent of diversity within these countries.

Language

The Spanish language is used by most Hispanic countries, with the exception of Brazil, where Portuguese is spoken. Historians point out that the Spanish language was brought to Mexico by Spanish Conquistador Hernando Cortez and his soldiers, sent by Queen Isabella of Spain to search for gold and silver. The formal Castilian Spanish language which originated in Spain serves as a model for modifications that have occurred since. Regional differences in the Spanish language have also evolved through influences of geography and acculturation over time.

Differences and Similarities

Cultural differences are particularly important to Hispanics. Not only are differences between Hispanics important for data clarification and health care, they are essential in research. Clinical investigations about Hispanics, their families, and their health are critically lacking. The need for research is spiraling with increasing population numbers.

Over time, some Hispanics have changed their behaviors to concur with others' perceptions of them. Behavioral changes may occur for acceptance or other more complex reasons such as fear of rejection, reprisal, or ridicule. Many Hispanic Americans have found it easier to adopt English over their primary Spanish language in the business world and have lost their Spanish-speaking abilities for lack of practice. Others have changed their names from Spanish to English versions for easier pronunciation or communication with non-Spanish speakers. This is especially common in communities where few or no Hispanics live or speak Spanish. A legal name change from an Hispanic surname to an English one is a more drastic step taken to blend in with an English-speaking majority.

In a recent study of cultural overlap and cultural distance concepts (Cox, 1993), differences described between Mexicans, Mexican-Americans, and Anglo-Americans included individual levels of cultural comfort in organizations and other personality variables. Impersonality was found to be more prominent among Anglo-Americans than Mexican-Americans (U.S. citizens), and Mexicans. Means were statistically significant at 1.67, 1.83, and 1.94, respectively. Conversely, Mexicans and Mexican-Americans placed a higher emphasis on personal alliances and friendship than on institutional obligation. Cox's data especially were collected in diversity-awareness workshops designed to illustrate cultural fit and acculturation. Participants were largely White males from organizations in the United States.

This study points out selected value differences important in nursing and in identifying preferred management styles of Anglo-Americans and their Mexican-American, or Mexican counterparts. Application to Hispanic health care is evident. An impersonal nursing approach could be satisfactory to a non-Hispanic or Mexican-American, for example, yet totally unacceptable to a Mexican citizen.

First-generation groups have stronger ties to traditions and customs from their country of origin than second and third generations. Persons living in countries other than their own for extended periods tend to reduce allegiance to their cultural customs and traditions without someone to share the customs. Researchers note that values change as new generations of a culture group adopt the new country views over time. However, this is not the case for Hispanics who retain strong cultural and family ties, especially Mexican-Americans who live along U.S.-Mexico border communities. Cultural ties remain strong because of the close proximity to Mexico and their families residing there.

Others' perceptions of Hispanics vary with their own sociocultural and religious upbringing, as well as linguistic and cultural influences that affect their view of Hispanic values, customs, and rituals. For these reasons, assumptions about Hispanics are often based on misperceptions and limited information that result in misunderstandings. Incorrect assumptions are also made about Hispanics based on miscommunication between the spoken language, written information, and nonverbal cues that differ significantly between cultures. Incorrect or inadequate information often leads to misperceptions and stereotyping.

The practice of labeling Hispanics broadly has created inaccurate and incomplete data for governmental agencies, researchers, and others. Inconsistencies and information gaps are evident to persons seeking reliable information about Hispanics. Especially affected by this information gap is the health care sector and care providers who need accurate data for making critical decisions to meet the needs of Hispanic groups. Accurate data are a prime concern for researchers who need reliable information for clinical studies. Basic data about Hispanics need to be obtained and research studies conducted to overcome these deficits. Until recently, data were unavailable about Hispanics by country of origin.

Hispanics themselves have differing opinions about the most appropriate self-report label, *Hispanic* or *Latino*. Hispanics are themselves acutely aware of the cultural differences within the Hispanic culture, and within the Mexican culture. These subcultural differences, too, are determined by social and economic status, education, country of origin, place of residence, and religious and political affiliation. The analogy of an inexperienced artist who would paint a landscape with a single brush stroke of color and the expert artist who would use varying shades and hues to define important details and clarify subtle differences is apt here. Without such shading, critical details would be lost. Differences need to be highlighted and models developed that depict Hispanics realistically.

However small cultural differences may appear to non-Hispanics, these subtleties are significant. Differences as well as commonalities are particularly important when determining relationships and communication patterns between Hispanics and others, especially in providing nursing care. These patterns and preferences are particularly relevant to nurses working with Hispanic populations because they serve as parameters of cultural expectations, and need to be considered when assessing the patient and providing needed care. Understanding the importance of cultural values that influence verbal and nonverbal communication is key to developing the trust needed by care providers to deliver quality health care to Hispanics.

Selected Values and Behaviors

Social values are rapidly changing in our society, yet essential values remain consistent for Hispanics. Valued behaviors include cooperation toward goal achievement, establishing positive interpersonal relationships, and concern for others. Cooperating with peers in working together to complete tasks is valued for the sense of camaraderie and a noncompetitive approach in business.

Research studies indicate that bicultural Mexican-Americans do well in a cooperative and competitive approach to goal achievement and task completion (Ramirez, 1979, p. 10). American society tends to value independence, assertiveness, and competition in achieving wealth, power, and positions of influence. Other studies indicate that positive interpersonal relationships are of great importance to Hispanics in business and other dealings. How these values are applied can mean the difference between success and failure in working with Hispanics. Additionally, concerns for family members and significant others are highly regarded and important to Hispanics. This knowledge is particularly relevant for health caregivers and nurses. The importance of establishing rapport and trust with the client and family is vital when providing direct care and care planning in the home. Bilingual providers can more readily facilitate the acceptance of care if they are also knowledgeable about the cultural aspects of care.

Courtesy, deference to authority, and modesty are but a few of the commonly valued behaviors instilled early in the lives of Mexican and Mexican-American children. Children are taught that courtesy and deference are demonstrated by allowing elders and other authority figures to speak first without interrupting them. Deference is also demonstrated by using the titles of Mister, Mrs., or Miss (Senor, Senora, and Senorita), with the person's last name often omitted. Professional titles are used to denote respect, followed by the person's last name. As in the case of attorney (Abogado), physician (Doctora), and nurse (Enfermera), the appropriate title is used followed by the person's last name: Doctora Martinez, Abogado Rodriguez, Enfermera Ramirez. A baccalaureate graduate in any other field is also addressed as Licenciado (Lic.) as a sign of respect and licensure. This is an expectation and custom in the Hispanic culture, especially in the middle-to-upper social classes. Conversely, it is considered extremely rude to refer to a person by their last name or given name without their approval to do so. If one addresses an individual using the first person, informal *Tu* (you) instead of the formal *Usted* (you), regardless of age, it is considered a lack of etiquette and cultural knowledge. These nuances are subtle differences and examples of appropriate behavior, valued and expected regardless of one's social class or educational status.

Placing others' needs above self is based on selected religious tenets and is carried through to daily life activities. Behaviors related to this thinking are often perceived by non-Hispanics as subservient and passive. For example, allowing a peer to enter an elevator first is a gesture of courtesy, respect, and selflessness for a Hispanic. To a non-Hispanic, this act may be considered subservient and passive. Hispanics view the same behaviors as courteous, respectful, and neutral and, if not carried out, aggressive and rude. These examples of cultural differences need to be identified and discussed with non-Hispanics to raise awareness. Expected behaviors vary between cultures. Judgmental non-acceptance of these behaviors by non-Hispanics is of particular concern to Hispanics and viewed as a lack of caring and understanding. There is a need to raise questions for clarification, information, and discussion regarding Hispanic values, beliefs, and related behaviors. Customs and health care practices, whether traditional or not, also need to be incorporated into care plans used by physicians, nurses, and social workers, as interdisciplinary teams working together with Hispanic clients and their families. All too often, judgmental approaches are used by health care providers when medical or nursing care is questioned or not readily accepted. Middle class values tend to be imposed by providers in health care environments and used to ensure compliance to treatment, care, or medication regimes.

Benevolent-authoritarian and paternalistic approaches are often used by non-Hispanic health care providers to address the health concerns of clients in their "best interests." However appropriate these approaches may seem, Hispanics as others have a right and responsibility to accept or reject personal care and treatment modes based on their knowledge and beliefs. Hispanics also have a right to culturally competent care that demonstrates a sensitivity and awareness of Hispanic cultural values, needs, health care practices, and physical aspects of care. Nontraditional health care practices are a major part of competent care.

Modesty considerations and spiritual care cannot be overstated for most Hispanics undergoing treatment and care. The inclusion of clergymen is emphasized in the health care of most Hispanics, regardless of their religion as an important and basic aspect of care. As such, religious affiliation and care data need to be obtained during the initial assessments of the patient or client.

Medicinal herbs and their use are less traditional behaviors or practices that also need to be considered in the care of some Hispanics. Of course, the use of medicinal herbs and nontraditional practices may cause discomfort in individuals whose strongly held beliefs preclude acceptance of these differing views and practices. Still, numerous individuals practice folk healing throughout the world, such as the practice of *curanderismo* in Mexico and other countries. The use of herbs for medicinal purposes is well recognized by researchers and practitioners in many countries as a respectable and effective practice to cure selected maladies and ills. One need only consider that selected and readily accepted medications, too numerous to count, hold Food and Drug Administration (FDA) approval in this country only after long-standing use by folk healers and subsequent studies. While these practices are not universal among Hispanics, information needs to be collected and considered in their health care planning.

UNDERSTANDING DIFFERENCES

Differences that exist between Hispanic groups are to be celebrated, not denigrated. Distinctions need to be made that establish a clear understanding about Hispanics and their culture. Differences between ethnic cultures and subcultures also need to be reconciled into a complementary whole, with Hispanic similarities and differences clearly delineated. This knowledge needs to describe true and accurate identities of often misrepresented ethnic groups. Society must reassess its perceptions of Hispanics based on accurate data and make plans for future health care needs.

The differences that exist between ethnic cultures and subcultures are based on ethnicity, economic advantage or disadvantage, such as the culture of poverty and other variables. Hispanics are often at a disadvantage by being placed in these categories through birth and circumstance, and a lack of education that locks them into a downward spiral. Although education is highly regarded and sought after by Hispanics, it may not be an option for many.

Cultural diversity encompasses more than the recognizable and described variables of skin pigmentation, language, country of origin, food preferences, and religious preferences. Social and economic variables considered important must also be viewed separately because Hispanics as a whole are a young and growing population, evolving through acculturation and age maturation.

In some minds, cultural diversity conjures images of major shifts away from the traditions and cultural norms of middle America and accepted health care practices. Traditional models and approaches to care are no longer effective nor efficient. However, health care and nursing care models previously held to be ideal need modification, not abandonment. Given current fiscal concerns and changing health care scenarios, cultural diversity can no longer be viewed as just another unpredictable variable.

Major population shifts taking place regionally, nationally, and internationally have affected the methods and protocols of health care required, especially in nursing.With these new challenges and opportunities for change, there is an even greater need for critical assessment of current and existing health care systems and models.

In an ideal world, clear definitions of ethnicity and Hispanic American culture may become a reality. In that ideal, individuals will be categorized according to ethnic origin, cultural group identity, and socioeconomic considerations. Clear insights and specific cultural knowledge about Hispanics will occur through open discussion and models will be developed that describe Hispanic identities with a high degree of accuracy. Perceptions about Hispanics will be based on complete data. Understanding the new culture and its members will be achieved through learning about another's cultural and individual needs. For equality to occur between cultures, understanding will need to occur between individuals and groups of different ethnicities and judgment withheld to reduce cultural barriers and increase trust.

REFERENCES

Cox, T., Jr. (1993). *Cultural diversity in organizations: Theory, research & practice.* San Francisco: Berrett-Koehler.

D'Souza, D. (1991). *Illiberal education: The politics of race and sex on campus.* New York: The Free Press.

El Paso offers good corridor for NAFTA superhighways. (1995, July). *El Paso Times.* p. 6A.

Castillo, M. H. M. *Perceptions of Mexican-American and Anglo-American nursing students toward an ideal leadership and followership style.* Unpublished doctoral dissertation, New Mexico State University, 1983.

Ramirez, C., & Collins, C. (1995, June). Fort Bliss to boast 500 new jobs. *El Paso Times.* p. 1A.

Bruhn, J. G., Chesney, A. P., & Salcido, R. (1995). Health and organizational issues in managing a multicultural work force. *Family and Community Health, 18*(2), 1-2.

UTMB to Host "NAFTA & HEALTH" Conference in December 1995. *NAFTA & HEALTH: Universities for a Healthier Border Environment,* 1-4.

Simmons, M. (1995, June). Pioneers used cultures, bible to pick baby names. *El Paso Times.* p. 3B.

Valdez, D. W., (1995, June). Tide of public opinion turns against NAFTA. *El Paso Times.* p. 2B.

CHAPTER TWO

Profile of the Hispanic Child

Mary Lou de Leon Siantz, PhD, RN, FAAN

*H*ispanic is a term officially created by the U.S. Census Bureau attributed to persons of Spanish origin or descent. The term barely existed prior to the 1970 Census and continues to be used to identify persons of Spanish origin in the United States. Another term preferred by some Hispanics, but not used by the Census Bureau, is *Latino,* which connotes Latin American rather than Spanish origin (The National Coalition of Hispanic Health and Human Services Organizations [COSSMHO], 1989). This paper describes Hispanics in the United States and presents a profile of the Hispanic child based on descriptive data from the Hispanic Health and Nutrition Examination Survey (HHANES).

With the exception of Mexican-Americans, data on various Hispanic origin populations were almost nonexistent prior to 1960 (Secretary's Task Force, 1986). Even for Mexican-Americans, nationally representative data were not available until 1970. However, as the Hispanic population in the United States has grown, both demographically and politically, available data suitable for national studies has also increased.

Hispanics are not a homogeneous group, despite the fact that they share a common language. Some are U.S. citizens, others are not. Some are recent arrivals to the United States, while others have been in this country for many generations. Many speak only Spanish, some are bilingual, others are monolingual in English (COSSMHO, 1988). Hispanics include a range of nationality subgroups: 62.8% Mexican-American, 11.6% Puerto Rican, 12% Central and South, 7.8% other (U.S. Department of Commerce, 1990). The differences between Hispanics are important. For example, Mexican-Americans living north of the Rio Grande River for several centuries,

This investigation was funded by a grant from the National Coalition of Hispanic Health and Human Services Organizations (COSSMHO), Washington, DC.

second-generation Cuban-Americans, and recent immigrants from El Salvador vary widely in their schooling, employment, and cultural norms.

Poverty Status

As a group, Hispanics are among the poorest people in the United States. In 1988, about one out of every six persons living in poverty was Hispanic (U.S. Department of Commerce, 1990). Hispanics comprise 7% of U.S. families with employed heads of households, but 17% of poor families with employed heads of households (National Council of La Raza, 1989). Almost 39% of the 5.4 million Hispanics living in poverty were children under 18 years of age. From 1978 to 1987, the proportion of Hispanic children living in poverty rose more than 45% (U.S. Bureau of the Census, 1988). In 1988, two out of five Hispanic children were living in poverty. Hispanic children make up 11% of all children in the United States, but they represent 21% of all children living in poverty.

Lack of Prenatal Care

According to the National Center for Health Statistics (1987), 13% of Hispanic mothers had late or no prenatal care compared to 12% of non-Hispanic Black mothers and 4% of non-Hispanic White mothers. Among Puerto Rican mothers, the incidence was much higher, with 17% either beginning prenatal care in the third trimester or not at all. Sixty-one percent of all Hispanic mothers began prenatal care in their first trimester of pregnancy, compared to 82% of White non-Hispanic mothers. Among Hispanic subgroups, only 57% of Puerto Rican mothers started prenatal care during the first trimester. As a result, there is an increased risk for complications during pregnancy and the perinatal period that can occur among these infants and mothers.

Risk for AIDS

While Hispanics constitute 8.2% of the population in the United States, since 1981, Hispanics have accounted for 13% to 17% of all AIDS cases in the United States, including the commonwealth of Puerto Rico. Of every hundred thousand Hispanics, 58 of them have AIDS. Of every hundred thousand non-Hispanic Whites, 21 of them have AIDS. Hispanic women account for 19% of all AIDS cases among women. Almost one in four (23%) cases of pediatric AIDS (children under 13 years) is Hispanic. The majority of these cases are infants born to mothers with HIV infection or AIDS.

THE HISPANIC CHILD

Hispanic children comprise over one-third of the Hispanic population of the United States. It is estimated that from 1985 to 2000 there will be 2.4 million more Hispanic children in the United States, compared to 66,000 more White non-Hispanic children. In 1986, Hispanic children comprised 32.9% of 0- to 17-year-olds in Texas, 29.3% in California, 16.2% in New York, 9.6% in Florida, and 9.2% in Illinois.

Educational Status

In 1986, only 28.7% of 3- and 4-year-old Hispanic children were enrolled in preschool programs of any kind compared to 39% of Whites and 43% of Blacks (U.S. Bureau of the Census, 1988). Nearly 30% of Hispanic children in grades 1–4 are enrolled below grade level (Select Committee for Children, Youth, and Families, 1989). The Hispanic dropout rate increased to 35.7% in 1988 from 28.6% in 1987. Nearly one-third of Hispanic dropouts have completed no more than six years of school (National Center for Education Statistics, 1989).

The importance of this data is that it identifies a growing population of children at risk for early parenthood and diminished opportunities throughout life. The available studies on Hispanic children do not discriminate across developmental periods. In them, childhood frequently refers to anyone under 17 years of age, although some distinctions are made between those 0–6 and 7–17 years (COSSMHO, 1988; Guerra, 1980). Such broadly defined categories both mask the possible developmental stages in a child's life when specific risk factors impact deferentially on their health, development, and school potential and make it difficult to identify developmentally appropriate strategies that enable Hispanic children to reach their potential at home, at school, and in their communities. In addition, most research has focused on specific communities or regional groups, with few studies on the national level available (Gundelman & Schwalbe, 1986).

To begin to address this lack of data, a secondary analysis of the Hispanic Health and Nutrition Examination Survey (HHANES, 1988) was undertaken. The HHANES was conducted by the National Center for Health Statistics (1984–1986) in response to the need for detailed health, nutritional status, and needs of Hispanics, and to investigate their access to health services. Additional goals for the survey included identification of information useful to public health planners and researchers as well as stimulation of research focused on Hispanic health issues.

Design

The HHANES design included a complex, multistage, stratified, cluster sample of individuals aged six months to 74 years of age. As it was neither feasible nor cost-effective to draw a probability sample of Hispanics from all groups in the entire United States, HHANES surveyed Hispanics from the three major Hispanic subgroups as indicated by the 1980 Census: Mexican-Americans, Puerto Ricans, and Cuban-Americans (Delgado, Johnson, Roy, & Trevino, 1990). The survey universe included approximately 76% of the 1980 Hispanic origin population in the United States. Even in areas defined for the survey, certain counties were excluded because of cost and logistics which may have resulted in some bias due to noncoverage. The sample weights created for analysis and estimation purposes attempted to take into account this issue of noncoverage (Delgado et al., 1990).

Sampling

The Mexican-American universe was composed of 193 primary sampling units (PSUs) in five southwestern states: Arizona, California, Colorado, New Mexico, and Texas. The Cuban-American universe consisted of one PSU in Dade County, Florida. The Puerto Rican universe consisted of 16 PSUs in the New York City metropolitan area including parts of New York, New Jersey, and Connecticut. The PSUs were stratified to group similar counties and one was selected from each stratum. Finally, segments and households were selected from each PSU. The HHANES survey was restricted to those areas of the country in order to allow an efficient operation of the survey from the standpoints of cost and logistics (Gonzales, Exxati, White, Massey, Lago, & Waksberg, 1985).

Within each PSU, block areas with less than a minimum number of eligible Hispanics were excluded due to the costs of interviewing ineligible households. This exclusion should be considered during interpretation of the results. Households that had at least one Hispanic member were eligible for participation. A small percent of non-Hispanics are included in the overall sample. Eligibility for the survey was determined by the family unit. A family was considered to be eligible if at least one family member's reported national origin or ancestry met the criteria for eligibility appropriate to the survey locations.

The HHANES was not designed to be representative of all Hispanics residing in the United States. Therefore, survey results can be generalized in the strictest sense to the three subgroups and geographic areas.

HHANES Child Sample

A total of 4,043 children six months to eleven years was sampled. Of these, 98% (3,966) were interviewed (mother or caretaker), and 88% (3,567) were examined in the HHANES. The sample size and response rate for each Hispanic subgroup are presented in Tables 2.1 to 2.3.

The HHANES used five data collection methods: interviews, direct physical examinations, diagnostic testing, anthropometry (body measurements), and laboratory analysis. Depending on the nature of the interviews, some were administered in the household and others were administered in private within a mobile examination center. All examinations and tests were performed in the mobile examination center located in the local community.

Attrition of sample persons occurred either during the interview or the physical examination. All interviewers were bilingual and most were bicultural.

Because the HHANES used a complex, multistage, stratified, survey design, instead of a simple random sample design, standard statistical methods were not appropriate. Sample weights were used to produce correct population estimates. This is because each sample person did not have an equal probability of selection. The weights incorporated the selection probabilities and adjustments for post-stratification (in the Mexican-American sample only), noncoverage, and nonresponse. In addition to the sample weights, the strata and the primary sampling units from the sample design were needed to estimate the sample variances and to test for statistical significance. Sample variances would be underestimated if calculated without incorporating the complex sample design.

A design-based approach considers both the sample weights and the complex design (Kovar, 1985). In a design-based approach, the design

Table 2.1 Sample Size and Response Rates by Age: Mexican-Americans

	Sample	Interviewed		Examined	
Age	Size	Number	Percent	Number	Percent
6 months–4 years	1,232	1,136	92.2	1,025	90.2
5-9 years	1,288	1,182	91.8	1,100	93.0
10–11 years	480	443	92.3	412	93.0
Total	3,000	2,761	92.0	2,537	84.5

Note: Data provided by NCHS and reflects estimate of children sampled.

Table 2.2 Sample Size and Response Rates by Age: Cuban Americans

	Sample	Interviewed		Examined	
Age	Size	Number	Percent	Number	Percent
6 months–4 years	144	122	84.7	85	69.0
5–9 years	134	115	85.8	93	80.8
10–11 years	65	54	83.0	43	79.6
Total	343	291	85.0	221	64.4

Note: Data provided by NCHS and reflects an estimate of children sampled.

effect is used to illustrate the impact of the complex sample design on the variance. The design effect is defined as the ratio of the variance of a statistic from a complex sample to the variance of the same statistic from a simple random sample of the same size as the following formula illustrates:

$$\text{Design effect} = \frac{\text{Variance complex sample}}{\text{Variance simple random sample}}$$

A design-based approach offers several advantages for developing exploratory models from survey data. These include consideration of weights that account for unequal probabilities of selection, adjustment for nonresponse, and adjustment for coverage of complex variances in the analysis. In addition, misspecification of error variances can be prevented. By considering the complex sample design, a design-based approach facilitates appropriate estimates of means, medians, and other descriptive statistics. The variance and covariance estimates of the design-based approach also facilitates more conservative inferences than those in a simple model-based approach (Kovar, 1985). A design-based approach was used to analyze the child data in the HHANES.

Table 2.3 Sample Size and Response Rates by Age: Puerto Ricans

	Sample	Interviewed		Examined	
Age	Size	Number	Percent	Number	Percent
6 months–4 years	424	388	91.5	335	86.3
5–9 years	411	374	90.9	338	90.3
10–11 years	162	152	93.8	136	89.4
Total	997	914	92.0	809	81.0

Note: Data provided by NCHS and reflects an estimate of children sampled.

Data analysis involved: (1) screening and factoring of variables, (2) descriptive analyses, and (3) inferential analyses—with the descriptive analysis reported in this chapter.

Incomplete Data

A major problem of health examination surveys such as the HHANES is the large number of sample persons who initially agreed to complete the household and health history questionnaire, but did not participate in the physical examination.

The completion rates ranged from a high of 93% to 69%. A minimum response rate of 73% and 75% for previous HHANES was acceptable. The completion rates for the subsample in the analysis was within the acceptable limits for Mexican-Americans and Puerto Ricans as Tables 2.1 and 2.3 illustrate. This was not the case for Cuban children. Their rate of completion was lower as illustrated in Table 2.2.

Results: HHANES Child Sample

Parent History. The average age for mothers of the child sample ranged from 24.1 years to 26.9 years with the Puerto Rican mothers being the youngest as Table 2.4 illustrates. Fathers of children sampled were somewhat older. Paternal age ranged from 27.2 years (Mexican-American) to 30.2 years (Cuban-American). The number of years in school for the head of the house varied (9.2 years–11.03 years) with Mexican-American heads of household the least educated. Family income also varied with the Puerto Rican household reporting the least income ($11,600). Family size ranged from 5.2 among the Mexican-American children sampled to 4.4 among the Cuban-American sample.

Table 2.4 Parent History Sample Child Means

	Mexican-American	Cuban-American	Puerto Rican
Mother's age	24.4 yrs.	26.9 yrs.	24.1 yrs.
Father's age	27.2 yrs.	30.2 yrs.	27.4 yrs.
Head of house years in school	9.2 yrs.	11.03 yrs.	10.06 yrs.
Family income	$14,900	$16,800	$11,600
Family size	5.16	4.4	4.7

Health Insurance. The results indicated that a little more than half of the Mexican-American and Cuban-American children had health insurance. Only one-third of Puerto Rican children from 6–35 months were insured. The likelihood of having health insurance somewhat increased for the Mexican-Americans and Cubans from 3–5 years of age but decreased among Puerto Rican children. Health insurance continued to slightly increase among Cuban-Americans and Puerto Ricans but decreased for Mexican-Americans 6–11 years, as Table 2.5 illustrates.

Among Mexican-Americans and Cuban-Americans, the lack of health insurance for children sampled was primarily due to the expense of such insurance. Puerto Ricans depended on Medicaid/Welfare for health insurance coverage.

Health Care. All three subgroups reported a high incidence of medical treatment for sickness among children 6 months to 11 years. Follow-up care was the least type of medical treatment sought. It increased only slightly for Cuban-Americans. Follow-up care was the highest among Puerto Rican children 6 to 35 months (Table 2.6).

Health Care Provider. A particular health care provider was not consistently seen by the sample children. For those children who did see a particular health care provider, visits decreased with the age of the child. Only 22.7% of the Mexican-American children 6 to 35 months saw the same person. The likelihood among Cuban-American and Puerto Rican children was slightly higher, 28.6% and 26.7%, respectively (Table 2.7).

Table 2.5 Insurance Coverage Sample Child

	Mexican-American	Cuban-American	Puerto Rican
Age (6–35 months)			
Insured	52.6%	53%	33%
Not insured	47.4	47	67
Age (3–5 years)			
Insured	58.0	59	27
Not insured	42.0	41	73
Age (6–11 years)			
Insured	56.0	62	34
Not insured	44.0	38	66

Table 2.6 Medical Treatment Sample Child

	Mexican-American	Cuban-American	Puerto Rican
Age (6–35 months)			
Sickness	85.90%	84.75%	72.80%
Injury	5.30	3.39	4.89
Follow-up	3.60	8.40	15.76
Other	5.20	3.50	6.50
Age (3–5 years)			
Sickness	83.74	80.95	80.27
Injury	9.69	4.76	4.04
Follow-up	3.60	9.52	8.07
Other	7.07	4.77	7.71
Age (6–11 years)			
Sickness	79.90	75.00	82.84
Injury	15.18	11.29	6.37
Follow-up	3.82	11.27	7.60
Other	1.10	2.44	3.19

DISCUSSION

The purpose of this paper was to describe the Hispanic population of the United States, with particular focus on a profile of the Hispanic child. The Hispanic population was described as growing, youthful, poor, lacking prenatal care, and at high risk for AIDS. The findings of the HHANES concerning the parental history of the children sampled paralleled other

Table 2.7 Same Professional Seen if Sick or Injured

	Mexican-American	Cuban-American	Puerto Rican
Age (6–35 months)			
Yes	22.73%	28.57%	26.67%
No	77.27	71.43	73.30
Age (3–5 years)			
Yes	5.56	0.00	28.57
No	94.40	100.00	71.43
Age (6–11)			
Yes	7.03	35.00	33.33
No	92.97	65.00	66.67

national data that has documented the low education found among Hispanics in the United States, particularly among Mexican-Americans. For example, in 1988, only 51% of Hispanics 25 years old and over had completed four years or more of high school, compared to 78% of non-Hispanics (U.S. Bureau of the Census, 1988).

The larger family size found especially among the Mexican-American (5.2 persons) and Puerto Rican (4.7 persons) subgroups was consistent with national trends that have been reported for Hispanic families. In 1987, 57% of Mexican-American, 44% of Puerto Rican, and 38% of Cuban families had four or more persons.

Family income was consistent with the higher risk for poverty that has been identified among Hispanics in the United States. In 1985, the median annual income in the United States was $26,000, compared to $19,000 among Hispanics. The income reported for the families of the sample children was significantly less, contributing to their poverty status.

Descriptive analyses revealed the low incidence of health insurance coverage for the children sampled. Previous research has documented 21.7% of Hispanics lack public or private health insurance compared with 10.1% of Blacks and 7.7% of Whites (Select Committee for Children, Youth, and Families, 1989). The low incidence of health insurance may be due to the fact that the head of the house did not have employment that offered health insurance for families or the opportunity to purchase it at group rates. Difficulties in determining eligibility and other bureaucratic obstacles may have further reduced the number of poor families who can pay for health services through Medicaid. A recent survey by COSSMHO, the National Coalition of Hispanic Health and Human Services Organizations, revealed that a third of the Medicaid application sites studied had no special services to help their staff work with Spanish-speaking clients. Puerto Ricans' higher prevalence of Medicaid coverage may be due to their likelihood of residing in states that provide greater optional coverage.

Of greater concern for the children sampled was the low incidence of follow-up care and the lack of a regular health care provider, particularly for a developing child. All children need health care. Follow-up care is important for prevention and early detection of health problems, in determining if acute conditions have been treated successfully, and to monitor a child's normal growth and development (American Medical Association, 1990). The absence of a regular health care provider may make it difficult or impossible for infants and children to receive the primary and specialized care they need. Conditions not treated promptly and followed up may worsen and become chronic. This may result in not only increasing the medical care expense, but potentially interfering with education and the child's eventual ability to earn an income (National Center for Children in Poverty, 1991).

Implications

National trends and the results from the HHANES underscore the educational, economic, and health risks that exist among Hispanic children, particularly Mexican-American and Puerto Rican. Poverty continues to widen the socioeconomic gap that exists among Hispanic children.

The American Academy of Pediatrics has reported that as many as 14% of Hispanic children 0–2 years have not been seen by a physician (American Medical Association, 1990; Secretary's Task Force, 1986). If their mothers are less likely to have a usual source of care, to be privately insured, and to initiate early and continuous prenatal care, it is not surprising that the children suffer a similar fate. In addition, children are even more unlikely to be uninsured or Medicaid insured than their adult counterparts (McManus, 1986). Medicaid is important to families with several young children because it helps to defray some personal health expenses and pay for the preventive and primary care services needed during childhood (Gundelman & Schwalbe, 1986).

With an increased trend in the poverty rate among Hispanic children and the stringent eligibility criteria for public programs, an Hispanic child's health is likely to worsen unless steps are taken to develop a national agenda that addresses the health care of Hispanic children in the United States. Unfortunately, there is little available research on the Hispanic child to guide the health care professional and health care policy maker in the development of such an agenda. Research is needed to identify the unique characteristics, norms, health behaviors, problems, and strengths of Hispanic children as they grow and develop (Siantz, 1990). It is both good public policy and sound science to prepare ourselves to meet the health and human service needs of Hispanic children by developing a sound base of research.

REFERENCES

American Medical Association. (1990). *Target 2000: A Newsletter of the AMA Healthier Youth by the Year 2000 Project, 1*(3), 1–8.

COSSMHO: The National Coalition of Hispanic Health and Human Services Organizations. (1989). *AIDS: A guide for Hispanic leadership.* Washington, DC: Author.

COSSMHO: The National Coalition of Hispanic Health and Human Services Organizations. (1988). *Delivering preventive health care to Hispanics.* Washington, DC: Author.

Delgado, J., Johnson, C., Roy, I., & Trevino, F. (1990). Hispanic health and nutrition examination survey: Methodological considerations. *American Journal of Public Health, 80,* 6–10.

Gonzales, E., White, M., Lago, & Waksberg. (1985). *Plan and operation of the Hispanic health and nutrition examination survey, 1982–1984.* (Programs and Collection Procedures). Vital and Health Statistics, Series No. 19, DHHS Pub. No. (PHS) 85-1321, Hyattsville, MD: U.S. Department of Health and Human Services. Public Health Service, National Center for Health Statistics.

Ginzberg, E. (1991). Access to health care for Hispanics. *The Journal of the American Medical Association, 262*(2).

Guerra, F. (1980). Hispanic child health issues. *Children Today, 9*(5), 18–22.

Gundelman, S., & Schwalbe, J. (1986). Medical care—how does it differ from black and white peers? *Medical Care, 24*(10), 925–937.

Kovar, M. (1985). *Approaches for the analysis of data. Plan and operation of the Hispanic health and nutrition examination survey, 1982–1984* (DHHS Publication No. (PHS) 85-1321). Hyattsville, MD: National Center for Health Statistics, pp. 56–67.

McManus, M. (1986). Evaluation of interventions to reduce racial disparities in infant mortality: Health insurance coverage of maternal and infant care for minority women, January, 1986. In U.S. Department of Health and Human Services, *Report of the Secretary's Task Force on Black and Minority Health* (Vol. VI, pp. 103–125).

National Center for Children in Poverty. (1990). *Five million children: A statistical profile of our poorest young citizens.* New York: Author.

National Center for Children in Poverty. (1991). *Alive and well? A research and policy review of health programs for poor young children.* New York: Author.

National Center for Education Statistics (1989, September 25). Hispanic children and their families: A key to our nation's future. A fact sheet for select committee on children, youth, and families, Washington, DC.

National Center for Health Statistics (1989). Advance report of final nationality statistics, 1987. *Monthly Vital Statistics Report. Vol. 38,* No. 3, Suppl. Hyattsville, MD: Public Health Service.

National Council of La Raza (1989, September 25). Hispanic children and their families: A key to our nation's future. A fact sheet for select committee on children, youth, and families, Washington, DC.

Secretary's Task Force. (1986). *Report of secretary's task force on Black and minority health.* U.S. Department of Health and Human Services.

Select Committee for Children, Youth, and Families. (1989, September 25). Hispanic children and their families: A key to our nation's future. A fact sheet. Washington, DC: U.S. House of Representatives.

Siantz, de Leon, M. (1990). Who is the Hispanic child? A preliminary analysis of HHANES statistical figures. *Pacesetter Newsletter of the Council on Psychiatric and Mental Health Nursing.* American Nurses' Association, *17*(1/1990), 5–7.

Trevino, F. (1983). Health insurance coverage and physician visits among Hispanic and non-Hispanic people. In *Health—United States, 1983*. DHHS Pub. No. (DHS) 84-1232. Washington, DC: Government Printing Office.

Trevino, F., & Ray, L. (1988). Health insurance coverage and utilization of health services by Mexican-Americans in Texas and the southwest. In *Hispanic Health Status Symposium Proceedings.* San Antonio, TX: Center for Health Policy Development.

U.S. Bureau of the Census. (1988). The Hispanic population in the United States: March 1989. *Current population reports,* p. 20, No. 444. Washington, DC: U.S. Government Printing Office, 1990.

U.S. Department of Commerce. (1990). *The Hispanic population in the United States: March 1989.* Washington, DC: Government Printing Office, 1991.

CHAPTER THREE

The Birth of a Premature Infant in a Puerto Rican Family

Evelyn Crouch-Ruiz, PhD, RN

When a woman delivers a baby, she expects that baby to be perfect. This is universally true for families. For Puerto Rican families, a healthy baby can be a symbol of the father's virility. It is also very important for a woman to demonstrate her fertility, strength, and success during and after birth.

Culture plays an important role in shaping an individual's view of the world. This includes values, how we interpret events, and how we adjust to new roles, especially in being a mother. For many Hispanics, a family is not considered a "real family" until after the children are born, the first child being ideally a male. A male baby is proof that the father is a real man (macho), whereas if the child is a female or a sickly child, the father may be seen as possessing only a weak seed. This unspoken expectation of machismo can be especially difficult when a couple's experience of gestation and childbirth is not going well.

Puerto Ricans have a family-oriented culture. They like to celebrate life; they also love to experience and sustain intimacy in relationships. This intimacy can be quite beneficial for a couple who are bearing a child, providing much needed support and hope. On the other hand, such intimacy can prove difficult for parents when their baby is not as perfect as everyone would wish. If the baby does not fulfill all expectations, it can be threatening to have family, friends, other relations simply drop by to see the baby. The intimacy sought can then become a confused, even painful, legacy of a promise gone awry.

Important here is a capacity to respond positively to stress. Certainly, this is influenced by the support available from family and community. The support that comes from community or is provided by health agencies is more formal. The informal support provided by friends and relatives is important as well. Other sources of informal support can also come from indigenous traditions of care, including spiritualists or *curanderos* (Delgado, 1985). These informal social support sources are, in fact, sometimes more important to Hispanics because of their openly intimate character.

Generally, Hispanics have a need to trust before they are able to seek formal support sources. Agencies that wish to help couples in adjusting to premature births need to ensure that such trust exists. Contacting and interacting with couples early on in the pregnancy provides time for trust to develop between couples and provider. Failure to do so may prove costly. Without early intervention, many sorts of complications can arise. In order to become proficient in attending to Hispanic families of childbearing age, health care agencies must first gain their trust, and do so consistently.

How dependable the social support systems are and how effectively the family can use them can influence a couple's responses to childbirth. Especially in cases of premature births, this support complements the couple's ability to cope. If the Hispanic couple feels that the support they have is trustworthy and adequate, no doubt they will be better able to handle the event. The resulting behaviors and emotions, however conflictive they may be, will not prove overwhelming. In seeking and finding assistance, they will be able to judge the event differently, perhaps even as an event to be thankful for.

With inadequate social systems, however, Hispanic couples may indeed have a hard time adjusting to the birth and the event. Some may even see the event as harmful, then decide if it is a threat or a challenge and, at that point, seek appropriate assistance. If a couple reacts to the birth of their premature infant by avoiding the infant, it does not mean that they do not love or want the child. Perhaps they are worried about the present and future suffering of the child and, more immediately, the reactions of their friends and relatives to the less-than-perfect infant. Shame can become a powerful barrier to other emotions just beneath the surface.

The event can be an opportunity for growth or, again, a hindrance to the development of the family. Cultural and economic states do play into this as well. We see many different reactions to the same event. Families which have more support systems available to them, both formal and informal, will respond differently; perhaps more positively. The child is theirs, and his or her disabilities are theirs, as well. But even very poor families, when faced with the same type of challenges, do not give up their preferences for family nor the values that support family as such. The difficulties remain "in the family."

Rituals are important for family unification. In Puerto Rico, rituals include baptism, confirmation, birthdays, quinceraneros, anniversaries, and wakes, to mention a few. There are many holidays also related to children such as Christmas, with both Santa Claus and Three Kings Day. These events can be stressful when a child is not perfect.

Puerto Ricans tend to make "promesas" or promises of a religious nature in response to stressful situations. These promises can be anything from a special prayer, a mass, a pilgrimage to a church or sacred place, to wearing a "habit" or special clothes in honor of a saint. Promises are made and used as a bargaining tool for the health of a loved one. When the request is granted, the promise must be kept, or something terrible will result. Some couples are content, for example, to place a medal or a figure at the crib or incubator of the premature infant. When the infant is well and can be taken home, the saint is thanked. But if the infant dies or does not recuperate, the parents may believe that it was not God's will for them to have this child. They thus attempt to alleviate their anguish and distress by placing the responsibility on an outside power.

When the threat of losing the infant is real, the affliction felt by the couple can alter the normal acquaintance process with the new family member—this can also extend to different family members as well. Couples can try to prepare for the loss of the ideal and the real infant, acknowledging their failure to produce a full-term healthy infant and understanding, as much as is possible, how their infant differs from a full-term infant. Religious promises and the help of relatives may help them, but this assistance is not always certain. They may gain greater protection if their support system includes additional, formal sources. Puerto Rican families that can trust community agencies and health care professionals when they need assistance will be in a better position to grow stronger and bond as a couple because of their experience.

REFERENCES

Crouch-Ruiz, E. (1987). *Puerto Rican mother's perceptions of and emotional, cognitive and behavioral responses to premature and full-term births.* Dissertation Abstracts International.

Crouch-Ruiz, E. (1991). *Percepciones y respuestas de las madres Puertorriqueñas al parto prematuro.* Science/Ciencia.

Guzman, M. (1994). *Puerto Rico: The meeting of the Hispanic and Anglo-Saxon cultures in the world of work.* Puerto Rico: Boriquen Corp.

CHAPTER FOUR

Health of Hispanic Adolescents

Antonia M. Villarruel, PhD, RN

The dreams of Hispanic youth:

- "I want to be a lawyer."
- "I want to be a teacher, elementary."
- "I want to be a veterinarian."
- "I want to have a family and my own house and a car."
- "I want to be a travel agent."
- "I want to be a secretary."
- "I want to be a singer. Just like Selena."
- "Go to college, get a good education."
- "Ever since two years ago, I wanted to be a doctor. I want to be a doctor, I want to finish school and go to college, get a good education."
- "Go to college to study . . . I don't know exactly what, but I want a job that has something to do with computers and business."
- "I want to be a . . . I don't know yet. I want to finish school. That's all I know for right now."
- "I want to be 15 so I can have my quinciñera . . . I think they'll (parents) treat me older. Because right now they see me as a little girl, but . . . I'm not a little girl anymore, I *actually know things* and they should treat me my age."
- "To get my driver's license and take my mom some places she wants to go because I hate when she walks in the night . . . She goes to meetings and sometimes she has to walk. So I want to get a car." (Villarruel, 1995)

The hopes and dreams of their parents:

- "Well, what I have said to my children, is that first they finish their education. Because for myself, I only finished grade school. Once you're finished with your education and you have your career, then you can think about marriage."
- "I tell my 16 year old . . . my son . . . that he has to finish his studies, because before, in Mexico, our parents couldn't provide us with that type of education."
- "My daughter is very smart and I don't want her to grow up like I did. I was married and divorced at 22. I don't want to wish that on you. I want you to go all the way. You have plenty of time for babies after a while. Go ahead and have a good time. But be careful." (Villarruel, 1995)

The realities confronted by Hispanic adolescents:

- "I'm worried because I'm pregnant right now and I have to worry about my kid's future and I need to know if my mom and dad are going to stand by me. . . . I need a job and I've got to go and look for a job and finish school. That's what I want, to finish school and go to college. And raise my kid up in the right community, because around here it's bad. The gangs. I got involved and I don't want any of my sisters or my kid getting involved in that."
- "I was in a gang because I wanted to be different. I was never like a little girl. . . . And it was something, I got hurt, I had a lot of pain inside me and it was like they [gang members] were the only people that I could relate to. Nobody understood me but them and they had the same pain. It was like they were like a family to me. That's what it is, like a family. . . . A lot of the females in my gang, they're all Latinos, they're all Mexicans and Puerto Ricans."
- "Because I was always hanging, I was always out with them [gang members]. And they're mad. They ask me, they tell me it's going to be hard raising a kid. It's like they always try to make me feel bad, 'Look, you ain't going to be able to go out with your girls and do the stuff that . . . ' I was like, 'Dang, that's true.' But to me it's kind of good that I'm having a kid because it's going to take me away from all that and put me where I should be, at home doing stuff that I have to do for myself and not being out there getting high and drinking all the time and jumping people for . . . you know, standing and putting my life on the line for them. I have to think about my life and my family's life." (Villarruel, 1995)

The challenges faced by Hispanic parents:

- "I want my daughter to be able to go to college. . . . She is the smartest one of all the children. But we just can't afford to send her. It's not just a question of the money . . . we need her here to help around the house and with the younger children, because I work too. She does it all . . . cooking, cleaning, baby-sitting. Because we don't speak English, she comes with us to the doctors, to school to see about the other kids. . . . I'd be lost, we'd all be lost without her."
- "I pray nothing goes wrong with my kids. We don't have any insurance. Just my husband with his work. We can't get assistance because they say we make too much, but it's not enough for us to have insurance. It's the choice you make between a house and food on the table and the chance that nothing is going to happen to them."
- "I took my 17-year-old out of the gang, and they didn't do anything to me . . . I sent him away, to Chicago. And I think if my other child, my daughter, gets into a gang, I'm going to send her to Puerto Rico, because, I don't want her to be involved in that . . . we want to lead them down a good road."
- "My oldest was an honor student and one day they got him . . . gang members . . . at school. They said that the first one that walked down the hall they were going to beat up. So his senior year, he dropped out of school, because of the fear he had. . . . We all had to get over what happened. So today, he is taking classes at the library so he can get his GED." (Villarruel, 1995)

Adolescence is a time of rapid and complex biological, cognitive, emotional, and social transitions. During this period, youth are particularly vulnerable as they begin to develop the skills and resources needed to deal with new demands and expectations. However, there also exists the opportunity for youth to learn to develop healthy lifestyle patterns that will endure throughout adulthood.

Hispanic adolescents, like other ethnic and racially diverse adolescents, are particularly vulnerable as these transitions are even more complex. The voices of these Hispanic adolescents and their parents provide an important context for discussing the health of Hispanic adolescents. For Hispanic youth, the distinctions and expectations between home, school, neighborhood, family, and peers become more apparent, often conflicting, and thus difficult to bridge. Further, the opportunities for Hispanic adolescents to develop healthy lifestyle patterns is compromised by the effects of poverty, discrimination, and the lack of access to community-based health and social services. In addition, the limited availability of culturally and linguistically appropriate services for adolescents and their families creates barriers to accessing needed resources and results in missed opportunities by health providers to further develop and enhance existing strengths of Hispanic adolescents.

This chapter profiles the challenges and opportunities confronting Hispanic adolescents, specifically as they relate to health status and behaviors. Of much importance as well are the commonalities and diversity that exist among Hispanic youth. Finally, barriers to health care are identified and recommendations for practice are offered.

HISPANIC ADOLESCENCE: THE DEMOGRAPHIC PICTURE

Growth trends suggest that Hispanic youth are and will continue to comprise a significant portion of this nation's population. By the year 2050, it is projected that 1 in 5 Americans will be of Hispanic origin. However, despite growing numbers, a significant portion of Hispanic youth continue to face the deleterious effects of poverty. While Hispanics are generally more likely to live in poverty (26.5%) than non-Hispanics (10.2%), the burden of poverty is disproportionately represented among children (U.S. Bureau of the Census, 1993a). Two out of every five Hispanic children under the age of 18 (39.9%) are currently living in poverty; a rate that is two times higher than for non-Hispanic youth (19.5%) (U.S. Bureau of the Census, 1993c). Among Hispanic youth, there are differential rates of poverty. Puerto Rican children living on the mainland have the highest proportion of children living in poverty (57.9%) as compared with Mexican-American (40%) and other Hispanic subgroups (approximately 33%) (U.S. Bureau of the Census, 1993b).

A major means for persons to escape the cycle of poverty is through educational attainment. The relationship between education, employment, and higher income status has been well established. However, among Hispanics educational attainment continues to be elusive. The low educational attainment of parents, the decay of urban schools where the majority of Hispanics reside, increasing violence in the schools, and discriminatory practices in schools are all factors that have been associated with the high drop-out rate among Hispanics. In 1990, 35% of Hispanics between the ages of 16 to 24 did not have a high school diploma (U.S. Department of Education, 1992). Hispanic youth are at higher risk for dropping out of school in general, and for dropping out at a younger age. Across all grade levels, Hispanic youth are twice as likely to drop out of school than non-Hispanic White youth (Bureau of the Census, 1991). In addition, Hispanic and Black youth are more likely than their White peers to be suspended or expelled from school (National Center for Health Statistics [NCHS], 1991).

This continued trend in school dropouts among Hispanic adolescents has important implications. In the work place today, there is no longer a need for the large number of unskilled laborers. Rather, workers are required to be highly skilled, trained, and technologically competent. Many entry-level jobs require persons to have some post-high school education, and that trend is likely to continue. Given the growing numbers of Hispanic youth, it is possible that one of the most important resources for the future will not be developed adequately to meet the challenges of the future.

Because of the increasing numbers of Hispanic youth, it is important that health care providers and policy makers recognize and address the health problems and barriers to health care confronted by these youth. The high rates of poverty and low educational attainment creates a number of barriers that can impede both health and development. Furthermore, these barriers will call for the creation or modification of existing programs to facilitate access to health and human services. The relationship between poverty, low educational attainment, and health and health services will be further explored.

HISPANIC ADOLESCENT HEALTH: AN INCOMPLETE PICTURE

Any discussion of health and health behavior related to Hispanic adolescents needs to be considered within the context of existing data. Unfortunately, there is a significant lack of data related to Hispanic health. Furthermore, the data available is based on the assumption that Hispanics are a homogeneous group. Thus existing data is not sufficient to examine differences among subgroups of Hispanics or to examine important intragroup differences related to generational distance or acculturation level. For example, in a recent survey of 21 major national data systems of the U.S. Department of Health and Human Services (DHHS), only the U.S. Vital Statistics System is designed to provide data on all four of the major Hispanic subpopulation groups (Delgado & Estrada, 1993). Furthermore, six of the data systems do not contain sufficient data on Hispanics to permit for adequate and meaningful analysis.

Specifically related to adolescents are national data systems such as the National Nutrition and Examination Survey (NHANES) that provide data on the nutrition and health status of children and adults. The National Survey of Family Growth (NSFG) that provides data on demographic and social factors associated with maternal and child health are not designed to provide sufficient data on all Hispanic subgroups. This holds true for other federally funded national surveys concerned with adolescents such as the National Longitudinal Survey of Youth (NLSY) that provides data on topics such as educational attainment, work experience, fertility, health patterns, and also the High School Senior Survey, which is an epidemiological survey on drug abuse.

Much of the existing data related to the health status of Hispanic adolescents was made available through the Hispanic Health and Nutrition Examination Survey (HHANES) which was conducted in 1982–1984 by the National Center for Health Statistics (1985). (See Chapter 2 for details of this study.) Despite the limitations of collecting regional data on Hispanic subgroups, this study provided a comprehensive look at health and nutrition indicators for Hispanic populations, including adolescents. Unfortunately, there are no plans to replicate this effort, with provisions being made within the current HHANES study to oversample only for Mexican-Americans.

Thus there is a lack of critical information on health, growth, and development indicators, such as health service utilization patterns, nutritional intake patterns, height and weight norms, the onset of pubertal development, age of first sexual intercourse, and prevalence of drug abuse for Hispanic adolescents. Clinicians and policy makers may only have data about Mexican-American adolescents to make decisions and design programs for Cuban, Puerto Rican, and Central and South American adolescents. The current lack and inadequacy of data leaves researchers, clinicians, and policy makers with an incomplete and skewed picture about the health of Hispanic adolescents.

The implications of this lack of data are best illustrated by examining *Healthy People 2000* (DHHS, 1991) objectives for Hispanic adolescents. The purpose of this important document was to provide a national framework for health promotion and prevention activities. Specific objectives comprising this initiative were derived for existing national data sources. However, because of the lack of available national data for Hispanics, there are no component objectives for Hispanic adolescents in the area of tobacco use, sexually transmitted diseases, substance abuse, violence and safety, mental health, or nutrition. The lack of specific objectives targeting Hispanic adolescents increases the likelihood that the needs of Hispanic adolescents may not be addressed in public health initiatives, and also implies that progress or its lack thereof may not be adequately monitored (National Coalition of Hispanic Health and Human Service Organizations

[COSSMHO], 1994). Thus, the cycle of exclusion for Hispanic adolescents from data collection and programmatic efforts is perpetuated.

HISPANIC ADOLESCENT HEALTH: A PROFILE

In order to provide a comprehensive overview of Hispanic adolescent health, several indicators of health including growth and development indicators, morbidity and mortality data, and the prevalence of health risk and protective behaviors will be presented.

Growth and Development

The growth patterns of children and the achievement of developmental milestones are basic indicators of health status for children and adolescents. The growth spurt and pubertal development are important milestones during the adolescent years. In an analysis of data from the HHANES, Hispanic youth 12 through 17 were more likely to be at low height for age as compared with non-Hispanic Whites. Further, among all Hispanic subgroups, the percentages of low height for age were higher among girls (4.6–8.8%) than boys (6.2–9.5%), and also higher among Mexican-Americans of both genders (Fanelli-Kuczmarski & Woteki, 1990). In relation to pubertal development, Puerto Ricans sampled in the HHANES reached stages of sexual maturation at rates similar to that of U.S. adolescents, while Mexican-Americans were moderately delayed in terms of development of secondary sexual characteristics (Martorell, Mendoza, Baisden, & Pawson, 1994). Thus on two critical indicators of development, Mexican-Americans lag behind the Hispanic and non-Hispanic populations.

What does this mean? It depends on whether the causes for these differences are genetic, related to poverty, and/or associated with poor nutrition. The relationship between poverty and ethnicity and short stature among Mexican-Americans (Martorell, Mendoza, & Castillo, 1989) and Puerto Ricans (Martorell et al., 1994) sampled in the HHANES was examined. In these analyses, poverty was not associated with differences in stature in Puerto Rican and Mexican-American youth between 12 through 17 years of age nor did poverty account for differences in stature between Hispanic and non-Hispanic Whites. However, poverty was a significant predictor of stature for Mexican-Americans between the ages 2 to 5 and 6 to 11 years. While the failure of poverty to account for differences in stature during adolescence may seem to provide support to the conclusion that differences in height are due to genetic factors, findings also provide support to the notion that actual growth retardation may have occurred at earlier ages (Mendoza, 1994). However, because the HHANES was a one-time study, it is not possible to determine whether these findings truly reflect changes over time.

Nutrition is another important factor to consider in determining growth and development trends as well as future health status. Two nutrition-related problems for Hispanic adolescents that affect health and growth are iron deficiency and obesity. In relation to iron deficiency anemia, prevalence was highest among Mexican-American adolescents, and across all groups, highest among girls. In relation to obesity, among Hispanic youth age 12 through 19, the percentage of Mexican-American children that exceeded a body mass index above the 90th percentile for non-Hispanic Whites was evident throughout most of childhood and during adolescence (Fanelli-Kuczmarski & Woteki, 1990). The prevalence of higher body mass index for females exceeded that of boys from ages 15 through 17. Thus Mexican-American adolescents, particularly females, are heavier than their Hispanic and non-Hispanic White peers.

As with short stature, poverty was not a predictor of overweight status. Again, the failure of poverty to account for differences in high body mass index might suggest a genetic predisposition to greater fat deposition among Mexican-Americans. However, the influence of specific diet and physical activity patterns common across all income levels of Mexican-Americans must also be considered (Martorell, Mendoza, & Castillo, 1989). The low rates of physical inactivity especially among female Hispanic adolescents (Centers for Disease Control, 1991d; Wolf et al., 1993) has been documented and lends support to the need to assess behaviors like diet and nutrition that can contribute to obesity.

In summary, specific growth and development trends, such as short stature, later pubertal development among Mexican-Americans, and nutrition related problems, including iron deficiency anemia and obesity, have been documented. While it has not been determined whether these trends are related to genetic, dietary, or activity patterns, these areas could impact future health status and thus should be important areas for health care providers to consider.

Morbidity and Mortality

In general, Hispanic adolescents are affected by similar chronic medical conditions, such as cardiovascular diseases, congenital anomalies, and central nervous system disorders, and experience them at comparable rates as their non-Hispanic peers, the one exception being mainland Puerto Rican children residing in New York (Mendoza et al., 1991). This group had a higher prevalence of chronic medical conditions than that of other Hispanic subgroups and for the national average. This difference may in part be accounted for by the high prevalence of asthma among mainland Puerto Rican children.

However, while the prevalence of chronic medical conditions are comparable to those of non-Hispanic children and adolescents, other conditions, such as sexually transmitted diseases, including HIV infection, is rapidly increasing among Hispanic adolescents. For example, rates of syphilis and gonorrhea among Hispanic adolescents and specifically among Hispanic males are higher than that for their non-Hispanic White peers (CDC, 1992). In relation to HIV infection, fast-growing rates are a problem among all adolescents. HIV-infected adolescents differ from adults in that adolescents are:

1. More likely to acquire HIV through heterosexual transmission;
2. More likely to be asymptomatic; and
3. More likely to be Black or Hispanic as compared with adults (Blair & Hein, 1994).

Similarly, Black and Hispanic adolescents are over represented among those with AIDS (CDC, 1991b). The primary mode for contracting AIDS among Hispanic females is through heterosexual contact with an infected partner, while for males homosexual/bisexual contact and intravenous drug use are the major modes of transmission (Gayle & D'Angelo, 1991; Holmes, Karon, & Kreiss, 1990).

While not immediately thought of as a morbidity factor, pregnancy affects both the growth and continued development of female adolescents. For example, young adolescents experience a maternal death rate 2.5 times greater than that of mothers ages 20 through 24 years of age (Morris, Warren, & Aral, 1993). In general, pregnancy rates are higher among Hispanic adolescents (13%) as compared with White adolescents (8%) (Alan Guttmacher Institute [AGI], 1994). However, there is much diversity in pregnancy rates and outcomes among Hispanic adolescents. For example, while pregnancy rates among Puerto Rican and Mexican-American adolescents are comparable, they are higher than rates among Cuban-American (Pletsch, 1990). In relation to live births, rates are highest among Puerto Ricans and again lowest among Cuban-Americans (NCHS, 1993).

Another important indicator of health is mortality data. Similar to all youth, the leading causes of death among Hispanic adolescents between the ages of 15 to 24 are accidents, homicides, suicides, and motor vehicle accidents (NCHS, 1993). Hispanic adolescents have rates similar to or below non-Hispanic Whites in relation to deaths resulting from accidents, suicides, and motor vehicle accidents. In relation to homicides, the rate among Hispanic youth (39.9/100,000) is nearly five times as high than that for non-Hispanic Whites (6.8/100,000) (NCHS, 1990). A health risk behavior associated with homicides is weapon possession. Hispanic and Black high school students were more likely to report having carried a weapon at least once in the last month than White peers (CDC, 1991c).

However, in relation to suicides, it is important to note that in a national sample of students in grades 9 through 12, Hispanic adolescents in general and Hispanic females specifically were more likely than Black or White adolescents to have reported at least one suicide attempt in the past year (CDC, 1991a). Because frequency of past attempts is a risk factor for suicide completion, suicide among Hispanic adolescents must be considered as an important issue.

Health Risk and Health Protective Behaviors

Genetic or physiological factors are not the major causes of morbidity and mortality among Hispanic youth. Rather, social, environmental, and behavioral factors must also be considered a high priority in promoting health among Hispanic adolescents. It becomes important then to examine both health risk and health protective behaviors, specifically as they relate to causes of morbidity and mortality among Hispanic adolescents.

For example, multiple sexual partners, intravenous drug use, early initiation of sexual behavior, and unprotected sex are risk behaviors associated with sexually transmitted diseases (including HIV/AIDS) and pregnancy. While only a few studies have examined the sexual behavior of Hispanic adolescents, several studies have found that Mexican-American female adolescents were found to initiate sexual activity later than non-Hispanic White groups (De Anda, Becerra, & Fielder, 1988) and at ages later than their male peers (Christopher, Johnson, & Roosa, 1993). Delaying sexual activity is a health protective behavior; however, specific health risk behaviors related to sexual behavior have been reported. Specifically among Hispanic adolescent females, low rates of contraceptive use have been documented (Hodges, Levy, Swift, & Gold, 1992; Norris & Ford, 1992; Padilla & Baird, 1991; Smith, McGill, & Wait, 1987). During 1983–1988, Hispanic (32%) and Black (58%) women were less likely to use contraception during their first reported premarital sexual intercourse than were White women (70%) (Mosher & McNally, 1991). Just as there is diversity among Hispanics in outcomes related to sexual behavior, there is also diversity in health behaviors. In one study, differential effects of birthplace among different groups of Hispanic adolescents in relation to HIV risk status (multiple sex partners, STD) were found. Adolescents born in Puerto Rico were at greater risk than non-U.S. born Hispanics; Hispanic adolescents born in the

United States were at increased risk as compared to those who were born outside the United States.

In relation to alcohol, cigarette, and marijuana, use rates among Hispanic youth sampled in the National Senior Survey (1980–1989) were higher among males than females, and lower than use rates among non-Hispanic White youth (Wallace & Bachman, 1993). However, Hispanic adolescents cannot be considered low risk based on findings from this survey. A major limitation of this study is that only persons in high school were surveyed. Given the high number of dropouts among Hispanics, the representativeness of this sample comes into question. However, despite these low documented rates of alcohol, cigarette, and marijuana use, Hispanic adolescents should not be omitted from prevention efforts. The use of these substances by Hispanic youth are more prevalent among Hispanics than are illicit substances. As in the instance of alcohol use, the transition from non-abusing behavior in adolescence to heavy use by Hispanics in adulthood is not clearly understood.

While illicit drug use, cocaine, and injecting drug use has been reported as low among all adolescents, it is highest among Hispanic youth (NCHS, 1993; Substance Abuse and Mental Health Services Administration [SAMSHA], 1993; Wallace & Bachman, 1993). As with risk behavior associated with sexual behavior, there is diversity among Hispanic adolescents as it relates to use of licit and illicit substances. In an analysis of data from the HHANES, reported drug and alcohol use among Mexican-Americans and Puerto Ricans were similar (25%), and higher than that for Cuban adolescents (16%) (Sokol-Katz & Ulbrich, 1992). Among Mexican-American and Puerto Rican youth, the proportion of persons reporting drug use was higher than those reporting alcohol use.

Several cultural factors, including gender-role expectations and *familism,* have been associated with both health risk and health protective behaviors. These factors can both aggravate and assuage situations leading to risk behavior. For example, among Hispanic females, the cultural values and expectations related to the role of women have been associated with higher rates of abstinence from alcohol (Rivas, 1987) and later initiation of sexual intercourse, particularly among Mexican-American adolescents (Hovell et al., 1994; Padilla & Baird, 1991). Further, the cultural value of *familism,* or importance of the family has been considered as a moderator of stressors confronted by adolescents and has been associated with a decreased influence by peers on certain risk taking behavior (Padilla & Baird, 1991). Hispanic adolescents express concern about how their behavior will affect their parents and siblings.

Conversely, these same cultural values and other behaviors believed to be common among Hispanic adolescents can also be considered as health risk factors. For example, the cultural imperative and desire to be a mother has been associated with higher birth and pregnancy rates among Hispanic adolescents (AGI, 1994; De Anda et al., 1988; Russell et al., 1993). The cultural value of *machismo* has also been associated with unprotected sexual behavior (Hodges et al., 1992), multiple sexual partners, and the tolerance of drinking among male adolescents (Beck & Bargman, 1993).

It is important to recognize that variation among and within Hispanic subgroups determines in part whether a behavior can be considered as risky or protective. An important factor that influences this variation is that of acculturation. It has been proposed that the longer the time spent by an individual in the host country, the more likely they are to adopt behaviors of the host country, and thereby diminish the influence of protective factors within their own culture. Similarly, as youth experience higher levels of acculturative stress, the more they are likely to engage in culture-based conflicts and behavioral expectations favoring experimentation with drugs and other risk behaviors (Vega et al., 1993). For example, in one study, Hispanic female adolescents who were acculturated significantly had engaged in intercourse at an earlier age than those who were less acculturated (Reynoso, Felice, & Shragg, 1993). In another study, acculturation scores were positively associated with smoking by Puerto Rican male, but not female students 14 to 20 years of age (Smith, McGraw, & Carillo, 1991). Higher acculturative level and English language use have also been associated with higher rates of alcohol, cigarette, and drug use among Cuban adolescents (Sokol-Katz & Ulbrich, 1992).

Thus it is important to recognize the diversity among and within Hispanic subgroups in relation to health behavior. Furthermore, it is important to understand the cultural context, that is, the cultural meaning and expectations associated with behavior. This is a critical factor in the design of culturally relevant health promotion programs.

Access to Health Care

In general, Hispanics and Hispanic adolescents face a barrage of financial, structural, and institutional barriers to primary and preventive health care services including, and most importantly, lack of health insurance. The rates of uninsured among adolescents is parallel to that of adults. Over one-third of Hispanic adolescents (32%) are uninsured as compared to non-Hispanic Black (21%) and non-Hispanic White (12%) adolescents (American Medical Association, 1991). In addition to the lack of employer-based or private insurance, Hispanics are less likely to receive public insurance, such as Medicaid. While in 1990 approximately 28% of Hispanics lived below the poverty level, only 18% received Medicaid benefits

(Bureau of the Census, 1991). In part, this low level of participation in public programs is due to the ineligibility of underemployed Hispanics for Medicaid benefits and also due to the fact that the majority of Hispanics live in states that have the most stringent Medicaid requirements (e.g., Texas, Florida). In addition, however, culture and linguistic barriers, discrimination, and the fear of deportation are other factors which influence the lack of participation of Hispanics in public insurance.

One consequence of the lack of insurance is that it acts as a barrier to health care for adolescents. This is reflected in low physician utilization rates for primary care services. In a secondary analysis of data from the National Health Interview Survey, insurance status, health status, and utilization of health services among 10- to 17-year-old White, Black, and Hispanic children and adolescents were examined (Lieu, Newacheck, & McManus, 1993). A higher proportion of Hispanics (28%) than Blacks (16%) and Whites (11%) were found to be uninsured. Using the number of school-loss days as an indicator of health status, Hispanic teens had the highest number of school-loss days (6.6 days per year) compared to Black (3.8 days per year) and White (5.2 days per year) teens. However, despite a higher number of school-loss days, Hispanic teens had significantly fewer physician contacts (1.7) for both routine (i.e., preventive) and sick (i.e., primary) care than did White (2.6) teens.

The fewer physician contacts by Hispanic adolescents reported in this study may also be related to the finding that Hispanic adolescents (19%) were significantly more likely to report that they had no usual source of sick health care. In this study, having insurance increased by 21% the chances of Hispanic students having a usual source of care. However, having insurance had less of an effect for Hispanics on having a source of care than it did for Hispanic adolescents. Thus an important finding from this study is that insurance reform alone is not sufficient to increase access to health care for Hispanic adolescents. In addition to considering access to primary health care, it is also important to consider access of Hispanic adolescents to mental health treatment and preventive services. No study was found in which utilization of mental health services by Hispanic adolescents was examined.

While there has been growing attention to preventive health care, the emphasis on health care services remains primarily on the treatment of disease. Thus, necessary preventive services for adolescents' mental health screening, STD, and family-planning counseling may not be reimbursable services. Second, while there has been a movement for the provision of school-based clinics as a means to make primary and preventive health care services more available to adolescents, many of these clinics are placed at the high school level. Given both the high and early drop-out rate among Hispanic adolescents, these initiatives may not be adequate to address the primary and preventive health care needs of Hispanic adolescents.

These financial, structural, and institutional barriers affect health promotion and prevention efforts and associated health outcomes for Hispanic adolescents. For example, access to family-planning, abortion services, and the use of contraception have been associated with differences in teenage pregnancy and birth rates by race and ethnicity (Mosher & McNally, 1991). For Hispanic adolescents, access to these and other primary, preventive, and mental health services is tied to cultural and linguistic barriers and the lack of physical availability of community-based services (COSSMHO, 1994).

Because of the multiple barriers that impede access to primary and preventive health care, the discussion and evaluation of both health risk and health protective behaviors of Hispanic adolescents must be considered in the context of access to health care services.

RECOMMENDATIONS FOR RESEARCH AND PRACTICE

From this profile of Hispanic adolescent health, it is clear that health promotion must be addressed within the context of poverty, limited access to health care, changing sociocultural norms, and other threats of the environment. Recommendations for policy and practice will be delineated.

As was stated previously, it is important that a more complete picture of Hispanic adolescent health be ascertained from current data systems and also future research. Given the diversity in health risks and health outcomes among Hispanic adolescents, it becomes necessary to include sufficient numbers of adolescents from different Hispanic subgroups in order to monitor health patterns and identify those who are most at risk. In addition to a profile of health, additional research is necessary to examine important questions such as: (1) to what extent do cultural values support or impede health protective behaviors? (2) how do factors such as acculturation and nativity influence health outcomes? (3) what are similarities and differences among Hispanic adolescent subgroups in relation to health risk and health protective behaviors? These questions are essential in order to design culturally effective health promotion activities.

Second, from this profile of Hispanic adolescent health and perhaps most importantly, from the voices of Hispanic adolescents and their families, the vulnerability of youth at this time should be recognized. High rates of poverty, school dropout, low access to primary and secondary health services place this group of youth at risk. However, it is equally important to recognize the strengths of this group. For example, despite being confronted with multiple risk factors, Hispanic adolescents fare as well as and sometimes better on a number of health indicators than their non-Hispanic peers.

Third, the design of primary and preventive health services for Hispanic adolescents must address the financial, structural, and institutional barriers to health care. The use of bilingual/bicultural providers, translators, community outreach, and peer educators are important strategies in order to establish confidence and trust for both Hispanic adolescents and their parents. Hispanic community-based organizations have incorporated many of these strategies in the delivery of health and social services and as such have played a critical role in prevention efforts in Hispanic communities. As expressed by an Hispanic mother:

> *My daughter says . . . "mom, I am so glad that I am coming to Latino Family Services because all of my friends are wearing colors. They are pregnant, they are doing drugs." I walked up to the library a couple of weeks ago. I saw all of my daughter's girlfriends outside smoking joints behind the library. (Villarruel, 1995)*

Partnerships with these established agencies would be useful in promoting Hispanic health among adolescents.

Fourth, cultural values must be incorporated in both individual and program strategies to promote safe sexual behavior. According to Marín (1993), components of culturally appropriate community interventions incorporate the following: (1) the intervention is based on the cultural values of the targeted group; (2) strategies that reflect the attitudes, expectancies, and norms regarding a particular behavior; and (3) the components that comprise the strategies reflect the behavioral preferences and expectations of group members. At a minimum, practitioners and educators should show respect for cultural values and practices held by Hispanic adolescents and parents. Making efforts to identify and understand values and beliefs of Latino adolescents and parents; acknowledging those beliefs and values as important; and attempting to find solutions or options within the cultural framework of adolescents and parents are a few examples that illustrate how respect can be communicated.

Consideration of Hispanic cultural values should also be given to program design. As an example, concepts of *machismo* can be integrated into programs related to conflict resolution and in promoting safer sexual programs. The values of courage and protection of others that are components of machismo can be used to support health protective actions such as walking away from a fight and in protecting a partner from pregnancy and sexually transmitted diseases. The *quinceñera,* an important rite of passage for Mexican-American female adolescents, may also be used as a strategy to promote the delay of sexual activity or as an opportunity to assist adolescents in developing skills to overcome sexual pressures. It is important that adolescents not just be imparted with knowledge, but also be assisted in the development of skills that are effective and congruent in the contexts in which they live.

Prevention efforts should include parents. Parents need not only to be informed, but supported in their efforts to provide an environment that will facilitate their adolescents' growth and development. One example of a successful program was directed at keeping adolescents in school. Both parents and teens attended similar classes and tutorial sessions. Parents were instructed on how to assist their sons and daughters and learned skills necessary for furthering their own education. Other specific strategies might be directed toward the facilitation of communication between parents and adolescents related to sensitive topics. Hispanic parents often express an interest in providing their adolescents with appropriate information; however, they also express concern as to how much and when they should know about certain issues, such as sex. Assistance in finding community-based services or other avenues in which their adolescent can be supported during this time is another strategy. Representatives of the Hispanic community, as well, including parents and adolescents, should be involved in the design of preventive efforts in order to ensure the cultural relevance of the program.

Finally, it is important to recognize that there are existing programs at both the national and community level that have been designed to address specific issues related to Hispanic adolescents (i.e., pregnancy and AIDS prevention; substance abuse prevention; stay in school initiatives). While few of these programs have been evaluated on a systematic basis, they are invaluable resources for the both the revision and design of similar preventive efforts. Sources are available that both identify and describe existing prevention programs (e.g., COSSMHO, 1993).

In summary, the challenges confronting Hispanic adolescents are both difficult and numerous. Researchers, practitioners, educators, parents, and adolescents must work together to develop culturally relevant and effective strategies to deal with these complex issues and to promote growth, development, health, and well-being. The hopes and dreams that these youth have can only be realized in this manner. Not only does their future depend on it, but our futures as well.

REFERENCES

Alan Guttmacher Institute [AGI]. (1994). *Sex and America's teenagers.* Washington, DC: The Allan Guttmacher Institute.

American Medical Association. (1991). *AMA profiles of adolescent health, Vol. 2.* AMA (No. OPO 18091).

Beck K. H., & Bergman, C. J. (1993). Investigating Hispanic adolescent involvement with alcohol: A focus group interview approach. *Health Education Research, 8*(2), 151-158.

Blair, J., & Hein, K. K. (1994). Public policy implications of HIV/AIDS in adolescents. *The Future of Children, 4*(3), 73-93.

Centers for Disease Control. (1991a). *The health of America's youth: Current trends in health status and health services.* Atlanta, GA.

Centers for Disease Control. (1991b). *HIV/AIDS surveillance: Year-end edition.* Atlanta, GA.

Centers for Disease Control. (1991c). Weapon-carrying among high school students—United States, 1990: Youth risk behavior surveillance system. *Morbidity and Mortality Weekly Report, 40*(40).

Centers for Disease Control. (1991d). Vigorous physical activity. *Morbidity and Mortality Weekly Report, 41*(3).

Centers for Disease Control. (1992). *Sexually transmitted disease surveillance. 1991.* Atlanta, GA.

Christopher, F. S., Johnson, D. C., & Roosa, M. W. (1993). Family, individual, and social correlates of early Hispanic adolescent sexual expression. *Journal of Sex Research, 30*(1), 54-61.

De Anda, D., Becerra, R. M., & Fielder, P. (1988). Sexuality, pregnancy, and motherhood among Mexican-American adolescents. *Journal of Adolescent Research, 3,* 403-411.

Delgado, J., & Estrada, L. (1993). Improving data collection strategies. *Public Health Reports, 108,* 540-545.

Fanelli-Kuczmarski, M., & Woteki, C. E. (1990). Monitoring the nutritional status of the Hispanic population: Selected findings for Mexican-Americans, Cubans, and Puerto Ricans. *Nutrition Today,* 6-11.

Gayle, J., Selik, R., & Chu, S. (1990). Surveillance for AIDS and HIV infection among Black and Hispanic children and women of childbearing age, 1981-1989. *Morbidity and Mortality Weekly Report, 40,* 41-44.

Hodges, B. C., Leavy, J., Swift, R., & Gold, R. S. (1992). Gender and ethnic differences in adolescents' attitudes toward condom use. *Journal of School Health, 62*(3), 103-106.

Holmes, K. G., Karon, J. M., & Kreiss, J. (1990). The increasing frequency of heterosexually acquired AIDS in the United States, 1983-1988. *American Journal of Public Health, 80,* 858-863.

Hovell, M., Blumberg, E., Atkins, C., Hofsetter, C. R., & Kreitner, S. (1994). Family influences on Latino and Anglo adolescents' sexual behavior. *Journal of Marriage and Family, 56,* 973-986.

Lieu, T. A., Newacheck, P. W., & McManus, M. A. (1993). Race, ethnicity, and access to ambulatory care among U.S. adolescents. *American Journal of Public Health, 83,* 960–965.

Marín, G. (1993). Defining culturally appropriate community interventions: Hispanics as a case study. *Journal of Community Psychololgy, 21,* 149–161.

Martorell, R., Mendoza, F. S., Baisden, K., & Pawson, I. (1994). Physical growth, sexual maturation, and obesity in Puerto Rican children. In G. Lamberty & C. G. Cole (Eds.), *Puerto Rican women and children: Issues in health, growth, and development* (pp. 119–136). New York: Plenum.

Martorell, R., Mendoza, F. S., & Castillo, R. O. (1989). Genetic and environmental determinants of growth of Mexican-Americans, *Pediatrics, 84,* 864–871.

Mendoza, F. S. (1994). The health of Latino children in the United States. *The Future of Children, 4*(3), 43–72.

Mendoza, F. S., Ventura, S. J., Saldivar, L., Baisden, K., & Martorell, R. (1993). The health of U. S. Hispanic children. In A. Furino (Ed.), *Health Policy and the Hispanic* (pp. 97–106). Boulder, CO: Westview Press.

Mendoza, F. S., Ventura, S. J., Valdez, R. B., Castillo, R. O., Salvidar, L. E., Baisden, K., & Martorell, R. (1991). Selected measures of health status for Mexican-American, mainland Puerto Rican, and Cuban-American children. *Journal of the American Medical Association, 265,* 227–232.

Morris, L., Warren, C. W., & Aral, S. O. (1993). Measuring adolescent sexual behaviors and related health outcomes. *Public Health Reports, 108 (Suppl. 1),* 31–35.

Mosher, W. D., & McNally J. W. (1991). Contraceptive use at first premarital intercourse: United States, 1965–1988. *Family Planning Perspectives, 23,* 108–116.

National Center for Health Statistics. (1985). *Plan and operation of the Hispanic health and nutrition examination survey, 1982–1984.* (DHHS Publication No. PHS 85-1321). Washington, DC: Government Printing Office.

National Center for Health Statistics. (1990). *Deaths of Hispanic origin, vital and health statistics,* Series 20, No. 18, December 1990.

National Center for Health Statistics. (1992). *Health, United States, 1992.* Hyattsville, MD: Public Health Service.

National Center for Health Statistics. (1993). Advance report of final natality statistics, 1991. *Monthly Vital Statistics Report, 41*(9) *(Suppl.)* Hyattsville, MD: Public Health Service.

National Coalition of Hispanic Health and Human Service Organizations [COSSMHO]. (1993). *Adolescent pregnancy prevention: Programs serving Hispanic communities.* Washington, DC: COSSMHO

National Coalition of Hispanic Health and Human Service Organizations [COSSMHO]. (1994). *Growing up Hispanic: A leadership report.* Washington, DC: COSSMHO.

Norris, A. E., & Ford, K. (1992). Beliefs about condoms and accessibility of condom intentions in Hispanic and African American youth. *Hispanic Journal of Behavioral Sciences, 14,* 373–382.

Padilla, A. M., & Baird, T. L. (1991). Mexican-American sexuality and sexual knowledge: An exploratory study. *Hispanic Journal of Behavioral Sciences, 13,* 95-104.

Pletsch, P. K. (1990). Hispanics: At risk for adolescent pregnancy? *Public Health Nursing, 7*(2), 105-110.

Recio Adrados, J. L. (1993). Acculturation: the broader view. Theoretical Framework of the acculturation scales. In M. R. De La Rosa & J. L. Recio Adrados (Eds.), *Drug abuse among minority youth: Advances in research methodology* (pp. 57-78). Rockville, MD: National Institute on Drug Abuse.

Reynoso, T. C., Felice, M. E., & Schragg, G. P. (1993). Does American acculturation affect outcome of Mexican-American teenage pregnancy? *Journal of Adolescent Health, 14*(4), 257-261.

Rivas, M. (1987). Similarities and differences in alcohol use and abuse among Hispanic and non-Hispanic drinkers. In M. Singer, L. Davison, & F. Yalin (Eds.), *Alcohol use and abuse among Hispanic adolescents, state of knowledge, state of need* (pp. 37-49). Hartford CT: Hispanic Health Council.

Russell, A. Y., Williams, M. S., Farr, P. A., Schwab, A. J., & Plattsmier, S. (1993). Patterns of contraceptive use and pregnancy among young Hispanic women on the Texas-Mexico border. *Journal of Adolescent Health, 14*(5), 373-379.

Smith, K. W., McGraw, S. A., & Carillo, J. E. (1991). Factors affecting cigarette smoking and intention to smoke among Puerto Rican-American high school students. *Hispanic Journal of Behavioral Sciences, 13,* 401-411.

Smith, P. B., McGill, L., & Wait, R. B. (1987). Hispanic adolescent conception and contraception profiles. A comparison. *Journal of Adolescent Health Care, 8*(4), 352-355.

Sokol-Katz, J. S., & Ulbrich, P. M. (1992). Family structure and adolescent risk-taking behavior: A comparison of Mexican, Cuban, and Puerto Rican Americans. *International Journal of the Addictions, 27,* 1197-1209.

Substance Abuse and Mental Health Services Administration. (1993). *1992 National Household Survey on Drug Abuse: Final Findings.* Washington, DC: U.S. Government Printing Office.

United States Bureau of the Census, Department of Commerce. (1991). *School enrollment, social and economic characteristics of students: 1990.* (Current Population Reports, Series P-20, No. 452). Washington, DC: U.S. Government Printing Office.

United States Bureau of the Census, Department of Commerce. (1993a). *Hispanic Americans Today.* (Current Population Reports, Population Characteristics, P23-183). Washington, DC: U.S. Government Printing Office.

United States Bureau of the Census, Department of Commerce. (1993b). *The Hispanic population in the U.S.: March 1992.* (Current Population Reports, Population Characteristics, P20-465).

United States Bureau of the Census, Department of Commerce. (1993c). *Poverty in the United States: 1992.* (Current Population Reports, Population Characteristics, P60-185).

United States Department of Education, National Center for Education Statistics. (1992). *The condition of education, 1992.* Washington, DC: U.S. Government Printing Office.

United States Department of Health and Human Services, Public Health Service. (1991). *Healthy people 2000: National health promotion and disease prevention objectives.* Washington, DC: U.S. Government Printing Office.

Vega, W. A., Zimmerman, R., Gil, A., Warheit, G. J., & Apospori, E. (1993). Acculturation strain theory: Its application in explaining drug use behavior among Cuban and other Hispanic youth. In M. R. De La Rosa & J. L. Recio Adrados (Eds.), *Drug abuse among minority youth: Advances in research methodology* (pp. 144-166). Rockville, MD: National Institute on Drug Abuse.

Villarruel, A. M. (1995). *Sexual behavior of Latina adolescents.* Unpublished raw data.

Wallace, J., & Bachman, J. G. (1993). Validity of self-reports in student based studies on minority populations: Issues and concerns. In M. R. De La Rosa & J. L. Recio Adrados (Eds.), *Drug abuse among minority youth: Advances in research methodology* (pp. 167-200). Rockville, MD: National Institute on Drug Abuse.

Wolf, A. M., Gortmaker, S. L., Cheung, L., Gray, H. M., Herzog, D. B., & Coldita, G. A. (1993). Activity, inactivity, and obesity: Racial, ethnic, and age differences among school girls. *American Journal of Public Health, 83,* 1625-1627.

CHAPTER FIVE

The Health of Puerto Ricans

Eugenia V. Pérez-Montijo, BSN, RN

Gloria E. Ortiz, EdD, RN

Elsie Méndez, MSN, RN

Alice Santiago, MSN, RN

The health problems of Puerto Ricans in the continental United States are intimately related to their health problems and general circumstances in their island of origin. In this chapter, we offer fellow nurses and health professionals in the United States an opportunity to understand this ethnic group so that they may be more empathetic to Puerto Rican clients' values, strengths, and their plight.

Initially, we assess this client noting two distinctions: *Puerto Ricans in Puerto Rico* and *Puerto Ricans in the United States.* The health status of Puerto Ricans on the island and an initial discussion of who they are and where they come from, historically and culturally, is provided.

In terms of the health situation of *Puerto Ricans in the United States,* we consider their migratory circumstances as the most important etiologic factor to their health status. Similarities, discrepancies, and relationships between the two groups of Puerto Ricans also became apparent.

Data analysis and diagnosis follow with a focus on collective *relocation stress syndrome* and *powerlessness.* Finally, suggested clinical interventions, as well as educational and professional strategies, show how nursing can make a difference in the lives of these two groups.

The authors gratefully acknowledge the assistance of Dr. Juan Flores, Director of El Centro de Estudios Puertorriqueños, Mr. Carlos Manzano of the Provost's Office and Desiree Ruz, student of Puerto Rican Studies, at Hunter College, CUNY. Thanks are also extended to *Niuyoricans* Mikey Rodríguez and Jenny Chicchelli for their most unselfish collaboration.

ASSESSMENT

Puerto Ricans in Puerto Rico

Over one-third of these Hispanic U.S. citizens—2.7 million—make up the second largest Hispanic group in the United States (12% of the total), spread out among the 50 United States. The other 3.8 million Puerto Ricans live in their island of origin. Ethnicity is based on language (Spanish) and culture; racial makeup is a mixture of European Caucasians (mostly Spanish), native *taíno* indians (long disappeared as a distinct group), and African slave descendants (who are mostly blended into the general population) (Commonwealth of Puerto Rico Office of Budget and Management, 1992; Institute of Puerto Rican Policy, 1994; Toro-Sugrañes, 1992; U.S. Public Health Service, 1990). Official languages are Spanish and English, but, "regardless of the law, less than a quarter of Puerto Ricans are completely bilingual" (Luxner, 1995, p. 15).

History. Puerto Rico is located in the Caribbean Sea, about 1,000 miles southeast of Miami and 500 miles north of Caracas, Venezuela. A Spanish colony for 400 years, the island is, since 1952, a *free associated state,* officially called a commonwealth, of the United States. Since 1898, when it was invaded by the United States during the Spanish-American War, Puerto Rico has been a U.S. "territory" for almost 100 years.

Puerto Ricans are U.S. citizens by birth since 1917 and bear U.S. passports. They elect their local government and participation in elections is strong. There is permanent debate on the status question, with statehood, commonwealth, and independence movements and sporadic outbursts of activism. Puerto Ricans do not vote in U.S. elections, but they have served in the U.S. armed forces since World War I (American Legion, 1995, cited in Reguero, 1995). "More Puerto Ricans died in Vietnam per-capita than soldiers from any state—all having been sent there by a president for whom none of them had voted. And in 1993, the first U.S. casualty in the war in Somalia was Puerto Rican" (Luxner, 1995, p. 14). In spite of this, benefits have been denied to Puerto Rican veterans although cases heard by the federal court have been awarded back payments of as much as $200,000 (Mulero, 1995c).

The island has a population density of 1,068 people per square mile, the tenth in rank worldwide. This concentration is higher in the cities, especially San Juan, the capital (Luxner, 1995, p. 14). While income is low, with an average of $6,300 a year, "people [still] enjoy the highest per-capita income in Latin America" but have to "make do with half the per-capita . . . of the poorest state, Mississipi" (p. 10). As a point of reference, the U.S. Public Health Service Office of Student Aid (1993) defined

$9,100-a-year for one person as low-income. The island is included in most federal educational and social service programs, though with special allocations lower than for the 50 states. Social program entitlements are sometimes applied as for any state of the union; sometimes they are applied with special restrictions or not applied at all; it is up to Congress or the U.S. Executive to decide on each occasion (lunch for school kids, for example, Mulero, 1995a).

Economy. Puerto Rico has the poorest economy within the United States. About three-fourths of the citizens depend on federal transfers for nutrition and social support. The economy relies principally on industry and business, a dramatic change from an agricultural base in the early decades of the century, which also forced the flow of population into the urban centers.

The island has modern business, tourism, education, and health facilities. There are also several active U.S. military bases. The currency is the U.S. dollar and it is the fifth largest United States market.

Residents of Puerto Rico pay local and Social Security taxes. Under a special code approved by Congress, some 2,000 American firms on the island are exempt from paying tax on profits, and account for almost 300,000 jobs. Environmental issues have brought fierce activism against U.S. companies and the military. Federal coasting laws also force Puerto Rico's imports and exports to be carried by expensive U.S. marine transport, taxing the island's economy and providing the United States with a yearly income above $300 million (Noriega, 1995).

Manufacturing jobs have grown little in the past 25 years and unemployment officially stands around 15%. The economy is a high-level one among the underdeveloped countries, but a very low-level one among the developed countries.

Culture. Puerto Rico is an Hispanic nation (Pérez, 1995). It has developed a rich culture of its own, being dominated by, but distant from, Spain. While other colonies obtained their independence, Puerto Rico obtained a short-lived autonomy in 1898 after a failed revolt. That same year the United States military took over the island.

In 1917, citizenship was "granted" to residents and all Puerto Ricans born thereafter. The U.S.-appointed government imposed an all-English school system.

Ironically, it was Puerto Rico's immigrants to the United States, especially in New York, who most preserved their traditions with music a significant source of celebrating and preserving ethnic pride (Glasser 1995a, 1995b).

Cultural identity has remained essentially the same, even though it has been greatly influenced by the United States during this century. Art has developed to a high level of sophistication. There are four university systems. Literacy is a high 92%; 33% of the population have completed high school and 8% have completed college (Millán-Pabón, 1995a). Education is conducted in Spanish.

There is racism, though more subtle than in the United States and other countries (Rivera de Ríos, 1995; Zenón, 1972). A disproportionate number of Black Puerto Ricans remain in the lower socioeconomic stratum.

Puerto Rico has enhanced its identity and relationship within the United States as well as internationally. Many entities, such as the American Medical Association, have a Puerto Rican chapter. There is also a Puerto Rican Olympic Committee.

Catholicism, brought by the Spanish *conquistadores,* inspired art, music, public festivities, celebrations, and literature. African and, to a lesser extent, Indian religious practices continue today. Recent literature continues to explore the relationship between religion and social forces.

Health. Puerto Rican residents have one of the highest health standards in Latin America. Their life expectancy, among the highest worldwide, is 75 years, slightly higher for women. They have a 19.5/1,000 birth rate. The population has a larger older component due to longer living, reduction in birth rate, and emigration of working age adults to the United States combined with a return of retired and aged people (Puerto Rico Planning Board, 1993).

Health problems greatly resemble those of highly developed nations. The general mortality rate is 7.4/1,000. Heart diseases (21.4%), malignant neoplasms (16%), diabetes mellitus (6.7%), HIV Infection (5.2%), cerebrovascular diseases (4.7%), and accidents (4.4%) are major causes of death. Hypertension and diabetes are among the most important factors in cardiovascular disease. There are close to 800,000 hypertensives and over 400,000 diabetics. Diabetes has gone from being the 17th cause of death in 1965 to the 3rd, and the first cause for nontraumatic amputations, blindness, and renal failure. Its prevalence was already 10.2% in 1986, with over 40% among the elderly. Traffic accidents are responsible for 17% of violent death, followed by 16% for homicide; suicide is the third. Infant mortality is 14%, down from over 50% in the 1950s (Pérez-Comas, 1993; Puerto Rico Department of Health [PRDH], 1992; Rodríguez, 1994; Toro-Sugrañes, 1992).

The major acute conditions (1.7 yearly conditions per person) are respiratory and infectious and parasitic diseases, with children younger than six the most affected group. The major chronic conditions (1.3 yearly conditions per person) involve the circulatory, respiratory, osteomuscular, and connective tissue systems with those 65 and older the most affected (PRDH, 1992). Obesity is a major problem—more among females—being addressed by health and legislative authorities (Reguero, 1995a, 1995b). Although smoking has been legally banned from public places, 28% of those 18 or younger smoke. Alcohol consumption has skyrocketed (66% of school age children); 13% have used "other drugs" (Fernández-Colón, 1995a). The use of toxic substances, which is of growing concern among all public and private entities (Martínez, 1995a, 1995b), is also closely related to traffic accidents and crime.

Single women, who represent 23% of all heads of household, are especially vulnerable to depression. They also are older, poorer, less educated, and living more in urban areas, and see themselves as less socially connected. Lifestyle-related problems are compounded by a 10.5% rate of functional illiteracy (Morales-Napoleoni, 1995). Women's health is further complicated by the generally authoritarian, male-oriented attitude toward women's health and social concerns, and rising rates of domestic violence. New, small, but very active groups and leaders are emerging to address these issues.

Mental health is recognized as a paramount health problem by itself and as the underlying cause of specific mortality and morbidity rates, such as homicides. Women who suffer mental health illness are especially discriminated against (Acevedo, 1995). Puerto Rico is lacking in professionals specializing in the mental health area, including nurses (Maldonado, 1995, cited in Millán-Pabón, 1995a).

In regards to AIDS:

> *In 1990, Puerto Rico had a higher incidence rate of AIDS among adult and adolescent males . . . and among women . . . than any of the 50 states in the United States Puerto Rican women have also had a higher proportion of AIDS cases caused by heterosexual transmission than any other race/ethnic female group in the United States. Moreover, the San Juan, Puerto Rico, metropolitan area had one of the highest AIDS incidence rates . . . compared to all U.S. metropolitan areas. (Menéndez, Blum, Singh, & Drucker, 1995, p. 15)*

Health Behavior. Puerto Ricans in general are sophisticated health consumers. Middle and upper income Puerto Ricans resemble U.S. citizens in their health behavior and consumer practices. They expect modern technology and highly trained physicians and staff. Most have private insurance for health coverage. There is a trend, which may reflect dissatisfaction with traditional medicine, to use alternative services and providers, such as chiropractic, massage, acupuncture, naturopathy and new-age, spiritual-religious, and self-help practices.

Lower income class members are less sophisticated but nevertheless acquainted with modern technology and health delivery systems. Many Puerto Ricans combine traditional natural indigenous practices and treatments such as herbs, teas, and treatments with plants. The services of *curanderos* (healers) have always been used. They prescribe natural, age-old homemade treatments and they manipulate body parts, in sprains, for instance.

There are also spiritual and religious healers; some from the African spiritual tradition, some from modern-day religious revival groups. These leaders and groups affect health perceptions and practices. Certain illnesses may be seen as caused by spiritual entities or causes, or as the outcome of sin. They are more common among the poor but they exist across social strata. Due to the influence of natural health tendencies, use of herbs and plants and self-help practices have grown in popularity and social acceptance, even though they have to be paid out-of-pocket.

Puerto Ricans of all classes tend to accept the patriarchal doctor figure. Doctor-shopping/hopping, the seeking of alternative medicine, and the attachment to the traditional healing approaches are a way of bypassing doctors' authoritarism and dissatisfaction with the system, without confrontation.

Health Resources and Services. Puerto Rico's Department of Health offers free service to all the medically indigent, such services being part of Puerto Rican life since the times of the Spanish-Catholic tradition. The philosophy of Puerto Rico's government is evident in the first draft of the Constitution's Section 20, which was eliminated by congressional mandate. It recognized the right:

> *of every person to enjoy an adequate level of life and to ensure for himself and for his family the health, the well being and especially the nutrition, the clothing, housing, medical assistance and necessary social services . . . to social protection in unemployment, in illness, in old life or disability . . . of every pregnant or lactating woman and . . . of every child, to receive special care and help . . . (Toro-Sugrañes, 1992, p. 179)*

Federal program funding, such as Medicare and Medicaid, apply to Puerto Rico with special lower allocation adjustments (Mulero, 1995a, 1995b; Romero-Barceló, 1995; Valdivia, 1995d, 1995f). U.S. federal jurisdiction is claimed on equal terms to the states in health as well as in other matters (Zayas-Torres, 1995a). Private insurance (a new concept that came with U.S. influence), facilities, and providers serve those with the ability to pay personally or through employment plans. In general, problems with the system reflect those in the United States—principally spiraling costs (Rivera-Marrero, 1995a, 1995c, 1995d). There is general agreement that there are two systems: a poor one for the poor, a not-so-poor one for the rest (Mayo-Santana, 1993; Puerto Rico College of Professional Nurses, 1993a; Puerto Rico Health Reform Committee, 1993; Rivera, 1993).

Correa de Jesús and Colón-Reyes (1991) state that the prevalent biomedical model of health denies existing relationships between individual and social health, and it does not take into consideration social, cultural, and economic factors that could affect health. Instead, it minimizes them as variables intervening in the process. In this biomedical model, the victim is often blamed for loss of health. The doctor-patient relationship is still traditionally authoritarian, requiring patient dependence. Psychological and emotional problems are treated separately and individually. In the disease process, the loss of autonomy is considered natural. People are apparently taught to accept whatever health care they receive without questioning its quality. There are also serious problems with compliance in treatment, especially among chronic hypertensives and diabetics—important factors in Puerto Ricans' health behavior patterns and contributive to rising costs. For instance, some practitioners have expressed concern over the rising numbers of diabetes-related amputations and there has been a sudden growth of the hemodialysis-related industry, mostly due to complicated diabetics.

Puerto Rico has 17.8 hospital beds per 10,000 persons (Toro-Sugrañes, 1992), similar to the United States. There are also three schools of medicine. All of these are accredited locally and by U.S. agencies and professional boards.

Malpractice insurance is compulsory for doctors. Nonetheless, a public entity had to be created because insurers had previously denied coverage due to high risks (Rivera-Marrero, 1995a).

Curanderos and *botánicas* (streetfront stores with a mixture of religious and traditional curative products) abound. Since nonmedical and alternative health service providers and literature have gained in acceptance and respectability, especially in the metropolitan urban areas, some controversy has begun to arise with the medical establishment. Some organizations are also offering women's health and social self-help assistance and support (Sloan-Altieri, 1995).

Nurses and Nursing. Puerto Rico has 34.6 RNs for each 10,000 persons, as compared to 83 for the United States (Puerto Rico Health Reform

Committee, 1993). Professional nurses are in great demand, and it is an occupational field expected to grow rapidly (De León, 1995). RNs are educated and licensed according to AD (associate), BSN (generalist), and MSN or higher (specialist) levels at institutions of higher learning since 1987 (Commonwealth of Puerto Rico, PL-9). There is no legal category for nurse practitioners (NPs) in Puerto Rico, although they are qualified as specialists. Nursing practice is essentially in bondage to physicians' orders within the traditional medical model. Generally, nurses appear to accept and support this model. Nonetheless, discussions continue to study nursing decision making across clinical settings in Puerto Rico.

With 15 baccalaureate, two masters' (MSN), and many associate and practical nursing programs in schools all over the island, educational resources are adequate. All schools must be accredited, with several accredited by NLN. Nursing education is conducted in Spanish. An all-English program will be offered at Inter-American University in San Juan, beginning fall 1995.

Nurses belong to a compulsory college and may not become members of the ANA (by ANA's disposition). Although there are small local chapters of the National League for Nursing and a few other U.S. nursing organizations, nurses in Puerto Rico—as a professional group—are essentially isolated from the United States, as well as from international organizations. There is no reciprocity of licensing with any state of the United States, and there is no direct reimbursement for nursing services. Nurses do take the U.S. NCLEX, offered by the Puerto Rico Board of Nurse Examiners. Some migrate, as other professionals do, looking for better living and/or working conditions. In fact, some institutions recruit nurses from Puerto Rico for work in the United States (Ortiz, 1989). Nurses working for the Department of Veterans Affairs may do so with their Puerto Rican license.

Back to the Future: Health Reform in Puerto Rico. Aimed principally at cost-containment and egalitarian health services, reform started in 1993 via elimination of public health facilities/providers and creating a government insurance entity to cover all the medically indigent who qualify under certain standards. This has created great controversy, but it is too soon for evaluation. Some issues related to nursing (home health, school nursing, nurse practitioners, direct reimbursement, etc.) have been left out with promises they would be taken care of with funds from reform pending in the United States. Puerto Rico may be substituting universal coverage for a *medigap* for those not poor enough to qualify for free insurance and those not able to buy it (Mayo-Santana, 1993; Puerto Rico College of Professional Nurses, 1993a, 1993b; Puerto Rico Health Reform Committee, 1993; Rivera, 1993; Rivera-Marrero, 1995d; Valdivia, 1995a, 1995b, 1995c, 1995e).

San Juan, the capital, has its own Department of Health and just started its own reform. It includes home health care and nursing clinics in a managed care model. However, according to local authorities, 30,000 potential buyers of insurance at a modest price were left out by the opposing party approving the reform plan (Blasor, 1995; Morales, 1995; San Juan Department of Health, 1995).

There is a growing gap between the haves and the have-nots with a large proportion of the population living in a socioeconomic limbo. Culturally speaking, Puerto Rico has more in common with Cuba, Venezuela, and the Dominican Republic than with the United States. From an economic perspective, however, it is almost completely tied to Washington. Dr. Pedro Cabán (1994) calls Puerto Rico "the United States' largest and most complex territorial possession," "a sophisticated society with a rich cultural history," and "a Latin American nation under the United States." Dr. Cabán states that "militarism, foreign capital, and dependence on federal transfers have coalesced to deform our society and transfigure our values" (p. 10).

The deformation of society referred to is reflected in the general health impairment of many Puerto Ricans, especially mental health, including use and abuse of toxic substances, related crime and injury, frustration and rage which bring traffic accidents, deaths, domestic and neighborhood violence, and cardiovascular and metabolic disease. The lesser educated, the women, and the poor—major victims of this system—are also the group which mostly immigrates to the United States, seeking opportunity in a country of which they are citizens and which, paradoxically, they can barely call their own.

Puerto Ricans in the United States

Migration. Puerto Ricans have been migrating to the United States mainly for economic reasons since the 1900s. By the middle of the twentieth century, a concentrated exodus began from the island. Although their migration has fluctuated, the flow has continued (Institute of Puerto Rican Policy, 1992). As a result, "by 1980, over 40% of the Puerto Ricans lived outside Puerto Rico, primarily on the U.S. mainland. Aldorondo (1990) projects that by the year 2000, 38.8% of Puerto Rico's population will have migrated to the mainland" (Rodríguez, 1994, p. 12).

The 1990 Census counted 2.7 million Puerto Ricans, the second largest group among Hispanics living on the U.S. mainland, close to 1% of the total United States and 12% of the total Latino population. Their birth rate is second among U.S. Hispanics, which are in general second only to Indian and Alaska natives (U.S. Public Health Service, 1989). Between 1980 and 1990, the Puerto Rican population in the United States grew by 32% (more than half a million) (Institute of Puerto Rican Policy, 1994a).

Puerto Ricans are heavily concentrated in New York (40%) and New Jersey (12%), but 9% are located in Florida; the remaining 40% are distributed among all the other states, mainly Illinois (Chicago) and Massachussetts (Boston-Cambridge). Even Hawaii, for instance, has a small but well-defined Puerto Rican community.

Recent trends in the increase of migration are better educated people—especially women—looking for job opportunities or professional development lacking on the island. Relocation is also changing from the traditional New York-New Jersey area to other areas of the United States.

Puerto Ricans in the United States are 52.5% female and have a median age of 27 years, very similar to the general Latino population and younger than the general non-Latino Whites (35.5 years median age). General demographic and social variables are likewise similar to those of other Hispanics.

In contrast to island residents, Puerto Rican participation in elections is regarded as poor. In fact, some U.S. residents travel to the island to cast their local vote whether they vote in the United States or not. The island commonwealth government sponsors the *Atrévete* campaign to engage Puerto Rican residents in the U.S. political process. It operates some offices in New York and Washington that deal with affairs of Puerto Rican residents in the mainland United States. Three U.S. Puerto Ricans have been elected to Congress and Puerto Rican politicians have been elected to local and state legislative bodies and serve on diverse types of boards in the United States.

In their effort to sustain identity, Puerto Ricans have retained essential elements of their homeland culture (e.g., the influence of religion in art) (Flores, 1995; Museo del Barrio, 1995). Community-wide visibility is also growing. Actors, writers, and community leaders have acquired national prominence. Jazz and Latin-sounding Puerto Rican musicians are well known in New York as well as internationally. Still, as with other Hispanic groups, it is said that Puerto Ricans lack focus and coherence as a community of U.S. citizens (Lopes, 1995). Pérez (1991) describes how in the early decades (around 1930s) of the *diaspora,* there were several organizations principally fighting for improvement of detrimental working, living, and health conditions, and against prejudice. These organizations gradually dwindled into oblivion.

There are now various organizations, from grassroots to academic/research centers, that address Puerto Rican needs and concerns (Cidoncha, 1995a). Some of them coalesce with larger Hispanic or Latino entities. In general, they seem to be small, somewhat scattered efforts. Recently, a Puerto Rican Studies Association was formed under the patronage of the

Institute of Puerto Rican Policy (IPR), an important research concern in New York. This new umbrella reunites college and university departments or centers of Puerto Rican studies nationwide. One of those, *El Centro de Estudios Puertorriqueños* (1995) at Hunter College, City University of New York, also conducts research on Puerto Rican issues, including the health of Puerto Ricans, and publishes a scholarly bulletin (Diálogo, 1993).

Socioeconomic Conditions. Half of Puerto Ricans in the United States are married and more than half have completed high school, 30% below non-Latino Whites (NLWs). Only 11% have post high-school education and only 8% have at least a bachelor's degree compared to 24% for NLWs. Homeowners are a low 13% (Institute of Puerto Rican Policy, 1994a, 1994b).

Puerto Rican participation in the labor force is 56% compared to 65% for NLWs; in both groups, males are employed 20% or more above females. Puerto Ricans have the lowest median household income for all Latinos and the highest poverty rates for persons and for families, these last being four times the percentages for NLWs. For instance, all Bronx, NYC, school districts have a higher percentage of poverty than the average for the state with the highest concentration (29%) of Puerto Ricans of all New York City boroughs (Cordero-Guzmán, 1995). Of all Latino firms in the United States (Institute of Puerto Rican Policy, 1987), Puerto Ricans have a small 6.5% share.

Puerto Ricans have a 60% rate of single female householders, 12% higher than for general Latinos, and 40% higher than for NLWs. Family size is about the same as for other Latinos, but only 23% of the families own a home, half as many for other Latinos and less than one-third as many for NLWs (Institute for Puerto Rican Policy, 1993, 1994b).

Health. "The health of the Puerto Rican community is in critical condition . . . data show (they) . . . are more likely to suffer acute ailments and to be hospitalized than White, Afro-American, Mexican, or Cuban Americans"; these words introduce El Centro de Estudios Puertorriqueños' (1991) special *Bulletin* issue on the health of Puerto Ricans (p. 4). The editorial adds: "This situation is not the result of mere happenstance but corresponds to the low socioeconomic position of Puerto Rican people in this country."

"The Hispanic health profile is marked by diversity" (U.S. Public Health Service, 1990, p. 34). In contrast with the fact that "Hispanics experience perhaps the most varied set of health issues facing a single minority population," data on Puerto Ricans are usually part of the general Hispanic population statistics, bypassing important differences. For instance, New York Puerto Ricans rate high in stroke whereas Mexican-Americans rate low.

There are marked differences in AIDS incidence and deaths among groups, but the government has been "talking about Hispanics as if they were an homogeneous group . . . dumping together different peoples from widely divergent regions . . . a simple fact of geography" (Culturelinc Corporation, 1988). Each Latin nation "has particular cultural characteristics, including diet, politics and rights, climate, degree of urbanization, etc."

Puerto Ricans share with Mexicans the lowest utilization rate of prenatal care and they also have an infant mortality rate higher than all Latinos, 12+ per 1,000 live births. Like Cuban Americans, teenagers 12 to 17 years old report higher rates of cocaine use than other minority groups. Puerto Ricans have the highest diabetes rate among Hispanics with a 13.2% prevalence among those living in New York in 1992 (Pérez-Comas, 1993; U.S. Public Health Service, 1990).

The *Healthy People 2000* (U.S. Public Health Service, 1990) document states that "barriers to care include language differences between Spanish-speaking patients and English-speaking health professionals, [and] logistical barriers posed by . . . costs of services" (p. 36). Its "Objectives Targeting Hispanics" include specific objectives for Puerto Ricans: reducing overweight to a prevalence of no more than 37% for women aged 20–74; infant mortality to no more than 8 per 1,000 live births; neonatal mortality to no more than 5.2 per 1,000 live births; postneonatal mortality to no more than 2.8 per 1,000 births; diabetes prevalence to no more than 49 per 1,000 (pp. 599–601). These targets point to the most pressing health issues affecting Puerto Ricans.

Eugenia Acuña-Lillo (1991), a health educator with the New York Department of Health, wrote about the reproductive health of Puerto Rican women. She quotes that "38% of all Puerto Rican women have been sterilized" and the proportion is the highest in the world (p. 29). "Puerto Rican women have a higher incidence of cervical cancer than any other group. . . . In New York, Puerto Rican women have a disproportionate share of teenage pregnancy, babies born with low birth-weight, and late or no prenatal care . . . and now . . . AIDS." She states that although Puerto Rican women have high rates of late or no prenatal care, for many, pregnancy will be the only time when they seek regular care, for the baby's sake—not for themselves (p. 33). Assessing prenatal care, she adds: "Social and emotional aspects, such as how she feels about her body, or about being pregnant are ignored. Most of the education is focused on 'pregnancy outcome'—the health of the baby—while the woman is treated as a receptacle" (p. 36).

Acuña-Lillo (1991) studied women's attitudes toward health, especially via her analysis of their socially assigned role as family caretaker. The

Puerto Rican woman is taught to think of everyone else before herself. The family, which for Puerto Ricans can be a very extended family, comes first; if there is time, she takes care of herself. Another contributing cultural perception is that Puerto Ricans may feel that the "doctor knows best." They have been taught to trust priests, ministers, teachers, and doctors—their authority is rarely questioned.

As in the island, Puerto Ricans in the United States use the services and products of *curanderos* and *botánicas.* This practice reflects tradition, established faith in alternative health care, and dissatisfaction with or inaccessibility to the health care system.

Lillian Martí (1991), a medical anthropologist who has researched teenage pregnancy in New York, analyzes that "there are serious misconceptions that influence public policy at the federal, state, and municipal levels" (p. 79). For example, the author gives a revealing cultural background on how "proper" or expected a teenage pregnancy and having large families may be. She also discusses the system's discouraging impersonal attitude.

Dr. Helen Rodríguez-Trías (1991) refers to the "diseases of oppression" of Puerto Ricans: "Diseases that are caused by social and economic inequities, and which are otherwise *preventable,*" she explains (p. 57). "If crack becomes epidemic because people are living in hotels where the crack dealers reign supreme," she points out, "that's totally preventable." Of the health system, she adds: "The notion that someone's going to pay attention to our health needs as such is misleading. That's not going to happen" (p. 58).

"In the case of AIDS," reports the U.S. Public Health Service (1990), "Hispanics' rate is nearly 3 times higher than for non-Hispanic whites with rates among Puerto Rican-born Hispanics as much as 7 times higher." "Puerto Ricans who immigrated to the mainland were experiencing higher AIDS rates in relation to all other foreign-born Hispanic groups . . . it also became manifest among Puerto Rico's resident population" (Menéndez et al., 1995, p. 15). Mortality rates were much higher among Puerto Rico-born male and female residents of New York City than for Puerto Rican residents and other Hispanic groups, sometimes 5 times the rate (pp. 15–16). Age-specific rate for those between 35–44 was 48%, followed by those between 25–34 years.

ANALYSIS AND DIAGNOSIS

In a review of recent journal entries (more than 400), the authors did not find literature that specifically addressed the Puerto Ricans' situation in the United States from the nursing perspective. Some references were obtained from the social sciences and psychology studies—some not too recent—at specialized centers cited in this work, and from U.S. government sources. For this attempt at assessment and diagnosis, the authors relied on general nursing and health literature.

Quo Vadis?

The health picture obtained for U.S. Puerto Ricans greatly resembles that of the island's residents in general, but problems seem to be more acute. This seems only logical if this immigrant group comes mainly from those on the island with the least favorable socioeconomic conditions and their related health problems, compounded by the immigration factor.

Puerto Ricans on the mainland have been in a most difficult and vulnerable economic situation. The experience of Puerto Rican migrants has been characterized by a succession of major social transformations such as industrialization, urban renewal, and other major economic changes, much like the thousands on the island who moved from the rural to metropolitan areas from which most of these immigrants come. With geographic mobility, as well, there comes severe disruption to existing, traditional social support systems, which when available serve to reduce the impact of stress. As a result, these transformations, whether beneficial or not, are doubly potential stress-inducers.

Increased rates of disease have also been associated with persons exposed to major social transformation (Canino, Earley, & Rogler, 1980). First-generation Puerto Rican migrants are, thus, at greater risks since they are compounding their potential source of stress through both social transformation experienced on the island and those experienced during and after migration.

Other sources of stress-inducing life events for Puerto Rican migrants besides social transformation include the need to learn a new language; the impact of bilingualism on information processing, memory, cognitive abilities, personality characteristics, and world view (prejudice and discrimination), adaptation to an impersonal, bureaucratized society, the demands of an agitated cycle of life; and the tribulations of daily interactions with persons outside the ethnic group. Not all Puerto Rican families are at equal risk nor will exposure to stress inevitably lead to pathological conditions. However, it is evident that Puerto Ricans are exposed to a variety of stress sources that can jeopardize their health, especially their mental health.

Relocation to a foreign land and cultural milieu, in spite of the *de jure* relationship to it, has constituted a major source of distress. Inability to healthfully cope with this reality compounded by structural biases has led to uneven social and health circumstances (Pérez, 1991; Zavala-Martínez, 1994).

Puerto Ricans have a higher rate of single women heading households than the general U.S. population. Their children are five times more likely to be poor, twice as likely to drop out of high school, and have a much higher probability of ending up in an orphanage or a penal institution. Their sons have a much higher probability of going to jail, being unemployed, and becoming indifferent to their own children in adulthood. Their daughters are three times as likely to become single adolescent mothers. This health problem is magnified by the established greater probability of premature or low-birth weight infants, regardless of income or social level (Douglas, 1995; Ward, 1995). The incidence of diabetes and hypertension is very high, with their devastating and costly consequences.

Among U.S. citizens 35 or older, Puerto Ricans rate the lowest in household income, in education, and in participation in the labor force, all widely used indicators of socioeconomic disadvantage. As Lamberty and García-Coll (1994) found: "The overall picture that emerges . . . is not a particularly enviable one. The worst maternal and child health. . . . This was expected, although not to the degree documented" (p. 10).

Diaspora and Alienation

Studies show that mental illness rates are higher among migrant groups than among nonmigrants, as measured by hospitalizations. Apparently, the transition from one society to another constitutes a major stress factor that leads to increased psychiatric hospitalization. Movement into new and unfamiliar environments increases susceptibility to psychological as well as physical problems. Since 1962, the Department of Health and Human Services has been operating migrant centers with a full range of services, including mental health, in 40 states and in Puerto Rico, especially for migrant and seasonal farmworkers (National Migrant Referral Project, 1989). In Puerto Rico, seven centers serve agricultural migrant and seasonal workers both working on farms in Puerto Rico and those returning from working on farms in the United States.

Many studies have examined the relationship between migration and mental illness. In the case of Puerto Rican migration, movement away from their place of origin will be felt as a loss which may lead to distress. Canino, Earley, and Rogler (1980) published a well-researched report and analysis on the subject. Rogler (cited in Canino et al., 1980) studied Puerto Rican migrants' view of their new life in the mainland. A majority evaluated their new situation as "better" in working conditions, opportunities for children, health care, and schooling. However, they evaluated the quality of life as "worse" regarding social contact, entertainment, way of life, neighborhood relations, and friendship. They longed for supportive social relations, the bond of primary-group contact, and a sense of communal living (*compadrazgo*) associated with life in Puerto Rico.

Puerto Ricans feel they must move to the mainland due to unsatisfactory employment opportunities on the island. However, this forced move becomes a source of extreme stress. The fact that they feel compelled to remain in the United States in spite of their longing for their homeland creates a sense of powerlessness that serves as an additional source of stress. Canino et al. (1980) suggest that social transformation increases psychological stress and vulnerability to illness, more so if it is an immediate change.

Despite the many variations that might exist among Puerto Rican families in terms of value and role behaviors, Puerto Rican families in general have been characterized by a strong patriarchal structure, where the man is recognized as the "authority" and breadwinner. This traditional role is undermined when families move to cities where there are high rates of male unemployment and the means of social support are more readily available to female single-parent families through Aid to Families with Dependent Children grants. This situation impacts children of both sexes, leading them to think that to be male is to be an authority with no economic potential and to be female is to be submissive but with financial alternatives. This conflict over sexually defined roles generates much stress for family members. The extent of change, quality of the new environment, and conditions related to the move are other variables affecting adjustments of Puerto Ricans (Canino et al., 1980).

Besides the external sources of change, Puerto Rican families also experience significant internal changes. Some of these internal changes affect secondary family functions, such as the transmission of family values and role behaviors. Here, discontinuity between the place of origin and destination puts the migrant family at a higher risk for mental health problems. When discontinuity has also been experienced for a prolonged time, traditional family values and role behaviors are made inappropriate by alternative social patterns from the area of destination. This family value conflict certainly places more stress on them.

A mental health profile of Puerto Rican children living in New York City showed that the rates of reported admission interviews for Puerto Rican and Black children are considerably higher than for those non-Hispanic White children. All three groups of children—White, Black, and Puerto Rican—reported similar problems of social performance in school, family, and social relations. However, Puerto Rican children demonstrated a higher frequency of symptoms in the categories of sleep disturbances, physical problems, inadequate intellectual development, problems with others in school, anxiety, fear, anger and belligerance, agitation and hyperactivity, and antisocial behavior.

Relocation Stress Syndrome and Powerlessness

Although Puerto Ricans in the United States recognize their political and legal rights by virtue of their citizenship, there is little true sense of belonging; there is a loss of identity. "Unfamiliar surroundings involving strange languages, customs, and modes of behavior are conducive to feelings of loneliness, isolation, and persecution on the part of the migrant" (Thomas & Lindenthal, 1989, cited in Louden, 1995). The authors have identified nonparticipative, behavioral patterns and cultural isolation, passed on to second and third generations, as individual/family/aggregate *relocation stress syndrome* (McFarland & McFarlane, 1993; Zavala-Martínez, 1994). Julia Bloch (1968, cited in Canino et al., 1980) stated: "Few escape the identity crisis that results from being in a society that depreciates their group" (p. 15).

The lack of identification and feelings of rejection have left Puerto Ricans in the United States with a perceived inability to pursue and reach higher levels of human dignity and accomplishment. The diagnosis of *powerlessness* is, hence, recognized as applicable to Puerto Rican individuals, families, and/or groups in their encounter with the U.S. society and with its health care system. Carpenito (1993) defines powerlessness as a "state in which an individual or group perceives a lack of personal control over certain events or situations which impact outlook, goals, and life-style" (p. 291). It is seen as related to a general and health system perceived as alien. The major defining characteristic of powerlessness is "overt or covert (anger, apathy) expressions of dissatisfaction over inability to control a situation (e.g., work, illness, prognosis, care, recovery rate) that is negatively impacting outlook, goals, and life-style" (ibid.). This characteristic is inferred from Puerto Ricans' health behavior and statistics indicative of dissatisfaction, rage, and self-destruction. Carpenito states that "a powerless person may see an alternative or answer to the problem, yet be unable to do anything about it because of perception of control and resources" (p. 592). This diagnosis may help explain, for example, poor educational outcomes and health behavior: "When an individual does not expect to be able to control outcomes, attention to and retention of information is poor" (p. 593).

Additional Inferences

In addition to the previous diagnoses discussed, the authors have made some additional diagnostic inferences which may be considered when caring for specific individuals, families, or groups. The major health problems of the Puerto Rican community have been identified. These tentative diagnoses have been categorized as potentially applicable to the Puerto Rican community as a collective client, to Puerto Rican families, or individuals, or to more than one of these three clients. They are presented in Table 5.1.

PLANNING AND INTERVENTION: NURSING CAN MAKE A DIFFERENCE

Planning and nursing interventions for *relocation stress syndrome* should be directed toward reducing anxiety, adjusting to changes, supporting clients through grieving, and increasing a sense of control. When the diagnosis of *relocation stress syndrome* is being considered, the nurse must make a culturally sensitive assessment. In order to do so, the nurse must receive special training to be sensitized. Such training, however, should include more than the study of cultural patterns, lifestyles, and Puerto Rican history (McFarland & McFarlane, 1993).

The preparation of the nurse who will care for Puerto Ricans in the United States must explore the impact of racism on the client and the nurse within the health care delivery system. It should also include an examination of the value system of the nurse and his or her Puerto Rican clients. The nurse should be sensitive to cultural and ethnic differences in matters such as child rearing, marital relations, interpersonal communication, sexuality, and recreation. Consideration must be given to other stressors brought about by the hospitalization experience, changes in health status and roles resulting from illness, alterations in cognitive functioning and degree of acculturation mastery. The coping capacity and adaptative needs of the Puerto Rican clients can be determined by interviewing at the time of admission to a facility or to a service. The nurse should gather information about the course of illness, emotional responses, and need for special support (e.g., language translator, bilingual staff, information written/said in Spanish when teaching). The patient and family perception about the move and changes in the environment are important pieces in determining the degree of disruption and vulnerability.

For the immigrant patient adjusting to a cultural move, admission to the hospital may heighten acculturation issues and relocation stress. The

Table 5.1 Additional Diagnostic Inferences

For the Puerto Rican community as an aggregate client:	*Ineffective community coping* ("pattern of community activities for adaptation and problem solving that is unsatisfactory for meeting the demands or needs of the community"). Defining characteristics that seem applicable: deficits of community participation, deficits in communication methods, excessive community conflicts, high illness rates, stressors perceived as excessive, expressed vulnerability (Gordon, 1995, p. 449).
For the Puerto Rican family/groups of families:	*Compromised family coping* ("usually supportive primary person providing insufficient, ineffective, or compromised support . . . to manage or master adaptive tasks" [p. 441).
	Disabling family coping ("behavior of significant person disables . . . own capacities . . . to effectively address tasks essential to adaptation" [p. 445).
	Impaired home maintenance management (mild, moderate, severe, chronic; "inability to independently maintain a safe, growth-promoting immediate environment" [Gordon, op. cit., p. 213).
For the Puerto Rican individual/family/group:	*Altered role performance* ("change, conflict . . . of role responsibilities or inability to perform role responsibilities [Ibid., p. 347).
	Support system deficit ("insufficient emotional and/or instrumental help from others" [p. 397).
	Spiritual distress ("a disruption in the life principle that pervades a persons entire being" [Gordon, op. cit., p. 455).
	Impaired social interaction ("insufficient or excessive quantity or ineffective quality of social exchange" [p. 357).
	Chronic low self-esteem ("long-standing negative self-evaluation about self or self-capabilities, which may be directly or indirectly expressed [p. 1329).

(Continued)

Table 5.1 *(Continued)*

For the caregiver (especially women and those who care for chronically ill elderly or AIDS clients):	*Risk for caregiver role strain* ("vulnerable for perceived difficulty in performing the family caregiver role" [p. 393).
For the diabetic individual/group:	Fear related to potential complications, insulin injections and the negative effect on life style. High risk for ineffective coping. Altered Nutrition. High risk for injury. High risk for altered sexuality patterns or function. Powerlessness related to the risk of complications. High risk for noncompliance related to complexity and chronicity of regimen . . . lack of knowledge (Carpenito, 1995, p. 137).
For the hypertensive individual/group:	High risk for noncompliance related to negative side effects of prescribed therapy versus the belief treatment is not needed without the presence of symptoms. High risk of ineffective management of therapeutic regimen related to lack of knowledge of condition, diet, restrictions, English, etc. (p. 84).
For clients with obesity:	Altered health maintenance related to imbalance between caloric intake and energy expenditure. Ineffective individual/group coping related to increased food consumption secondary to response to external stressors (Carpenito, p. 165).
For clients/family with AIDS:	Altered family processes related to the nature of AIDS, role disturbance, and uncertain future. High risk for infection transmission. High risk for ineffective management of therapeutic regimen related to insufficient knowledge of condition, medications, English language, etc. High risk for altered nutrition. High risk for ineffective individual/family coping. High risk for caregiver role strain related to shame/stigma, etc., and demands on caregiver (p. 370).

Table 5.1 *(Continued)*

For the alcohol consumer Puerto Rican individual/ group:	Ineffective coping: anger, dependence, or denial related to inability to constructively manage stressors without alcohol (p. 420).
For ill/hospitalized Puerto Rican clients:	Anxiety related to unfamiliar environment and routines, insufficient knowledge of English, condition, tests, treatments, surgery, etc., and loss of control (p. 768).

nurse should assess degree of acculturation and fluency with the English language, identify patient's beliefs about health and health practices, and social support that could promote comfort and culturally sensitive care.

For Puerto Rican children and adolescents affected by geographical mobility with their families, it is useful to assess the history of recent and multiple moves. The type, frequency, and significance of major attachment losses (e.g., siblings, biological parents, extended family, grandparents, neighbors, schoolmates, or pets) should be determined, as well as the developmental level of the child or adolescent for a better understanding of age, appropriate coping, and emotional expression of relocation stress.

Establishing a supportive relationship with the client experiencing relocation stress syndrome is essential to maintaining a sense of trust, continuity, and security. Allowing Puerto Rican clients/groups time to establish a relationship with the staff in the new setting would be helpful in reducing anxiety. If they are not fluent in English, orientation or teaching should be provided in Spanish. It is important to remember that anxiety will decrease the client's ability to learn new behaviors and coping skills.

When caring for clients/families coping with a loss or bereavement, the nurse must consider that the demands of resettlement may delay grieving or interfere with the process. Helping the Puerto Rican client identify these losses and stimulating verbalization of emotional discomfort promote coping and problem-solving abilities.

The *Puerto Rican Task Force Report* (Family Service Association of America, 1979) proposed an excellent "model for mental health services to the Puerto Rican community (in New York)" (p. 15). Its rationale is still valid and applicable to all health phenomena discussed. Nurses must work with interdisciplinary teams and strategies directed at helping to empower Puerto Ricans and to "address social issues like lack of food, jobs, housing" (Rodríguez-Trías, 1991).

"Not all Puerto Ricans need specially designed programs. There are and will continue to be clients who have a middle-class orientation and who seek agency services in the same manner as all other clients. They can easily maneuver the agency system and adapt to its formalities. They speak English well and can relate to treatment methods. . . . It should, however, be understood that no course of treatment with these clients will be complete without dealing with the identity issue."

Nursing should help U.S. residents/citizens of Puerto Rican descent realize they are part of U.S. society. Fortunately, in addition to NANDA's nursing diagnoses, advances in nursing science have developed the Nursing Interventions Classification (NIC) (Iowa Intervention Project, 1994, 1993, 1992; McCloskey & Bulechek, 1992), which identifies and delineates our discipline providing a practice-based guide for action. Interventions have been defined, described in terms of activities, categorized into dimensions and classes, and linked to NANDA diagnoses (Iowa Intervention Project, 1994, 1993, 1992; Tripp-Reimer, Woodworth, McCloskey, & Bulechek, 1994). These are powerful tools to be utilized when caring for these clients.

Table 5.2 presents principal and additional nursing interventions for the diagnoses identified in Puerto Ricans as an aggregate, as a group client. Likewise, they may be applied to Puerto Rican individuals and families. Table 5.3 presents selected additional interventions, as categorized by NIC, which may also be used to intervene with the individual, family/aggregate Puerto Rican clients, as other diagnoses are identified and dealt with.

There are examples of new, innovative and successful outreach programs/strategies to care for deprived community groups. For instance, the Clínica Sierra Vista Maternal Child Outreach Program has "dramatically reduced the disastrously high infant mortality rate among African Americans" (Comer, 1995, p. 18). Besides holistic nursing care, they effectively utilize trained community members to actually recruit women into the prenatal clinic. Nurses caring for Puerto Ricans must be aware of these projects and replicate and test them with these clients.

EVALUATION

Evaluation of clinical outcomes must be incorporated into the nursing plan of action. Periodic and systematic assessment of rates of prevalent conditions and diseases among Puerto Ricans are essential. The evaluation of outcomes related to the Puerto Rican clients' diagnoses should be validated with the client, client's family, special groups, or representatives.

Table 5.2 Suggested Nursing Interventions for the Selected Diagnoses

Diagnosis	Principal Interventions*	Additional Interventions*
Relocation Stress Syndrome (Physiological and/or psychological disturbances as a result of transfer from one environment to another)	Coping Enhancement Discharge Planning Hope Instillation Self-Responsibility Facilitation	Counseling Delirium Management Emotional Support Family Involvement Family Mobilization Family Support Mutual Goal Setting Patient Rights Protection Security Enhancement Sleep Enhancement Socialization Enhancement Spiritual Support Support System Enhancement Visitation Facilitation *Optional Interventions:* Activity Therapy Admission Care Animal Assisted Therapy Anticipatory Guidance Anxiety Reduction Art Therapy Humor Music Therapy Nutritional Monitoring Nutrition Therapy Presence Recreation Therapy Reminiscence Therapy Risk Identification Touch

(Continued)

Table 5.2 *(Continued)*

Diagnosis	Principal Interventions*	Additional Interventions*
Powerlessness (Perception that one's own action will not significantly affect an outcome; a perceived lack of control over a current situation or immediate happening.	Self-Esteem Enhancement Self-Responsibility Facilitation	Cognitive Restructuring Crisis Intervention Decision-Making Support Emotional Support Health System Guidance Learning Facilitation Mutual Goal Setting Presence Values Clarification *Optional Interventions:* Activity Therapy Anticipatory Guidance Anxiety Reduction Art Therapy Assertiveness Training Environmental Management Meditation Patient Contracting Progressive Muscle Relaxation Reminiscence Therapy Support Group Teaching: Individual/Group

*NIC provides definitions and activities for each intervention label.

Source: Iowa Intervention Project (1994, 1993, 1992), The University of Iowa, College of Nursing.

Special attention must be given to the measurement of the specific impact of individual nurses' interventions, as well as systematic nursing strategies. *Healthy People 2000* (U.S. Public Health Service, 1990) is an excellent reference for evaluation of outcomes. Successful interventions will be evidenced by clients' reduced problem/disease rates, social attachments and participation in activities, decision making, and performance of expected roles. Outcomes must also be measured in nursing

Table 5.3 Additional Suggested Nursing Interventions*

Domain	Class	Interventions**
Physiological: Basic—Care that supports functional health status	Nutrition Support: Interventions to facilitate change in nutritional habit patterns or provide methods for nutritional intake	Nutritional Counseling Teaching: Prescribed Diet Weight Reduction Assistance
	Self-Care Facilitation: Interventions to provide, facilitate or assist with routine, basic activities of daily living	Oral Health Maintenance Oral Health Promotion Oral Health Restoration
Physiological: Complex—Care that supports homeostatic regulation	Medication Management: Interventions to facilitate desired effects of pharmacologic agents	Medication Management Teaching: Prescribed Medication
Behavioral—Care that supports psychological functioning and facilitates life style changes	Behavior Therapy: Interventions to reinforce or promote desirable behaviors or alter undesirable behaviors	Behavior Management Behavior Modification Limit Setting Milieu Therapy Play Therapy Self-Modification Assistance Smoking Cessation Assistance Substance Use Prevention Substance Use Treatment
	Cognitive Therapy: Interventions to reinforce or promote desirable cognitive functioning or alter undesirable cognitive functioning	Anger Control Assistance Bibliotherapy Reality Orientation

(Continued)

Table 5.3 *(Continued)*

Domain	Class	Interventions**
	Communication Enhancement: Interventions to facilitate interaction with a patient who has difficulty delivering or receiving verbal or non-verbal messages	Communication Enhancement Music Therapy Play Therapy
	Coping Assistance: Interventions to assist another to build on own strengths, to adapt to a change in function or achieve a higher level of function	Role Enhancement Security Enhancement Self-Awareness Enhancement Sexual Counseling Spiritual Support Therapy Group Truth Telling
	Patient Education: Interventions to facilitate learning	Parent Education: Adolescent & Childbearing Family Teaching (in Spanish if necessary) individuals and groups about: Disease Process AIDS, cardiovascular disease, diabetes Prescribed Activity/ Exercise Prescribed Diet Prescribed Medication Procedure/Treatment Safe Sex
	Psychological Comfort Promotion: Interventions to promote comfort using psychological techniques	Anxiety Reduction Biofeedback Calming Technique Distraction Simple Guided Imagery Simple Relaxation Therapy

Table 5.3 *(Continued)*

Domain	Class	Interventions**
	Childbearing Care: Interventions to assist in understanding and coping with the psychological and physiological changes during the childbearing period	Anticipatory Guidance Birthing Bottle Feeding Childbirth Preparation Family Integrity Promotion Family Planning: Unplanned Pregnancy Genetic Counseling Infant Care Lactation Management Newborn Care Parent Education: Childbearing Family Postpartal Care Prenatal Care Risk Identification: Childbearing Family Teaching Infant Care
Family—Care that supports the family unit	Family Care: Interventions to facilitate family unit functioning and promote the health and welfare of family members	Caregiver Support (especially women) Family Integrity Promotion Family Process Maintenance Family Therapy Home Maintenance Assistance Parent Education: Adolescent Child Rearing Family Respite Care (especially women) Role Enhancement Sibling Support

(Continued)

Table 5.3 *(Continued)*

Domain	Class	Interventions**
Health System—Care that supports effective use of the health care delivery system	Health System Management: Interventions to enhance environmental support services for the delivery of care	Critical Path Development Examination Assistance Health Care Information Exchange (Spanish if necessary) Multidisciplinary Care Conference
	Health System Mediation: Interventions to facilitate the interface between patient/family (and aggregates) and the health care system	Culture Brokerage Patient (Family/Group) Rights Protection Referral Sustenance Support
Safety—Care that supports protection against harm	Crisis Management: Interventions to provide immediate, short term help in both psychological and physiological crises	Suicide Prevention Triage
	Risk Management: Interventions to initiate risk reduction activities and continue monitoring risks over time	Abuse Protection Environmental Management: Violence Prevention Health Screenings Infection Control Risk Identification Suicide Prevention Surveillance

* NIC provide definitions and specific activities for each intervention label.

** Interventions may be included in more than one class.

Source: Iowa University Nursing Interventions Project, 1993.

terms, evaluating the reduction/elimination of conditions which have served as cues for diagnosis.

A FINAL WORD

The use of nursing diagnoses and interventions offers the Puerto Rican client the opportunity to receive quality holistic services. Nonetheless, caution should be taken when applying them to this group. Expressions of health care, wellness, and illness have to be understood from the perspective of the individual Puerto Rican or group. "Nursing diagnoses . . . are used primarily on Anglo-American cultural values, norms, and standards" (Carpenito, 1993, p. 42). Nurses who care for Puerto Rican clients must examine if the diagnostic systems in use are relevant to Puerto Rican culture.

Since "research has found that there is a tremendous impact made when a Hispanic health care provider treats a Hispanic population," nursing service administrators serving Puerto Ricans must make deliberate efforts to recruit nurses from their community (Baye, 1995, p. 52). Also, since "there is still a very small number of Hispanic nurses," schools of nursing must encourage admissions of Puerto Rican students and help them through with their education. The severe shortage of nurses in Puerto Rico may mean that recruitment of student nurses within this group requires special approaches. Educators should also incorporate "social, cultural, and behavioral issues into the curriculum" (Rodríguez-Trías, 1991, p. 62). Partnerships and coalitions with agencies/institutions serving Puerto Ricans ought to be established. Arrangements for special care projects may also be carried out with Puerto Rican community groups, such as recommended at the U.S. Public Health Service Nursing Division's (1993) Invitational Congress on strategies for minority health issues. Nurse education administrators in areas of Puerto Rican concentration must procure faculty that may serve as role models (Coles, 1995, cited in Townes 1995). Researchers must identify and encourage validation of nursing diagnoses and nursing interventions with Puerto Rican clients. They may also offer tutoring/mentoring to engage more Puerto Rican nurses to pursue graduate studies and/or to study their group's concerns and effective approaches to care. Nurses, as a professional group, may support policies that enhance the well being and appropriate care of Puerto Rican clients, at the individual institution, as well as the larger community setting. They may also organize conferences/forums to address Puerto Rican health and nursing issues. Empowering Puerto Ricans using such a humanistic approach will lead to a positive outcome for clients, for nursing's mission, and for the betterment of the nation.

REFERENCES

Acevedo, C. E. (1995, July 12). The Department of Health accepts that it discriminates. San Juan: *El Nuevo Día,* p. 24.

Acuña-Lillo, E. (1991). The reproductive health of Latins in New York City: Make a difference at the individual level. *Bulletin, II*(4). New York: Centro de Estudios Puertorriqueños.

Aldorondo, E. (1990). *Profile of the Puerto Rican Community in the United States.* Commonwealth of Puerto Rico, Department of the Puerto Rican Community in the United States Affairs (abolished by the present pro-statehood island administration).

American Legion. (1995, May 29). In J. R. Reguero, Justice for Boricura Veterans, *El Nuevo Día,* p. 7. San Juan: El Nuevo Día.

Andreu-Cuevas, L. A. (1995, May 21). Navy denies Noriega's claims. In The Associated Press, *El Nuevo Día,* p. 17.

Baye, A. L. (1995). Managing minority healthcare. *Minority Nurse,* Winter–Spring 1993–94, pp. 52–53.

Bhatia, E. (1995, July 22). A culture of self-improvement and work. *El Nuevo Día: Perspective,* p. 66. San Juan.

Blasor, L. (1995, April 27). Acevedo health plan gets qualified OK: 30,000 slashed from program. In *The San Juan Star,* p. 2.

Cabán, P. (1994). In *The Plebiscite and the Diaspora,* Institute for Puerto Rican Policy Forum Proceedings. New York: Author.

Canino, I. A., Earley, B. F., & Rogler, L. H. (1980). *The Puerto Rican child in New York City: Stress and mental health.* Monograph Number Four. New York: Hispanic Research Center, Fordham University.

Carpenito, L. J. (1993). *Nursing Diagnosis.* 5th ed. Philadelphia: Lippincott.

Carpenito, L. J. (1995). *Nursing Care Plans & Documentation.* Philadelphia: Lippincott.

Centro de Estudios Puertorriqueños. (1991). *Bulletin. II*(4). New York: Author, Hunter College, CUNY.

Centro de Estudios Puertorriqueños. (1995). *Bulletin. VI*(1 & 2). New York: Hunter College, CUNY.

Cidoncha, I. (1995a, Mar. 6). Cultural link of those here with those there. San Juan: *El Nuevo Día,* pp. 46–47.

Cidoncha, I. (1995b, June 26). Looking for a future full of hope. San Juan: *El Nuevo Día,* pp. 52–53.

Cidoncha, I. (1995c, July 26). Cultural journals. San Juan: *El Nuevo Día,* p. 107.

Coles, A. B. (1995). A numbers game. In Glenn Townes (interview), *Minority Nurse,* Winter/Spring, pp. 39–41.

Colombani, J. (1995, May 14). Flamingo Beach closed for removal of explosives. San Juan: *El Nuevo Dia,* p. 16.

Comer, R. J. (1995). Caring on the mean streets. *Minority Nurse,* Winter/Spring 1994–95, pp. 18–21.

Commonwealth of Puerto Rico. (1987, October 11). *Public Law 9, Nurse Practice Act.*

Commonwealth of Puerto Rico, Office of Budget and Management. (1992). *Population Data by Municipality, 1990 Census.*

Cordero-Guzmán, H. L. (1995, June 30-July 6). Our Bronx. *Claridad,* p. 11. San Juan.

Correa de Jesús, N., & Colón-Reyes, L. (1991). Notes for the study of the health crisis in Puerto Rico. *Boletín, II*(4), pp. 63-70. New York: Centro de Estudios Puertorriqueños.

Coss, L. F. (1995, Feb.). Vieques belongs to us. In *Diálogo,* pp. 7-11. San Juan: University of Puerto Rico.

Culturelinc Corporation. (1988). *Cultural factors among Hispanics: Perception and prevention of HIV infection.* New York: AIDS Institute, NY State Department of Health.

De León, A. J. (1995, June 4). Employers have it their way. San Juan: *El Nuevo Día,* p. 6.

Diálogo. (1993). Alert to the Puerto Rican community. San Juan: University of Puerto Rico, Author.

Douglas, N. (1995, Apr. 24). In B. Vobejda Increase in number of women as heads of households (Report of Annie E. Casey Foundation). San Juan: *El Nuevo Día,* p. 40.

El Nuevo Día. (1995a, June 9). pp. 88-89. San Juan: Author.

El Nuevo Día. (1995b, June 9). pp. 90-91. San Juan: Author.

El Nuevo Día. (1995c, June 10). p. 25. San Juan: Author.

El Nuevo Día. (1995d, July 9). Specialized Employment. pp. 136-160. San Juan: Author.

El Nuevo Día. (1995e, July 12). Closer ties with the exterior. p. S-31. San Juan: Author.

El Nuevo Día. (1995f, July 12). Enterprise free of drugs and alcohol. p. S-31. San Juan: Author.

El Nuevo Día. (1995g, July 12). Referendum, yes or no? p. S-30. San Juan: Author.

El Nuevo Día. (1995h, July 12). The system ignores psychiatric female patients (editorial), p. 26.

El Nuevo Día. (1995i, July 20). Telecommunications (special supplement). San Juan: Author.

El Nuevo Día. (1995j, July 23). (Puerto Rico) National team to (head for) the Olympics. San Juan: Author.

Family Service Association of America. (1979). *Puerto Rican Task Force Report.* E. Mizlo (Ed), Project on ethnicity. New York.

Fernández-Colón, J. (1995a, May 7). Alarming alcohol consumption among minors. San Juan: *El Nuevo Día,* p. 17.

Fernández-Colón, J. (1995b, May 20). Nuclear experiments confirmed in local forests. San Juan: *El Nuevo Día,* p. 25.

Flores, J. (1995, Feb.). *Diálogo.* San Juan: University of Puerto Rico.

Glasser, R. (1995a, May 28). In Hernández, My Music is My Flag. Puerto Rican Musicians and their New York Communities, 1917-1940 (book review). *El Nuevo Día,* p. 22.

Glasser, R. (1995b, June 4). *Cubanacán* (radio program). Music & interview by Cristóbal Díaz-Ayala. Río Piedras, PR: WRTU-FM.

Gordon, M. (1995). *Manual of Nursing Diagnosis: 1995-1996.* St. Louis: Mosby.

Hernández, J. A. (1995, May 26-June 1). Dubious and risky function of the radar in Lajas. *Claridad*, p. 5.

Hernández-Hernández, J. (1995, July 12). Ours in Congress. San Juan: *El Nuevo Día,* p. S-18.

Homar, S. (1995, May). Julio Rivera, of Moca and New York. *Diálogo: Dance.* San Juan: University of Puerto Rico.

Institute of Puerto Rican Policy. (1987, Aug.). *Datanote,* Number 6. New York: Author.

Institute of Puerto Rican Policy. (1992, Oct.). *Datanote,* Number 12. New York: Author.

Institute of Puerto Rican Policy. (1993, April). Latino national political survey: Citizens vs. noncitizens. *Datanote,* Number 13. New York: Author.

Institute of Puerto Rican Policy. (1994a). *Latino population growth in the United States, 1980-90.*

Institute of Puerto Rican Policy. (1994b, June). *Datanote,* Number 16. New York: Author.

Iowa Intervention Project. (1992). *Nursing Interventions Classification (NIC): Taxonomy of Nursing Interventions.* The University of Iowa, College of Nursing.

Iowa Intervention Project. (1993). *NIC Interventions Linked to NANDA Diagnoses.* The University of Iowa, College of Nursing.

Iowa Intervention Project. (1994). *Nursing Interventions Classification (NIC).* J. C. McCloskey & G. M. Bulechek (Eds.), (list to be included in forthcoming 2nd. ed. in 1996). St. Louis: Mosby-Year Book.

Jordán-Molero, J. (1995, June 23-29). Mining exploitation: Beyond economics. *Claridad: In the nation.*

Lamberty, G., & García-Coll, C. (Eds). (1994). *Puerto Rico women and children: Issues in health, growth, and development.* New York: Plenum.

Lopes, T. (1995, April 16). Hispanics lack focus on Congress reforms. San Juan: *The San Juan Star,* p. 16.

Louden, D. M. (1995). Epidemiological findings in understanding mental illness in ethnic minorities: The case of schizophrenia. In R.W. Johnson (Ed.), *African American voices: African American health educators speak out,* Ch. 8. New York: NLN Press.

Luxner, L. (1995). *Insight Pocket Guide: Puerto Rico.* Boston: Houghton Mifflin.

Martí, L. (1991). Teen pregnancy propaganda and the Puerto Rican adolescent. *Bulletin, II*(4). New York: Centro de Estudios Puertorriqueños.

Martínez, A. (1995a, Mar. 5). The vice of greed. San Juan: *El Nuevo Día,* p. 6.

Martínez, A. (1995b, July 17). Proliferation of tricks to introduce drugs. *El Nuevo Día,* p. 17. San Juan.

Mayo-Santana, R. (1993, Oct.). Brief background of health reforms. *Diálogo,* p. 18. San Juan: University of Puerto Rico.

McCloskey, J. C., & Bulechek, G. M. (Eds.). (1992). *Nursing Interventions Classification.* St. Louis: Mosby.

McClintock, K. (1995, June 9). Opposition to radars in Lajas. *El Nuevo Día.* p. 16.

McFarland, G. K., & McFarlane, E. (1993). *Nursing Diagnosis and Intervention,* 2nd. ed. St. Louis: Mosby.

Menéndez, B., Blum, S., Singh, T. P., & Drucker, E. (1995). Puerto Ricans and AIDS: Research and Policy. In B. Vázquez (Ed), *Puerto Ricans and AIDS: It's time to act!, Bulletin, VI*(1 & 2). New York: Centro de Estudios Puertorriqueños.

Millán-Pabón, C. (1995a, June 4). Careers without a future. San Juan: *El Nuevo Día,* pp. 4-5.

Millán-Pabón, C. (1995b, June 8). Agriculture in peril if school lunch funds lack. San Juan: *El Nuevo Día,* p. 21.

Morales-Napoleoni, G. (1995, April-May). Alarming functional illiteracy. In *Interamericana,* p. 25. San Juan: Inter American University of Puerto Rico.

Morales, J. (1995). Presentation of the health reform plan for San Juan to the Board of Governors of the Puerto Rico College of Professional Nurses.

Mulero, L. (1995a, June 6). School lunch program funds in danger. *El Nuevo Día,* p. 16.

Mulero, L. (1995b, July 11). Medicare adjustments urged. San Juan: *El Nuevo Día,* p. 10.

Mulero, L. (1995c, July 23). Funds usurped from *boricua* veterans asked. San Juan: *El Nuevo Día,* p. 18.

Museo del Barrio (1995, June 23). From the *Barrio* Museum. *El Nuevo Día,* p. 80. San Juan.

National Migrant Referral Project, Inc. (1989). *Migrant Health Centers Referral Directory.* Austin, TX: Author.

Negrón-Negrón, A. (1995, May 7). In J. Fernández-Colón, Alarming alcohol consumption among minors. *El Nuevo Día,* p. 17.

Noriega, D. (1995, July 17). The hidden tax. San Juan: *El Nuevo Día: Perspective,* p. 39.

Ortiz, G. (1989). *Proposal: Baccalaureate degree program in sciences of nursing* (unpublished). Caguas, PR: Universidad del Turabo.

Pérez, L. N. (1995, June 30-July 6). Puerto Rico IS a nation. San Juan: *Claridad,* p. 10.

Pérez, N. (1991). A community at risk. *Bulletin, II*(4). New York: Centro de Estudios Puertorriqueños, pp. 16-27.

Pérez-Comas, A. (1993). Puerto Rico Report. San Juan: Puerto Rico Society of Endocrinology and Diabetology-handout.

Puerto Rico College of Professional Nurses. (1993a). *Presentation at Legislative Public Hearings on S400 on Health Reform* (unpublished). San Juan.

Puerto Rico College of Professional Nurses (PRCPN). (1993b). *Press Release: PRCPN opposed to health reform legislation.*

Puerto Rico Department of Health. (1992a, March). *Information Bulletin.* Series C-2, No. 16.

Puerto Rico Department of Health (1992b, March). *Information Bulletin.* Series C-2, No. 17.

Puerto Rico Department of Health (1992c). *Vital Statistics, 1992.*

Puerto Rico Department of Health. (1995, April 23). *AIDS Surveillance Report.*

Puerto Rico Health Reform Committee (1993). *Report to the Governor on Health Reform,* unpublished.

Puerto Rico Planning Board, Office of the Governor. (1993). *1990 Socioeconomic Indicators of the Aging Population.*

Ramos-Comas, A. (1995, June 8). United front in favor of 936 (special IRS code). San Juan: *El Nuevo Día.* p. 16.

Ramos-Mimoso, H. (1995, June 2). The Revolution of 1950. San Juan: *El Nuevo Día.* p. 71.

Reguero, J. R. (1995a, May 28). Bills on obesity to be considered. San Juan: *El Nuevo Día,* p. 26.

Reguero, J. R. (1995b, May 28). More 'fatties' in Puerto Rican population. San Juan: *El Nuevo Día,* p. 28.

Reguero, J. R. (1995c, July 19). To study radar project in depth. San Juan: *El Nuevo Día,* p. 32.

Rivera, O. (1993, Oct.). Reaction to *boricua* health plan. *Diálogo,* pp. 16–17. San Juan: University of Puerto Rico.

Rivera de Ríos, T. (1995, June 3). San Juan: *El Nuevo Día* (retort against Police Superintendent Toledo's comment on Dominicans and crime in San Juan).

Rivera-Marrero, M. (1995a, May 29). SIMED bled due to medical malpractice. San Juan: *El Nuevo Día,* p. 75.

Rivera-Marrero, M. (1995b, June 9). Agriculture declines. San Juan: *El Nuevo Día,* p. 14.

Rivera-Marrero, M. (1995c, June 10). Increase in medical insurance. San Juan: *El Nuevo Día,* p. 14.

Rivera-Marrero, M. (1995d, June 19). Chained future for hospital industry. San Juan: *El Nuevo Día: Business,* p. 83.

Rodríguez, C. (1994). A summary of Puerto Rican migration to the United States. In G. Lamberty & C. García-Coll (Eds.), *Puerto Rican Women and Children: Issues in health, growth and development.* New York: Plenum.

Rodríguez, J. (1994). *Demographic Data on Mortality and Morbidity due to Diabetes Mellitus in Puerto Rico.* San Juan: University of Puerto Rico Medical Sciences Campus, School of Public Health Department of Social Sciences.

Rodríguez-Trías, H., (1991). *Mi gente* (My people). *Bulletin, II*(4). New York: Centro de Estudios Puertorriqueños.

Romero-Barceló, C. (Puerto Rico's Resident Commissioner to Congress). (1995, June 5). In L. Blasor, (Ed.) Romero eyes parity in Medicare. San Juan: *The San Juan Star,* p. 3.

Romero-Barceló, C. (1995b, June 8). Romero firm on status debate. San Juan: *El Nuevo Día.* p. 16.

San Juan Department of Health. (1995). *Proposal for Health Reform in the Municipality of San Juan.* Unpublished document.

Schwartz, D. L. (1995, June 2). In Mulero, Pharmaceutical sector accused. San Juan: *El Nuevo Día.* p. 6.

Sloan-Altieri, A. (1995, July 26). Women and the law. San Juan: *El Nuevo Día,* p. 96.

Toro-Sugrañes, J. A. (1992). *Almanaque Puertorriqueño.* Río Piedras, Puerto Rico: Editorial Edil, Inc.

Tripp-Reimer, T., Woodworth, G., McCloskey, J. C., & Bulechek, G. (1994). *The dimensional structure of nursing interventions.* The University of Iowa College of Nursing.

U.S. Public Health Service, Centers for Disease Control. (1992). *Economic aspects of diabetes services and education.* Atlanta: National Center for Chronic Disease Prevention and Health Promotion, Division of Diabetes Translation.

U.S. Public Health Service, Health Resources & Services Administration, Bureau of Health Professions, Division of Student Assistance. (1993). *Program Guide, 1992–93: Scholarships for disadvantaged students, section 760, Public Health Service Act.*

U.S. Public Health Service, Health Resources & Services Administration, Bureau of Health Professions & Office of Minority Health. (1993). *Caring for the emerging majority: Empowering nurses through partnerships & coalitions* (Nurse leadership '93 Invitational Congress proceedings).

U.S. Public Health Service. (1990). *Healthy people 2000.*

U.S. Public Health Service, Health Resources & Services Administration, Bureau of Health Professions, Division of Disadvantaged Assistance. (1989). *Health status of minorities and low-income groups: Third edition.*

Valdivia, Y. (1995a, June 2). Reduction of services with health reform. San Juan: *El Nuevo Día,* p. 26.

Valdivia, Y. (1995b, June 6). Necessary measures in the Department Health. San Juan: *El Nuevo Día,* p. 12.

Valdivia, Y. (1995c, June 7). Complaints about the (medical) card. San Juan: *El Nuevo Día,* p. 16.

Valdivia, Y. (1995d, June 10). Medicare payments' budget increased. San Juan: *El Nuevo Día,* p. 16.

Valdivia, Y. (1995e, June 19). Health (Department) advised not to underestimate (reform) costs. San Juan: *El Nuevo Día,* p. 16.

Valdivia, Y. (1995f, July 26). Federal halt on health system privatization. San Juan: *El Nuevo Día,* p. 24.

Varela, L. R. (1995, July 23). Offended by treatment as a colony by the Navy. San Juan: *El Nuevo Día,* p. 12.

Ward, R. (1995, April 20). New England Journal of Medicine. In D. Q. Haney, Young mothers face double risk of premature births. *The San Juan Star,* April 27, 1995, p. 33.

WRTU, Universidad de Puerto Rico. (1995, June). Special program on black racism and discrimination.

Zavala-Martínez, I. (1994). Entremundos: The Psychological Dialectics of Puerto Rican Migration and Its Implications for Health. In G. Lamberty & C. García-Coll (Eds.), *Puerto Rican women and children: Issues in health, growth, and development,* Chapter 2. New York: Plenum.

Zayas-Torres, E. (1995a, Mar. 5). Sale of drugs by mail under judicial scrutiny. San Juan: *El Nuevo Día.*

Zayas-Torres, E. (1995b, May 3). Don Q rum readied for exportation. San Juan: *El Nuevo Día,* p. 141.

Zayas-Torres, E. (1995c, May 3). Knowledge and resources: Keys for exportation. San Juan: *El Nuevo Día,* p. 125.

Zenón, I. (1972). *Narciso descubre su trasero.* San Juan, Puerto Rico: Universidad de Puerto Rico.

CHAPTER SIX

The Aged Population in Puerto Rico: Its Characteristics, Present Health Status, and Health and Nursing Needs

Myrtha I. Díaz de Torres, MSN, RN

Puerto Rico is the smallest island of the Greater Antilles located in the Caribbean Sea. When Christopher Columbus discovered the island, Boriquén (its original name) was inhabited by several Indian groups, the largest of which were approximately 30,000 Taino Indians. As a consequence of battles between the Taino and the Spanish invaders, their numbers dwindled—and by 1582 they had almost disappeared. Thereafter, the population grew slowly and life expectancy was low due to unhealthy living conditions, poverty, lack of health education, high incidence of infectious diseases, and high rates of maternal and infant mortality.

Spectacular demographic changes have occurred in Puerto Rico during this century. With 953,000 habitants at the beginning of the century, by 1990 that number grew to 3,522,000, representing a ratio of 1.4% growth factor per year through 91 years. The greatest change has been in the 65-years-of-age and older population group, with an increase from 19,000 to 341,000 through those same 91 years. The rate of growth per year for this group has been 3.2%. Consequently, by the 1990 census, the 65-years-of-age and older group represented 9.7% of the total population of Puerto Rico while, in the 1899 census, it constituted only 2% of total population (Carnivali, 1992; U.S. Dept. of Commerce, 1990).

Various factors are responsible for the significant changes in the composition of the Puerto Rican population and for the dramatic increase in the aging group. Improvement in the health care system generally has been prominent here. A municipal health system provides primary and, in some cases, secondary care to people in each of the 78 towns that compose the Island. Secondary and tertiary care services are provided through eight regions. Both are organized with an island-wide referral and counter-referral system to the corresponding level of service.

Since the late 1950s, the Puerto Rico Health Department has been providing health care that is accessible and available to all people regardless of their ability to pay or if they possess health insurance. This has contributed, together with increased health education, sanitation, and increased nutrition factors, to significant reductions in rates of infectious diseases, diarrhea-enteritis, maternal and infants deaths, fertility rates, and death rates (Vázquez-Calzada & Carnivali, 1986).

Another very important factor that explains the significant increase in the aging population of Puerto Rico is the migratory status of its people (Carnivali, 1992). The migration stream to the United States began on a large scale during the 1940s, reached its peak in the 1950s, and extended well into the 1960s; eased in the 1970s, and spiked again in the 1980s. Migration activity has occurred mainly as a function of economic factors. It is the young and working groups that invariably travel to the mainland in search of jobs and better work opportunities, thus increasing the percentage representation of the aging population remaining on the Island.

The characteristics of the aging population in Puerto Rico reveals (Carnivali, 1992):

- The average life expectancy is 74.21, being higher for females and lower for males.
- The percentage of elders (9.7%) is lower than those of European countries and the United States and Canada, but significantly higher than those of Latin American countries.
- 54% are females.
- The predominant marital status of males in this age group is married (71%); while for females, it is widowed (46%).
- Nearly 80% of the elderly live in homes either with a family member or independently. Less than 2% are in institutional settings. This may be attributed to the strong sense of bonding and cohesiveness still prevailing in Puerto Rican families. The concept of extended family is maintained among many families. Grandparents are viewed as a source of emotional support within the family. Many are still exercising roles as caretakers for the children of families where both parents work.
- 51.2% of the males and 56.4% of the females in the 65–74 age group are below poverty level in terms of income. The situation is more

> critical for those 75-years-of-age and older (63% of the males and 62.4% of the females fall within that range). The average per capita income in Puerto Rico presently is slightly over $4,000; 58.9% of the general population are below the poverty level and 64% are considered medically indigent.

The first five causes of death in Puerto Rico in 1992 for the general population were heart diseases, malignant tumors, diabetes mellitus, acquired immunodeficiency disease (AIDS), and cerebrovascular conditions (CVA) (Saliceti et al.,1993). In the 65-years-of-age or older group, the first three account for the majority of deaths. However, CVAs represent the fourth cause up to 79-years-of-age. In people 80 years and over, pneumonia and influenza take the lead as the fourth cause. Chronic obstructive pulmonary disease (COPD) occupies the fifth place as cause of death of the 65-and-older age group until 79-years-of-age. Pneumonia occupies that position for the 80- to 84-years-of-age group, while diabetes mellitus does so for the 85-and-over-age group.

A Puerto Rico Department of Health (PRDH) morbidity report established that, while the rate of chronic diseases present in the population under 65-years-of-age was 225 per 1,000 persons, the 65-years-and-older age group rose to 318.8. The most common conditions present in the latter were reported as circulatory (78.4%), osteomuscular (55.2%), endocrine (25.2%), and digestive (21.8%). In terms of physical disabilities, the most prevalent were visual (22.2%), hearing impairment (10.1%), and absence or loss of a body part (7.8%). For their younger counterparts, the first two limitations differ significantly with only a 6.9 and a 2.2 ratio per 1,000 persons, respectively. The impairment related to visual deficit correlates with the fact that Puerto Ricans have a high incidence of diabetes mellitus (DM), approximately 13% in 1991. The relationship between DM and blindness was well-established in the Diabetes Control and Complications Trial (DCCT) carried out in the United States and Canada (Pérez-Comas, 1994). Another reason for the visual impairment in the Puerto Rican population is the high and continued exposure to solar rays in a tropical country with warm and sunny temperatures the year through.

Provided with adequate conditions, the aging population is capable of self-care, of maintaining functionality, and, thus, of fulfilling the developmental tasks of that stage of growth and development. It is nursing's responsibility to assist human beings to achieve the highest level of health of which they are capable. The application of Orem's Self-Care Theory (Orem, 1980) has proved its utility in working with aging populations in Puerto Rico. Since 1983, an assessment tool based on Orem's

Theory was developed to be applied in scenarios where the aged live by themselves (Torres, 1983). Thereafter, it has been used repeatedly, not only in those settings, but also with hospitalized and institutionalized aged individuals.

The Self-Care Assessment Tool for the Elderly (SCATE) has three parameters, namely: Universal Self-Care (USC), Developmental Self-Care (DSC), and Alterations in Health Status Self-Care (AHSSC). Each parameter contains indicators derived from Orem's proposed assessment areas. The categorization identifies each individual's potential to assume responsibility in the three areas.

The first parameter addresses oxygenation, nutrition, hydration, elimination (both urinary and intestinal), level of physical activity and exercise, sleep and rest pattern, circulation and neuromuscular status, skin integrity, ability to carry out activities of daily living (ADL), protection from physical and emotional harms, and sexuality. The second parameter which addresses developmental tasks explores the person's level of self-care in adjusting to physical changes, to a reduction or change in roles, to widowhood, to feeling useful. This area also includes items to assess: life satisfaction and life review, adequacy of self-image, and presence of a philosophy of life in which spiritual transcendence of life is acknowledged. Furthermore, this parameter assesses levels of interaction with primary and secondary groups and the balance between use of leisure time and loneliness. The third and last parameter explores the individual's knowledge about his or her health problems by including etiology, signs and symptoms, treatment, medications and their desired as well as untoward effects, and compliance with all aspects of treatment regime (including diet). The potential for self-care in this area is also assessed especially if the person needs to carry out specific activities on his or her behalf; adequacy of family or secondary group's support for physical, economic, psychologic, and social implications of his or her condition.

A scale was developed for the SCATE where 0 implies that the individual is capable of self-care in the specific area and only requires educational support to maintain his or her functionality. Another possible score is 1 in which the individual may have some deficit but with educational support and some nursing interventions is capable of self-care. A score of 2 indicates that the person's deficits are of a nature that require total nursing intervention.

After applying the SCATE, it is then necessary to determine each person's potential for self-care and the existing interferences. The causes must be specified, be it lack of knowledge, lack of skills, or attitude. Thereafter, nursing's efforts are geared to assist the aged person to participate actively in the search and implementation of strategies to conquer or reduce the deficit in an effort to maintain his or her functionality, independence, and self-esteem.

The SCATE was first utilized in 1983 with 11 persons of low income who attended a day-care center funded jointly by municipal and federal funds. In 1984, it was again applied to a group of 48 senior citizens in a similar day-care center. However, the economic level of this group was upper middle class. Both groups attended the center for socialization and nutrition purposes and spent approximately six to seven hours, five days a week there. The SCATE was most recently applied (1995) to a group of 52 senior citizens who resided in an elderly apartment housing facility for individuals capable of self-care. The results of application in the three instances have been similar. In the three groups, the largest number of participants who utilized the facility were widows with an average age of 70, most reported being Catholic, received their income from social security or other retirement funds and family support. Most knew how to read and write but few had formal education past junior high school. This finding is comparable to the general characteristics for this age group (Carnivali, 1992).

In regard to their ability for self-care, the results were compared with the previously established scale as follows (Torres, 1983):

0–0.55 Optimum potential for self-care. Requires only educational support.

0.56–1.25 Partial compensatory. Requires simple or minor nursing intervention or that of a substitute agent to assist the individual in self-care.

1.26–2.00 Total compensatory. Intense nursing intervention is required. There is a need to identify a substitute agent to satisfy the self-care needs of the individual either temporarily or permanently.

The following table depicts the findings for each group:

Comparison of the Averages for Self-Care Obtained by Persons 65 Years of Age and Older in Three Sites in Puerto Rico (1983–1995)

Group	Year	USC	DSC	AHSSC	X
1	1983	0.56	0.31	0.69	0.53
2	1984	0.14	0.07	0.16	0.12
3	1995	0.24	0.17	0.25	0.33

An analysis of the scores obtained by the three groups reflects that:

- All were capable of self-care either with educational support or minor nursing interventions. This correlates with findings regarding non-institutionalized elderly (U.S. Dept. of Commerce, 1990) in Puerto Rico that reported only 16.5% had difficulty with self-care.
- The group that evidenced scores needing more intervention was Group 1, which was also the group with the lowest income level. The most capable of self-care was Group 2 whose socioeconomic status was the highest of the three. This could probably correspond to availability of resources (economic and services) as well as a slightly higher level of education in the latter.
- The parameter that reflected most need for nursing intervention in the three groups was the AHSSC. This finding could imply that patient education by health care professionals is either not given, adequate strategies are not utilized for the education of this population, or not enough follow-up and reinforcement is provided to assist them in maintaining their adequacy as self-care agents. This finding could also be related to resources available to them for that purpose.

Although the averages for each item within the three parameters are not presented, the areas which revealed more deficit in USC were intestinal elimination, activity and exercise, sleeping patterns, circulatory status, and the special senses of sight and hearing. Chronic morbidity data for this group reported for 1988 indicated hearing and visual impairments as the two highest handicaps. The only area that fell under the category of partial compensatory was circulatory status. This could correlate with the high incidence of DM and cardiovascular conditions present in this age group in general.

The DSC parameter was, in all three groups, the most adequate. Nevertheless, some individuals expressed a sense of loneliness and inadequate use of leisure time. This could be explained by the observations made in all three sites in relation to insufficient occupational and recreational activities available to participants.

In the AHHSC, the most significant findings were lack of knowledge related to their multiple conditions and of the side effects of medications prescribed. This could be attributed to the factors mentioned previously in the analysis of this area.

The interventions and nursing diagnosis for individuals and groups in the three settings consisted mainly of education to increase self-care potential, especially in the management of chronic illness (DM and hypertension) and for the maintenance of functionality. To achieve the latter, participants were assisted in identifying alternatives to satisfy their activities of daily living. Consultation with or referral to other health professionals were sought as deemed necessary.

The recipients of nursing care expressed the need for having a qualified nurse available to them in the day-care center or living complex. However, health care was not the mission and objectives of any of the settings.

Based on the discussion related to Puerto Rico's aging population characteristics, present health status, and the data collected by intervening with groups who are capable of self-care, it is appropriate to consider the present and future implications of the gerontology field for nursing practice in this location. These encompass education, practice, and research components.

Since the aging population on the island will continue to increase, particularly those in the 75-and-older group, all nursing programs must incorporate gerontology and geriatric content. Furthermore, continued education and inservice activities must be provided to nurses who work in hospital, home care, and community settings. Both current students and practicing nurses must keep their knowledge and skills updated. It is of utmost importance to explore feelings and attitudes toward this age group as these affect the quality of care given.

Specific assessment and evaluation tools must be designed and utilized to identify each elderly person's strengths and weaknesses and their ability for self-care. Many such instruments are already available; however, they need to be tested as to their applicability and validity to this particular population.

The health care reform on the island is well under way. Although Puerto Ricans have virtually no problem with access to care, there is a need to improve its quality. Thus, the health care reform is geared toward having a uniform private system for the delivery of care instead of two parallel systems (one private and one public). The shift from curative to preventive care is important. These changes will definitely impact nursing as a whole and particularly on nurses' involvement in the care of special at-risk groups, one of which is the aged population. The scope of practice must necessarily include nurse-managed clinics to address wellness issues, as well as maintenance of persons with chronic illnesses free of complications stemming from lack of knowledge or ability for self-care.

CONCLUSION

Although the data presented regarding the ability for self-care from the three groups studied cannot be generalized for all of the Puerto Rican elderly population, it is suggestive of a tendency for their self-care potential. Demographic changes forecast that the percentage representation of this group will surpass the present 9.7% by far. Much of the care and education needed by this population is within the scope of nursing practice. Through education, service, and research, we can meet the challenge of assisting this important group in society to maintain their functional capacity and capability of self-care.

REFERENCES

Carnivali, J. (1992). *Demographic profile of the 65 years of age and older population of Puerto Rico: 1990.* (Unpublished). June, 1992; San Juan, PR.

Carnivali, J. (1993). *The 65 years and older population of Puerto Rico.* (Unpublished). Seminar on the Rights of the Elderly Population held at the Turabo University, Caguas, PR.

Orem, D. (1980). *Nursing: Concepts and practice.* 2nd ed., New York: McGraw-Hill.

Pérez-Comas, A., (Ed.). (1994). *Manual for the sixth course for diabetes educators.* San Juan, PR.

Saliceti, J., et al. (1993). *Statistics report of Puerto Rico health care agencies for 1991-92.* San Juan, PR: Puerto Rico Department of Health.

Saliceti, J., et al. (1993). *Preliminary 1992 selected statistics and demographic characteristics of the Puerto Rican population.* San Juan, PR: Puerto Rico Department of Health.

Torres, M. (Díaz de). (1983). *An assessment tool based on Dorothea Orem's self-care theory applied to the aged.* (Unpublished). San Juan, PR.

U.S. Department of Commerce. (1990). *Federal census of 1990;* General characteristics of the population of Puerto Rico.

Vázquez-Calzada, J., & Carnivali, J. (1986). *Sociodemographic profile of the aged in Puerto Rico.* (Unpublished). San Juan, PR.

CHAPTER SEVEN

The State of Hispanic Health: Cardiovascular Disease and Health

Teresa C. Juarbe, RN, PhD

Because cardiovascular disease (CVD) is the major cause of death in the United States and accounts for the majority of the deaths in minority populations (United States Department of Health and Human Services [USDHHS], 1986), there is increasing interest in the cardiovascular health of Hispanics. Despite this interest and the growing awareness of how CVD has impacted the health of Hispanics, efforts toward understanding this health issue are lacking.

This chapter has three purposes: (1) to provide information regarding the cardiovascular health of Hispanics in the United States, (2) to increase awareness and understanding of the sociocultural issues embedded in the promotion of heart health, and (3) to provide information that may improve the health care delivered by nurses and other health care professionals. In the first section, I discuss aspects related to CVD (Coronary heart disease, atherosclerosis), CVD and Hispanics, and CVD mortality among the Hispanic population in the United States. In the second section, I discuss the three major risk factors for CVD: hypertension (HTN), elevated serum cholesterol levels, and smoking. In the third section, I consider other significant predisposing risk factors for CVD in Hispanics, including diabetes, lack of exercise, and obesity. I conclude with a recognizance of the challenges regarding, and recommendations for, improving the heart health of Hispanics in the United States. We'll begin with two case studies.

Case Study

Mr. Rivera is a 53-year-old Cuban male, married, and an assistant in a small grocery store. He has high blood pressure, hyperlipidemia, and borderline diabetes. He was prescribed medical treatment and counseled to follow a heart healthy lifestyle. Over time none of the above were followed successfully. After a hypertensive crisis and hospitalization, Mr. Rivera's oldest daughter requested information about her father's condition and an appointment was set up with the family and the nurse educator.

After the meeting, they both found that: (1) some of the medications were not covered by the health insurance; (2) Mrs. Rivera was not informed about the dietary and lifestyle changes needed, because the information and counseling were given to her husband and the educational materials were in English; and (3) much of the information given to him was focused towards dietary patterns of another Hispanic subgroup.

After the meeting, a support system was created by the family to ensure the availability of financial resources for the medical treatment. With assistance of the nurse educator, the family negotiated for a medical treatment that was both effective and covered by medical insurance. Mr. and Mrs. Rivera then participated in a follow-up heart education program in Spanish. Their awareness and knowledge of risk factors improved. Mrs. Rivera was able to describe learning different ways to prepare meals and the reduction of sodium and fat intake in their diets. Mr. Rivera explained that the knowledge helped him, but that the greatest help was having support from his wife and family.

The Rivera family was able to develop strategies for those risk factors that could be changed by obtaining culturally relevant knowledge and awareness of the risk factors. Prudent dietary and lifestyle changes were accomplished with culturally sensitive methods and the involvement and support of the family.

Case Study

As part of a University health project, a community health assessment was conducted. Heart disease risk factors were found to be a significant health issue in this community in which 89% of the population was Hispanic. Project planning involved both Hispanic health care professionals in partnership with men and women from the community. The members of the project reviewed all aspects of the project including gender issues, Hispanic subgroups in the community, cultural values and beliefs, community resources, and educational materials. Other issues such as length of the program, attendance, evaluation, and outcomes were also addressed. Several community agencies and schools were informed and involved in the program.

The three largest Hispanic subgroups were targeted for the program, while aimed to reach families within specific communities, but considering each family member (children, men, and women) in the program. All project personnel were bilingual and bicultural. The materials used were assessed for cultural relevance and adequacy, in addition to psychometric properties. Issues regarding acculturation, education, language, cultural beliefs, and values were considered for the nutrition, fitness, and physical activity interventions plans.

The project had great community response and support, with receptivity and interest from individuals and families. The program was successful in many of its goals and provided information and grounds for further community-based assessment and interventions.

CARDIOVASCULAR HEART DISEASE AND HEALTH

Coronary Heart Disease and Atherosclerosis

Coronary heart disease (CHD) describes a disease of the heart caused by impaired coronary blood flow, and that can result in heart failure, myocardial infarction, angina, cardiac dysrhythmia, conduction defects, and sudden death. Most of the time its specific cause is atherosclerosis.

Atherosclerosis is a hardening of the arteries characterized by the formation of fatty tissue in artery linings, such as the aorta and the coronary and brain arteries. The condition is directly related to the onset of strokes and heart attacks. Atherosclerosis develops as a covert process, and its manifestations do not become evident for 20 to 40 years, or even longer.

There are many risk factors for the development of CVD. Heredity, gender, and age are among those risk factors that cannot be changed. Hypertension, smoking, and elevated blood cholesterol levels are major risk factors that can be changed. Contributing risk factors for the development of CVD include diabetes, lack of physical activity that promotes heart health, and obesity.

Cardiovascular Heart Disease and Hispanics

Heart disease is the leading cause of death in Hispanics (National Center for Health Statistics, 1987). Nonetheless, most relevant epidemiological studies have been done in the Hispanic population at large with partial or no information on Hispanics subgroups. Over the last decade, researchers have conducted large epidemiological studies, mostly with Mexican-Americans in Texas and California. These studies have used explanatory-predictive models suggesting that knowledge, education, attitude, self-efficacy, and acculturation are factors that may influence health behaviors.

A major deficiency in epidemiologic research on CVD in the United States is the limited, reliable information published about Hispanics. With the literature on prevalence and incidence incomplete and inconsistent (USDHHS, 1986), large epidemiological studies related to CVD and its risk factors have also included only a small number of Hispanic respondents, most of whom are Mexican-Americans. *Hispanic* itself has been inconsistent and unclear, creating unreliable statistics and other findings. For example, population-based studies often include many Hispanic-origin participants under the category of White, Black, or "other," or they do not include Hispanics because of uncommon surnames, limiting the reliable information available about CVD in Hispanics in the United States.

Studies of CVD and its risk factors in Hispanics have been conducted mainly in Texas among Mexican-Americans (Reichley, 1984; Stern et al., 1975; Stern & Gaskill, 1978; Stern et al., 1981a., 1981b; 1982; Stern et al. 1984) as this group represented 92% of the Hispanic population in that state during the period over which the studies were conducted (U.S. Bureau of the Census, 1986). A review done by the USDHHS (1986) of recent studies among Hispanics with CVD showed that with respect to hypertension and CVD risk factors, Hispanics have poorer understanding, less information, and more dangerous misconceptions than do Anglo-Americans.

Cardiovascular Disease Mortality

Although CVD is one of the leading causes of death, the incidence of CVD in Hispanics is less than among non-Hispanic populations (Friis, Nanjundappa, Prendergast, & Welsh, 1981; Schoen & Nelson, 1981; Stern & Gaskill, 1978). Despite extensive studies during the last decade, we lack knowledge about the incidence, prevalence, and mortality of CVD in Hispanics. A review of the mortality data available since 1950 demonstrated that Hispanic men and women had lower life expectancy and higher age-adjusted mortality than Anglo-Americans (Roberts & Askew, 1972). A classical and earlier study from Ellis (cited in Markides & Coreil, 1986) showed that Hispanics had slightly lower rates of CVD mortality than other non-Hispanic populations, but that Hispanic women had higher mortality rates than other non-Hispanic females. Similarly, Roșenwaike (1987) found that the incidence of CVD age-adjusted death among Cuban, Puerto Rican, and Mexican-Americans between 1979 and 1981 was lower than that of Anglo-Americans. Over the 30-year period between 1950 and 1980, Hispanics have shown a decline in mortality rates related to CVD (Becker, Wiggins, Key, & Samet, 1988). However, the Stern and Gaskill (1978) study of the secular trends in ischemic CVD mortality of people in Bexar County, Texas, from 1970 to 1976 found that the mortality rates from ischemic heart disease continued to decline for Anglo-American men and women, whereas for chronic ischemic heart disease, it declined only for Hispanic women.

Overall, the data that exist for Hispanics in the United States indicate that Hispanics have a lower mortality rate from CVD than do Anglo-Americans. Nevertheless, that limited mortality information shows that CVD is by far the leading cause of death among Hispanics in the United States.

MAJOR RISK FACTORS FOR CARDIOVASCULAR DISEASE

Hypertension

Hypertension (HTN) is one of three major risk factors for CVD, and it is "the major risk factor for premature death and disability from CVD, cerebral and renal disease" (Perloff, 1989, p. 207). It is estimated that over 62 million Americans have HTN; its prevalence is higher in Black than in any other subgroup, and it is higher in men than in women. HTN is a major cause of stroke and the third most frequent cause of death and disability in adult Hispanics in Mexico and South America (Yatsu, 1991).

Due to the prevalence of obesity among Hispanics, particularly Mexican-Americans (Stern et al., 1981a; Stern, Gaskill, Hazuda, Gardner, & Haffner, 1983), many health care professionals initially theorized that Hispanics would have a higher prevalence of HTN than Anglos. However, studies have shown that in general, the prevalence of HTN among Hispanic men and women is comparable to that of Anglo-Americans (Burchfiel et al., 1990; Franco et al., 1985; Stern et al., 1981). A more recent study of Hispanics in Brooks County, Texas (Webber et al., 1991), found that levels of blood pressure among the three groups studied were comparable to those of the Anglo-American population.

A more ambitious analysis of blood pressure levels in Mexican-Americans was conducted by Sorel, Ragland, and Syme (1991), who assessed the Second National Health and Nutrition Examination Survey and the

Hispanic Health and Nutrition Examination Survey (HHANES). These authors also found that blood pressure levels and HTN prevalence among Mexican-Americans were lower than in the Anglo-American and Black populations studied.

Although many studies have assessed the association of genetic influence, socioeconomic status (SES), education, employment, and acculturation with hypertension, they have reached inconclusive results. With exception of Ailinger (1982), who found Hispanics to have adequate knowledge of HTN and the risk factors for CVD, the only common factor among the different Hispanic subgroups is a lack of awareness, knowledge, and control of hypertension. Knowledge of risk factors and treatment was adequate.

Serum Cholesterol Levels

A person's level of serum cholesterol is affected by age, diet, exercise, and heredity. An elevated cholesterol level increases the risk of CVD; for example, levels above 240 mg/dl double the risk of CVD. The "Expert Panel on Detection, Evaluation, and Treatment of High Blood Cholesterol in Adults" (National Institutes of Health, 1989) suggests that the desirable blood cholesterol level should be less than 200 mg/dl. Levels higher than that require intervention from health care practitioners.

An early study of Mexican-Americans and other Whites in Northern California (Stern et al., 1982) found that while Hispanic men have cholesterol levels similar to those of Anglo men, Mexican-American women have somewhat lower levels than Anglo-American men and women. These results are similar to those of the Orange county study (Friis et al., 1981), the San Antonio Heart Study (Stern, Rosenthal, Haffner, Hazuda, & Franco, 1984), and the Laredo study (Stern et al., 1981). However, the San Luis Valley diabetes study (Burchfiel et al., 1990) reported that the Hispanic women studied had slightly higher total serum cholesterol levels than the Anglo women. Unfortunately, this study identified no subgroup for the Hispanics involved, which could have differed in many of the key sociocultural factors, including acculturation levels.

There is some disagreement in the literature regarding the dietary patterns of Hispanics and the influence of those patterns in serum cholesterol levels. Lack of knowledge regarding diets that are low in cholesterol and/or saturated fats has been mentioned as one factor that affects the serum cholesterol levels of Hispanics. Stern (American Heart Association, 1987), who described and compared diet, lifestyle, and heart health of Mexican-Americans and Anglo-Americans, said that while being Hispanic does not mean that a person will necessarily get heart disease, group knowledge about the risk factors and the need for lowering them does lag.

Other researchers (Ramírez, Herrick, & Weaver, 1981) have found that a substantial portion of the Mexican-American community lacks the fundamental knowledge necessary for adopting risk-reducing behaviors, such as following a heart healthy diet. It seems from most studies that Hispanics eat more meat and saturated fat than do Anglo-Americans (Stern et al., 1975) and that they are less likely to recognize dietary sources of cholesterol (Knapp, Hazuda, Haffner, Young, & Stern, 1988).

The HHANES (see Chapter 2), one of the most recent health analyses among Hispanics, provided data showing that Mexican-Americans had higher levels of elevated serum cholesterol than Cubans and Puerto Ricans. The only exception was among Puerto Rican women, who had higher cholesterol levels than Mexican-American women and men.

The challenge posed by elevated levels of serum cholesterol extends beyond problems associated with adult Hispanics. Because of findings of higher levels of low density lipoprotein (LDL) cholesterol and triglycerides among Hispanic children, some scientists are becoming more involved in looking at dietary patterns since childhood (Webber et al., 1991). Elevated levels of serum cholesterol in childhood are of concern since the risk may continue to be present into adulthood. In addition, their dietary pattern might be related to the tendency of Mexican-American children to be shorter but fatter and heavier than other groups of the same SES (Baumgartner et al., 1990; Ryan, Martínez, & Roche, 1990; Ryan et al., 1990).

Overall, the serum cholesterol levels of Hispanic men and women are lower than or similar to those of other groups studied (Stern et al., 1981, 1987). Further studies should assess the cholesterol-avoidance behaviors of different subgroups of Hispanics. The understanding of these nutritional behaviors might assist Hispanics in modifying eating patterns that lead to high levels of serum cholesterol and triglycerides.

As is true with hypertension, SES, education, acculturation, and gender are also strongly associated with the behavioral avoidance of cholesterol. It has been noted that with rising SES, higher education, and acculturation, there are differences in the overall cholesterol-avoidance behaviors of Hispanics. While SES has been seen as an important factor in cholesterol dietary knowledge, it is not as significant as some have predicted (Hazuda et al., 1984). On the other hand, because it has been able to explain more CVD-related behaviors than SES alone, acculturation might be the strongest predictor of diet-related knowledge in Mexican-Americans (Atkins et al., 1987). In addition, since most studies report that "men lag behind women in making prudent dietary and lifestyle changes" (Knapp et al., 1988, p. 175), it is important to consider gender differences in the development of community intervention programs that are focused toward the reduction of cholesterol intake.

Smoking

It is widely known that smoking carries severe and detrimental consequences for one's health, such as bronchitis, emphysema, CVD, and lung cancer. For many years, it was believed that the smoking habits and patterns of Hispanic men and women were the cause of their higher risk levels for many diseases, such as those mentioned above. However, a literature review in this area demonstrates that Hispanic men and women smoke less than Anglo men and women do.

Cigarette smoking patterns of Hispanics have been assessed in several studies in Texas, New Mexico, and California (Haynes et al., 1990; Holck, Warren, Rochat, & Smith, 1982; Humble, Samet, Pathak, & Skipper, 1985; Marcus & Crane, 1985; Marín, VanOss-Marín, & Pérez-Stable, 1986; Stern et al., 1975). Most studies arrived at the same conclusion: Hispanic women, whether Mexican, U.S.-born Hispanic, or other Hispanic, smoke fewer cigarettes than do Hispanic men, and Anglo men and women. The lower prevalence of smoking among Hispanics at large has been attributed to the lower prevalence of smoking among Hispanic women.

Results from the HHANES demonstrate significant differences in the patterns of cigarette smoking of Cuban, Mexican-American, and Puerto Rican men and women (Haynes et al., 1990). Puerto Rican women were found to smoke more than the Cuban women, and the Cuban women more than the Mexican-Americans. There was special concern about the smoking rate for Puerto Rican men and women in the 20 to 34 age group. Marcus and Crane (1985) have reported that the prevalence of smoking among Hispanic young men matches, if not surpasses, that found in the Black and Anglo youth population. Hispanic women's daily consumption of cigarettes is lower than that of Hispanic men, but as acculturation increases, that consumption increases. Indeed, the smoking habits of Hispanics of both sexes have been explained mainly as being part of the process of acculturation (Pérez-Stable, 1987). The age and rate differences for women are discussed in detail elsewhere (Juarbe, 1995a).

The study by Marín et al. (1986), which included a sample of Mexican-Americans and a large sample of Hispanics from Central and South America, also supports these previous findings, but it was especially relevant in its cross-cultural perspective and in identifying the variations in smoking patterns according to the acculturation of the Hispanic group studied.

Particularly for women, as acculturation to the mainstream culture occurred, the prevalence of cigarette smoking was higher. In a later study, acculturation was also found to influence Hispanics' self-efficacy perception in avoiding cigarette smoking in cessation programs (Sabogal et al., 1989). Given the potential negative impact of smoking rates and frequency in early ages among the Hispanic population, it is important to focus further research and further interventions in community-oriented programs.

CONTRIBUTING FACTORS FOR CARDIOVASCULAR HEART DISEASE

Diabetes Mellitus

Diabetes mellitus is a chronic disease that is the seventh leading cause of death in the United States. There is a significant lack of information about its determinants and frequency among the population at large. The disease predominantly affects obese individuals, and it is more common among men than among women. Its relevance for present purposes is that diabetes mellitus is a factor that increases mortality and morbidity among Hispanics. There are few studies that have assessed the incidence, prevalence, and etiology of diabetes in the Hispanic populations, and those that have assessed this risk factor for CVD have been limited to the Mexican-American population.

In general, most studies have shown that Hispanics have a higher prevalence of diabetes mellitus than in the Anglo-American population (Hazuda et al., 1984; Hazuda, Haffner, Stern, & Eeifler, 1988; Stern et al., 1981, 1984). Analysis of the San Antonio Heart Study (Hazuda et al., 1988; Stern et al., 1984) showed Mexican-American men with higher levels of acculturation had lower prevalence of diabetes, and among the Mexican-American women studied, both SES and acculturation influenced the prevalence of diabetes, with acculturation having the greater influence.

Similarly, a high prevalence of diabetes was noted in the Laredo study by Stern et al. (1981), who argued that it was perhaps related to the lack of diabetes awareness, diagnosis, and treatment. While diabetes has been thought to be an extremely relevant factor in CVD mortality, an analysis of the CVD mortality difference for Cubans, Puerto Ricans, and Mexicans from 1979 to 1981 (Rosenwaike, 1988) showed only that compared to Cuban women, Puerto Ricans suffered an excess of mortality due to diabetes.

Overall, diabetes is a well-established risk factor for CVD in the U.S. Hispanic population. The potential benefits from changes in exercise, diet, and weight need further studies among the different subgroups of Hispanics.

Exercise

Exercise and dynamic physical activity are recognized not only for their benefits to the overall physical health of the individual, but also for the perceived benefits to psychological and mental health. The benefits of exercise are related to the reduction of HTN, cholesterol, obesity, and stress (Leaf, 1991). Very few studies have assessed the impact of heart healthy exercise in Hispanics.

Early studies showed that Hispanics tend to engage less in recreational activities than do members of other groups, do not exercise on a regular basis, are less likely than others to do physical activities at work (Burchfiel et al., 1990; Hazuda et al., 1983; Shea et al., 1991), and live sedentary lifestyles (Friis et al., 1981; Stern et al., 1975; Stern et al., 1981). In this regard, education (Shea et al., 1987), SES (Hazuda et al., 1983), and acculturation (Vega et al., 1987) have been associated with engaging in regular exercise. Their lack of physical activity increases Hispanics' risk for developing CVD. This particular risk is related to the reduction of HTN, serum cholesterol levels, and obesity. In addition, since physical activity also promotes psychological and mental health, it is essential to assess the cultural lifestyles, health beliefs, and practices that enhance or hinder exercise.

In general, there is limited information regarding the factors that influence exercise behaviors in Hispanics. Further descriptive and exploratory studies are needed to gain an understanding of exercise practices and beliefs. These studies should include the assessment of Hispanic family support systems and their impact on exercise. Also, to encourage exercise that promotes heart health among Hispanics, health care providers should consider approaches that are focused on the family system and the community.

Obesity

Obesity is an excessive accumulation of body fat due to an imbalance between the number of calories consumed and the amount of physical activity. Overweight refers to weight that is in excess of standards determined for weight and height. The body mass index is the most commonly used standard for determining weight status (underweight, normal weight, overweight, and obesity). It is widely acknowledged that obesity is related to the development of several chronic diseases, such as CVD. The National Institutes of Health Consensus Development Conference

Statement asserts that weight 20% above ideal body weight is a risk factor for cardiovascular disease (USDHHS, 1985).

Among Hispanics obesity has been attributed to physical inactivity and poor eating patterns (Kumanyika, 1990), low levels of knowledge about health behavior, risk factors, foods that are sources of fat, and cholesterol (Delapa et al., 1990; Hazuda et al., 1983; Knapp et al., 1988; Vega et al., 1987), low socio-economic status (Ford & Jones, 1991; Mueller et al., 1984; Stern et al., 1981), and income (López & Massé, 1993).

Results from the Laredo Study (Stern et al., 1981), the San Antonio Heart Study (Stern, Rosenthal, Haffner, Hazuda, & Franco, 1984), the Northern California study (Stern et al., 1975), the San Luis Valley study (Burchfiel, 1990), the HHANES (1990), and others (Diehl & Stern, 1989; Mueller et al., 1984) demonstrate that a large proportion of Mexican-Americans are overweight and lacking in physical activity. In addition, an analysis of the Hispanic Health and Nutrition Examination Survey (Fanelli-Kuczmarski & Woteki, 1990) showed that the population of Cuban, Puerto Rican, and Mexican-Americans studied (ages 20 to 74) had a higher than normal prevalence of being overweight, and in these three groups, Mexican-American men and women were more overweight than the Cuban and Puerto Rican populations studied.

Pawson, Martorell, and Mendoza (1991) found that Puerto Ricans, Mexican-Americans, and Cubans in the National Health and Nutrition Examination Surveys (1971 to 1974 and 1976 to 1980) carry significantly greater amounts of adipose tissue than non-Hispanic populations. In particular, older adults among the three groups had high levels of obesity. Hispanic women in these three groups were found to have an above-normal prevalence of being overweight and obesity as determined by body mass index, triceps skinfolds thickness, subscapular skinfolds thickness, and the subscapular-to-triceps skinfolds-thickness ratio. However, some argue that Mexican-American women eat a less atherogenic diet (Stern et al., 1981) and make more dietary and lifestyle changes than do Hispanic men (Knapp, Hazuda, Haffner, Young, & Stern, 1988).

The role of SES (Malina et al., 1983), education (Ford & Jones, 1991; Stern et al., 1984), and acculturation (Vega et al., 1987) in the etiology of obesity is controversial. With exception of Pawson et al. (1991), it has been found that as acculturation, educational, and socioeconomic levels increase, the prevalence of obesity among Hispanics decreases. However, it is often difficult to identify the specific relationship of any of these three factors alone since they are found to correlate highly with each other. For instance, acculturation has often been found to have high correlations with education (Vega et al., 1987) and increased SES

(Stern et al., 1984). It has also been argued that regardless of SES, education, or acculturation levels, Hispanic groups that maintain traditional dietary practices will continue to be at risk for being overweight or obese.

There are many factors that contribute to an excessive accumulation of body fat. The literature has shown that independent of SES, education, and acculturation, culturally defined body weight images and dietary behaviors also play important roles in the development of obesity. Some researchers have found that Puerto Ricans (Massara, 1989) and immigrant Mexican women (Juarbe, 1994) perceive a cultural environment that favors an overweight body image. Cultural diet and cooking practices that include canned meat, sausages, and sauces and seasonings that are high in sodium need further assessment and understanding before community intervention programs can be successful at changing these lifestyles.

Last and to a lesser extent, the prevalence of obesity or being overweight, especially among the Mexican-American population, has been attributed to Native American genetic influences (Samet, Coultas, Howard, Skipper, & Hanis, 1988). However Stern (AHA, 1984) has argued that it is lifestyle, rather than genetic factors, that is the primary explanation of weight problems.

SUMMARY

Although the impact of CVD is widely acknowledged in the Hispanic population, data on the mortality of CVD and on risk factors among this group are lacking in the literature. Studies on cardiovascular disease risk factors (Schoen & Nelson, 1981), hypertension (Barrios et al., 1987; Stern et al., 1981), blood cholesterol levels (Stern et al., 1981), diabetes (Sahagun, 1983; Stern et al., 1981, 1982), obesity (Reichley, 1984; Stern et al., 1984), and smoking (Marcus, 1984; Marcus & Crane, 1985) imply that compared to the Anglo-American population, Hispanics (1) have more of the risk factors attributable to the incidence and prevalence of CVD (Derenoski, 1990), (2) have less knowledge about CVD-related risk factors, and (3) engage less in heart healthy diet and exercise (Hazuda et al. 1983).

The literature on knowledge of CVD and risk factors among Hispanics is limited to Mexican-Americans; knowledge of the other subgroups is lacking. Moreover, the available information is inadequate and confusing; some study findings suggest adequate knowledge while others suggest the opposite, and in many of the studies it is not clear which subgroup of

Hispanics was represented in the samples. The number of Hispanic respondents is relatively small in comparison with the total sample size, and it is unclear to what extent respondents who indicated that they are "other" or "Black" were in fact Hispanic. This inconsistency suggests the need for research that produces valid data based on consistent criteria, a clear definition of "Hispanic," and an adequate number of subjects who represent the population.

Regarding HTN, further studies should analyze how other sociocultural factors and psychological stress impact the cardiovascular risk. The existing data cannot fully explain the issues of HTN awareness and treatment. There is also a need to study the impact of HTN on the quality of life of Hispanic men and women since treatments for HTN have adverse effects on neurological, sexual, and physical functional capacities.

The development of culturally sensitive education and awareness programs may reduce the prevalence of HTN and the development of heart disease. These programs should include health beliefs and folk treatment assessment of the specific Hispanic subgroups. Access to health care for Hispanic men, and for women (Juarbe, 1995b), is also considered pivotal when addressing the diagnosis of HTN and its treatment.

While all the factors that impact the development of CVD are related to SES, education, and acculturation, there is a great possibility that these factors influence each other. These factors have been found to correlate with each other, and when interpreting the findings from acculturation scales, researchers need to be aware of the confounding effects of education and SES, which must be accounted for before conclusions can be reached about the effects of acculturation on health behaviors.

Also, although education, SES, and acculturation may be important conditions for behavioral changes (Vega et al., 1987), the literature suggests that there are also other factors that may impact the health behavior of Hispanics. For example, how do access to health care, language, familism, group cohesiveness, ethnocentrism, lack of confidence in Anglo physicians, and cultural expectations of the physicians affect the heart health of Hispanic men and women? What specific barriers to promoting heart health exist in the health care system? What health and illness perceptions are most significant to promote heart health? What does heart health mean for the Hispanic population?

The absence of answers to these questions, the disparity of results in the studies that have been done, and the prevalence of the risk factors among the Hispanic population are compelling reasons to assess the CVD knowledge, attitudes, beliefs, and behaviors of different groups of the Hispanic population, with an emphasis on specific gender differences.

RECOMMENDATIONS

The state of knowledge presented in this chapter calls for the promotion of community-oriented models for CVD and health. There are limited projects/programs in the literature that demonstrate successful accomplishments in preventing CVD or in promoting heart health. Community participation, social support, gender, Hispanic subgroups, and developmental differences are essential concepts to be considered in the development of community-oriented projects.

Community participation implies that in the planning, implementation, and evaluation of projects, the specific Hispanic community is involved. This involvement allows for community expression of factors that may hinder or enhance a project. Active participation of Hispanics enhances partnership and ownership over such programs, and it affords a sense of appreciation for Hispanics' roles, responsibilities, values, and beliefs. The project of Domel and co-workers (1992) is an example of the challenges involved when community participation is not sought. While careful attention was given to the cultural sensitivity of all aspects of the project, it is not clear that community participation from Hispanic women in the community was sought in an effort to assess the barriers that could have impacted the intervention.

There is a great body of literature suggesting that social support is an essential concept in community-oriented programs. Social support includes aspects embedded in emotional, financial, educational, and informational resources. Risk factor modification, heart disease treatment, and quality of life are areas that need many of these components of social support interventions. For instance, many cardiovascular clinicians find that having support systems or stable family situations is more important in treatment and health promotion than knowledge and awareness of the risk factors.

Financial and community resources, other components of social support, are also essential. For instance, a lack of economic resources and health care insurance may be the major barrier to obtaining treatment for HTN, hyperlipidemia, angina, and other CVD conditions. The Hispanic community is often accused of failing to comply with medical treatment, but this accusation is typically made by persons who fail to understand that for therapeutic interventions, as well as lifestyle modifications, to be effective, they must be tailored to meet family and client needs. These recommendations are specially important for Hispanic patients with HTN, angina, hyperlipidemia, and for those diagnosed with CVD.

Social support interventions for lifestyle changes (such as regular exercise, heart healthy behavior, and the maintenance of normal weight) need to use family rather than individualistic approaches to promote heart health. The dynamics of Hispanic families occur in environments that may have (1) traditional-to-nontraditional health beliefs, practices, and values, (2) decreased availability to extended social networks, and (3) both traditional and nontraditional dietary and cooking practices. The work of Nader and colleagues (1989), who developed a family approach to reduce risk factors among Hispanics in an area of San Diego, is one of the few examples in which "family" was the community unit of intervention.

Informational support resources that are difficult to read or are too long become a source of indifference or frustration rather than a source of support for families and communities. Regardless of the careful translation and use of adequate Spanish materials, many community and family projects for Hispanics have experienced client difficulties in using, understanding, and remembering essential information in educational materials (Domel et al., 1992). Stressful or difficult experiences with dietary guidelines or exercise routines and Spanish language differences are all barriers to the success of community-oriented projects. For instance, clinicians in California deal with Hispanics from all over Latin America. The available resources often use words that are complex or that are recognizable by only one Hispanic subgroup. Thus, clinicians and community workers are often puzzled about the names of food items required for specific dietary modifications. Other educational and teaching strategies are needed to overcome these barriers.

The length of community-oriented interventions to make lifestyle changes is also an issue. If longer periods of time are needed within Hispanic communities and among health care professionals to support lifestyle changes, serious alterations are needed in the ways cardiac primary care is currently given. Cost-containment issues, the limited availability of health care personnel, and health insurance requirements might make these interventions unrealistic. Does the current health care system possess the manpower and time for cardiovascular disease prevention and heart health promotion? What other approaches, such as media, audiovisual, and written materials, are needed to effectively reach communities and families? Can community health workers be trained to meet these lengthy educational needs? This is clearly a field in need of further assessment and action.

The literature cited in this chapter demonstrates that there are differences in the prevalence of and risk factor behaviors for CVD for Hispanic men versus Hispanic women. Community-oriented projects must consider which factors enhance lifestyle changes in Hispanic men and women. Rather than considering the "family" as the unit of project interventions, some projects should implement gender-focused heart health promotion projects. However, much information is needed to understand the possible benefits of programs restricted to Hispanic women. Several Hispanic women's health advocates have argued that Hispanic women are limited in promoting their health due to the lack of social support from partners/spouses, children, and other family members (Juarbe, 1994; Zambrana, 1982). Hispanic women's multiple roles may result in lack of time, finances, and physical energy to make changes in behavior involving regular exercise or dietary changes. Community-oriented projects must consider these challenges during the planning, implementation, and evaluation of interventions since success might depend not on Hispanic women's decisions but, rather, on the social support available to them from partners/spouses and family members.

For community-oriented projects to be effective, the specific Hispanic subgroups involved need to be identified. Recently, a community-oriented project on saturated fat modification was developed in a Hispanic community. Excellent audiovisuals and personal resources were utilized. There was excellent response from the community which was mostly Cuban and Puerto Rican. However, the American Heart Association materials, dietary practices, and cooking suggestions related to the Mexican population only.

While there are great similarities among Hispanic subgroups, differences do exist, and they are critical for heart health promotion. Cubans, Puerto Ricans, Mexicans, and Central Americans differ in many behaviors, as well as in issues regarding access to health care, socioeconomic status, traditional medicine notions, and health beliefs and practices. Weight reduction, diet, and physical activity may also need different focus among these groups.

Children are an integral part of Hispanic communities and they are pivotal to the prevention of heart disease and promotion of heart health in future generations. Since the prevalence of risk factors in Hispanic children is increasing and these trends continue into adulthood, long-term effects of community-oriented education projects for children are critical. The concepts of heart healthy nutrition, fitness, and physical activity must be integrated within a culturally sensitive framework in schools, and after-school programs should implement culturally and linguistically appropriate projects for these children and their families. While further studies are needed to assess the best community-oriented interventions for Hispanic children, at present there is no evidence that existing programs, such as those of the American Heart Association, are effective.

It is also imperative to consider the heart health needs of the Hispanic elderly population. "Quality of life" has become a battle cry for those concerned with the heart health of the Hispanic elders. This is one area in which knowledge for interventions and programs is adversely affected by unawareness of the issues that pertain to this group. Better understanding is needed regarding lifestyle behavior, treatment, social support, and health beliefs of the elderly. State-of-the-art assessments that integrate physiological and psychosocial issues will stimulate additional work for community-oriented interventions.

Overall, community-oriented programs cannot be successful without state and local policy changes. Community coalition for heart health promotion should be encouraged and strengthened to develop dietary, exercise, and weight education programs.

Finally, it is necessary to change from individually-based to community-based paradigms of health for Hispanics. This paradigm change calls for health promotion and disease prevention projects in schools, the workplace, women's organizations, and other community-based organizations. It is only by moving *with* and *inside* Hispanic communities that CVD will be improved.

REFERENCES

Ailinger, R. (1982). Hypertension knowledge in a Hispanic community. *Nursing Research, 31,* 207-210.

American Heart Association. (1987, Spring). Researchers discuss risk factors at San Antonio Forum. *Cardiovascular Research Report,* No. 24, p. 6.

Atkins, C. J., Senn, K., Rupp, J., Kaplan, R. M., Patterson, T. L., Sallis, J. F., & Nader, P. R. (1990). Attendance at health promotion programs: Baseline predictors and program outcomes. *Health Education Quarterly, 17,* 417-428.

Barrios, E., Iler, E., Mulloy, K., Goldstein, J., Chalfin, D., & Muñoz, E. (1987). Hypertension in the Hispanic and Black population in New York City. *Journal of National Medicine Association, 79,* 749-752.

Baumgartner, R. N., Roche, A. F., Guo, S., Camerón-Chumlea, W., & Ryan, A. (1990). *American Journal of Clinical Nutrition, 51,* 936-943.

Becker, T. M., Wiggins, C., Key, C., & Samet, J. (1988). Ischemic heart disease mortality in Hispanics, American Indians and non-Hispanic Whites in New Mexico, 1958-1962. *Circulation, 78,* 302-309.

Burchfiel, C. M., Hamman, R. F., Marshall, J., Baxter, J., Kahn, L. B., & Amirani, J. (1990). Cardiovascular risk factors and impaired glucose tolerance: The San Luis Valley study. *American Journal of Sociology, 131*(1), 57-70.

Delapa, R. M., Mayer, J. A., Candelaria, J., Hammond, N., Peplinsky, S., De Moor, C., Talavera, G., & Elder, J. (1990). Food purchase patterns in a Latino community: Project Salsa. *Journal of Nutrition Education, 22,* 133-136.

Derenoski, J. (1990). Coronary artery disease in Hispanics. *Journal of Cardiovascular Nursing, 4*(4), 13-21.

Diehl, A. K., & Stern, M. P. (1989). Special health problems of Mexican-Americans: Obesity, gallbladder disease, diabetes mellitus, and cardiovascular disease. *Advances of Internal Medicine, 34,* 79-86.

Domel, S. B., Alford, B. B., Cattlett, H. N., Rodríguez, M. L., & Gench, B. E. (1992). A pilot weight control program for Hispanic women. *Journal of the American Dietetic Association, 92,* 1270-1271.

Fanelli-Kuczmarski, M., & Woteki, C. E. (1990). Monitoring the nutritional status of the Hispanic population: Selected findings for Mexcican Americans, Cubans, and Puerto Ricans. *Nutrition Today, 5,* 6-11.

Ford, E. S., & Jones, D. H. (1991). Cardiovascular health knowledge in the United States: Findings from the National Health Interview Survey, 1985. *Preventive Medicine, 20,* 725-736.

Franco, L. J., Stern, M. P., Rosenthal, M., Haffner, S. M., Hazuda, H. P., & Comeaux, P. J. (1985). Prevalence, detection, and control of hypertension in a biethnic community. *American Journal of Epidemiology, 121,* 684-696.

Friis, R., Nanjundappa, G., Prendergast, T., & Welsh, M. (1981). Coronary heart disease mortality and risk among Hispanics and non-Hispanics in Orange County, California. *Public Health Reports, 96,* 418-422.

Haynes, S. G., Harvey, C., Montes, H., Nickens, H., & Cohen, B. H. (1990). Patterns of cigarette smoking among Hispanics in the United States: Results from the HHANES 1982-1984. *American Journal of Public Health, 80,* 47-53.

Hazuda, H., Haffner, S., Stern, M., Rosenthal, M., & Franco, L. (1984). Effects of acculturation and socioeconomic status on obesity and glucose intolerance in Mexican-American men and women. *American Journal of Epidemiology, 120,* 494.

Hazuda, H. P., Haffner, S. M., Stern, M. P., & Eifler, C. W. (1988). Effects of acculturation and socioeconomic status on obesity and diabetes in Mexican-Americans. *American Journal of Epidemiology, 128,* 1289-1301.

Hazuda, H., Stern, M., Gaskill, S., Haffner, S., & Gardner, L. (1983). Ethnic differences in health knowledge and behaviors related to the prevention and treatment of coronary heart disease: The San Antonio Heart Study. *American Journal of Epidemiology, 117,* 717-728.

Holck, S. E., Warren, C. W., Rochat, R. W., & Smith, J. C. (1982). Lung cancer mortality and smoking habits: Mexican-American women. *American Journal of Public Health, 72* (1), 38-42.

Humble, C. G., Samet, J. M., Pathak, D. R., & Skipper, B. J. (1985). Cigarette smoking and lung cancer in Hispanic whites and other whites in New Mexico. *American Journal of Public Health, 75*(2), 145-148.

Juarbe, T. C. (1994). Factors that influence diet and exercise experiences in immigrant Mexican women. Doctoral Dissertation, University of California, San Francisco. University Microfilms.

Juarbe, T. C. (1995). Access to health care for Hispanic women: A primary health care perspective. *Nursing Outlook, 43,* 23-28.

Juarbe, T. C. (in press). Risk factors for cardiovascular disease in Hispanic women. *Progress in Cardiovascular Nursing.*

Knapp, J. A., Hazuda, H. P., Haffner, S. M., Young, E. A., & Stern, M. P. (1988). A saturated fat/cholesterol avoidance scale: Sex and ethnic differences in a biethnic population. *Journal of the American Dietetic Association, 88,* 172-177.

Kumanyika, S. (1990). Diet and chronic disease issues for minority populations. *Journal of Nutrition Education, 22,* 89-96.

Leaf, D. A. (1991). *Exercise and Nutrition in Preventive Cardiology.* W.C.D. Brown & Benchmark Publishers.

López, L. M., & Masse, B. (1992). Comparison of body mass indexes and cutoff points for estimating the prevalence of overweight in Hispanic women. *Journal of the American Dietetic Association, 92,* 1343-1347.

Malina, R. M., Little, B. B., & Stern, M. P. (1983). Ethnic and social class differences in selected anthropometric characteristics of Mexican-American and Anglo adults: The San Antonio Heart Study. *Human Biology, 55,* 867-883.

Marcus, A. (1984). Smoking behavior among Hispanics: A preliminary report. In P. E. Engstrum, H. Anderson, & Mortenson (Eds.) *Advances in cancer control: Epidemiology and research,* (pp. 141-151). New York: Alion R. Liss, Inc.

Marcus, A., & Crane, L. (1985). Smoking behavior among U.S. Latinos: An emerging challenge for public health. *American Journal of Public Health, 75*(2), 169-172.

Marín, G., Otero-Sabogal, R., Pérez-Stable, E. J., Sabogal, F., & VanOss-Marín, B. (1987). Development of a short acculturation scale for Hispanics. *Hispanic Journal of Behavioral Sciences, 9,* 183-205.

Markides, K. S., & Coreil, J. (1986). The health of Hispanics in the U.S.: An epidemiological paradox. *Public Health Reports, 101,* 253-265.

Massara, E. B. (1989). *!Qué Gordita!: A study of overweight among Puerto Rican women.* New York, NY: AMS Press.

Mueller, W. H., Joos, S. K., Hanis, C. L., Zavaleta, A. N., Eichner, J., & Schull, W. J. (1984). The diabetes alert study: Growth, fatness and fat patterning, adolescence through adulthood in Mexican-Americans. *American Journal of Physical Anthropology, 64,* 389-399.

Nader, P. R., Sallis, J. F., Patterson, T. L., Abramson, I. S., Rupp, J. W., Senn, K. L., Atkins, C. J., Roppe, B. E., Morris, J. A., Wallace, J. P., & Vega, W. (1989). A family approach to cardiovascular risk reduction: Results from The San Diego Family Health Project. *Health Education Quarterly, 16,* 229-244.

National Center for Health Statistics. (1987). Advance report of final mortality statistics. *Monthly Vital Statistics Report, 36*(5). Supp. Department of Health and Human Services, Publication No. (PHS) 87-1120. Hyatsville, MD.

National Institutes of Health. (1989). *Expert panel on detection, evaluation, and treatment of high blood cholesterol in adults.* (DHHS Publication No.89-2925). Washington, DC: U.S. Government Printing Office.

Pawson, I. G., Martorell, R., & Mendoza, F. (1991). *American Journal of Clinical Nutrition, 53,* 1522-1528.

Pérez-Stable, E. (1987). Issues in Latino health care. *The Western Journal of Medicine, 146*(2), 213-218.

Perloff, D. (1989). Hypertension in women. *Cardiovascular Clinics, 19*(3), 207-241.

Ramírez, A., Herrick, K., & Weaver, F. (1981). El asesino silencioso: A methodology for alerting the Spanish-speaking community. *Urban Health*, 44-48.

Reichley, K. (1984). Centralized obesity & cardiovascular disease risk in Mexican-Americans. *American Journal of Epidemiology, 125*(3), 373-386.

Roberts, R. E., & Askew, C. (1972). A consideration of mortality in three subcultures. *Health Services Report, 87*, 262-270.

Rosenwaike, I. (1987). Mortality differences among persons born in Cuba, Mexico, and Puerto Rico residing in the United States, 1979-1981. *American Journal of Public Health, 77*, 603-606.

Ryan, A. S., Martínez, G. A., & Roche, A. F. (1990). An evaluation of the associations between socioeconomic status and the growth of Mexican-American children: Date from the Hispanic Health and Nutrition Examination Survey (HHANES 1982-1984). *American Journal of Clinical Nutrition, 51*, 944-952.

Ryan, A. S., Martínez, G. A., Baumgartner, R. N., Roche A., Guo, S., Camerón-Chumlea, W., & Kuczmarski, R. J. (1990). *American Journal of Clinical Nutrition, 51*, 925-935.

Sabogal, F., Otero-Sabogal, R., Pérez-Stable, E. J., VanOss-Marín, B., & Marín, G. (1989). Perceived self-efficacy to avoid cigarette smoking and addiction: Differences between Hispanics and non-Hispanic Whites. *Hispanic Journal of Behavioral Sciences, 11*, 136-147.

Sahagun, L. (1983). Diabetes: A special risk for Latinos. *Los Angeles Times*, April 20, Part I, p. 11.

Samet, J. M., Coultas, D. B., Howard, C. A., Skipper, B. J., & Hanis, C. L. (1988). Diabetes, gallbladder disease, obesity, and hypertension among Hispanics in New Mexico. *American Journal of Epidemiology, 128*, 1302-1311.

Schoen, R., & Nelson, V. (1981). Mortality by cause among Spanish-surnamed Californians, 1969-1971. *Social Science Quarterly, 62*, 259-274.

Shea, S., Stein, A. D., Basch. C. E., Lantigua, R., Maylahn, C., Strogatz, D. S., & Novick, L. (1991). Independent associations of educational attainment and ethnicity with behavioral risk factors for cardiovascular disease. *American Journal of Epidemiology, 134*, 567-582.

Sorel, J. E., Ragland, D. R., & Syme, S. L. (1991). Blood pressure in Mexican-Americans, White, and Blacks. *American Journal of Epidemiology, 134*, 370-378.

Stern, M., & Gaskill, S. (1978). Secular trends in ischemic heart disease and stroke mortality from 1970-1976 in Spanish surname and White individuals in Bexar County, Texas. *Circulation, 58*, 537-543.

Stern, M., Gaskill, S., Allen, C., Garza, V., Gonzalez, J., & Waldrop, R. (1981a). Cardiovascular disease risk factors in Mexican-Americans in Laredo, Texas. Prevalecence of overweight diabetes and distribution of serum lipids. *American Journal of Epidemiology, 113*, 546-555.

Stern, M., Gaskill, S., Allen, C., Garza, V., Gonzalez, J., & Waldrop, R. (1981b). Cardiovascular risk factors in Mexican-Americans in Laredo, Texas. Prevalence and control of HTN. *American Journal of Epidemiology, 113,* 556–562.

Stern, M., Haskell, W., Wood, P., Osann, K., King, A., & Farquhar, J. (1975). Affluence and cardiovascular risk factors in Mexican-Americans and other Whites in three northern California communities. *Journal of Chronic Disease, 28,* 623–636.

Stern, M. P., Gaskill, S. P., Hazuda, H. P., Gardner, L. I., & Haffner, S. M. (1983). Does obesity explain excess prevalence of diabetes among Mexican-Americans? Results of the San Antonio Heart Study. *Diabetologia, 24,* 272–277.

Stern, M., Reletithford, R., Ferrel, R., Gaskill, S., Hazuda, H., Haffner, S., & Gardner, L. (1982). *Diabetes and genetic admixtures in Mexican-Americans: The San Antonio Heart Study.*

Stern, M., Rosenthal, M., Haffner, S., Hazuda, H., & Franco, L. (1984). Sex differences in the effects of sociocultural status on diabetes and cardiovascular risk factors in Mexican-Americans: The San Antonio Heart Study. *The American Journal of Epidemiology, 120,* 834–851.

United States Bureau of the Census, Vital Statistics Report. (1986). Washington, DC: U.S. Government Printing Office.

United States Department of Health and Human Services. (1986). *Report of The Secretary's Task Force on Black and Minority Health. Ischemic heart disease in Hispanic Americans,* Vol. IV, 1986. Washington, DC: U.S. Government Printing Office.

United States Department of Health and Human Services. (1985). *Health status of minorities and low-income groups.* Department of Health and Human Services Publication No.(HRSA) HRS-P-DV 85-1. Washington, DC: U.S. Government Printing Office.

Vega, W., Sallis, J., Patterson, T., Rupp, J., Atkins, C., & Nader, P. (1987). Assessing knowledge of cardiovascular health-related diet and exercise behaviors in Anglo and Mexican-Americans. *Preview of Medicine, 16,* 696–709.

Webber, L. S., Harsha, D. H., Phillips, G. T., Srinivasan, S. R., Simpson, J. W., & Berenson, G. S. (1991). Cardiovascular risk factors in Hispanic, White, and Black children: The Brooks County and Bogalusa heart studies. *American Journal of Epidemiology, 133,* 704–713.

Yatsu, F. M. (1991). Strokes in Asians, and Pacific Islanders, Hispanics, and Native Americans. *Circulation, 83,* 1471–1472.

Zambrana, R. E. (1982). *Work, family and health: Latina women in transition.* Monograph Series # 7, MH 30569-05. Bronx, NY: Fordham University Press.

CHAPTER EIGHT

Bridge to Socially Competent Quality Care for Diabetics in the Hispanic Community

Blanca Rosa Garcia, PhD, RN, FNP

Maryann Yzaguirre, MSN, MS, RN

REVIEW OF FACTORS AFFECTING CARE OF HISPANIC DIABETES

Historical Factors

While this chapter will not provide a discussion of the pathophysiology of diabetes mellitus, a review of the historical development will serve as a backdrop to the care of affected Hispanic clients.

The diabetic symptoms are said to have been described centuries before the time of Christ. The first clinical description of diabetes was made by Celsus, while the name *diabetes* was introduced by Aretaeus, a Roman physician in the first century. Knowledge of diabetes continued to be scanty until the 17th century when Sir Thomas Rollo noticed the sweet taste of urine in a person with diabetes and was the first to recommend a dietary treatment (Thomas, 1974). During the 19th century, multiple contributions were made, especially Von-Mering and Minkowski, who in 1869 induced experimental diabetes by removing the pancreas in dogs (Thomas, 1974). It was not until 1921, however, that Banting and Best discovered a method of extracting insulin from the pancreas (Thomas, 1974). In 1897, Dr. Elliott Joslin treated the first diabetic patient and started a diabetes mellitus program to teach his patients how to care for themselves. In 1919, five years before the discovery of insulin, he wrote the Joslin manual. Dr. Joslin, who hired and trained a nurse to do diabetes mellitus teaching at the Joslin's Clinic, is also credited with understanding the importance of nursing to the diabetic. This "wandering nurse," as she was soon to be called, would return home with the patient for the first few days to help patient and family adjust to the therapeutic routine (Marble, Krall, Bradley, & Stuart, 1985). The importance of the educational component of diabetic care has continued in modern community-based models such as "Operation Defeat Diabetes in Texas, Corpus Christi" (1995). These programs seek to reduce diabetic complications and long-term effects through ample educational campaigns with nurses as key to diabetes management. In this chapter, other influencing factors in diabetes mellitus, especially in Hispanics, are discussed.

Societal Factors

In diabetes mellitus, quality care includes patient education to increase self-care management. Anderson, Nowacek, and Richards (1985) state that patient education will lead to changes in knowledge and skills that will contribute to better self-care behaviors, resulting in improved blood sugar glucose levels, decreased complications, reduced utilization of health care services, and ultimately improved quality of life. In 1985, the American Diabetes Association (ADA) set national standards for diabetes patient education, including standards for the diabetes nurse. The ADA board recognized that the diabetes nurse should be an RN holding certification status in diabetes. Recertification every five years includes an examination process. Continuing education, a vital ongoing need, is not mandatory (American Diabetes Association, 1986). A societal expectation of nurses to promote high quality education programs and care remains, however.

Diabetes mellitus affects 13 million people in the United States with Mexican-Americans being twice as likely to be affected (American Diabetes Association, 1993). About 650,000 people will be diagnosed yearly with diabetes mellitus, the fourth leading cause of death by disease in the United States. In 1990, some 39,000 people lost their sight because of diabetes mellitus, while 13,000 people initiated treatment for kidney failure. Some 54,000 people lost a foot or leg due to amputation There are 77,000 deaths annually due to heart disease related to diabetes mellitus, and those patients are five times more likely to suffer a stroke. In communities with high minority populations, diabetes mellitus is one of the leading causes of death. Nueces County in Texas, for example, lists diabetes mellitus as the third leading cause of death with at least 190 people dying of diabetes-related complications in 1992 alone (Huff, 1994). Given such incidence, this large effect on health has amplified the need for socially competent nursing care in reducing the relative cost of complications to communities, particularly in minority population groups such as Hispanics. Both social and political pressures emerge along with the health care challenges requiring nurses' awareness and seeing beyond an individual client focus.

In caring for Hispanics, Stasiak (1991) offers four universal themes that should be seen as social factors of importance: the strong influences of religion, cultural values, kinship, and language. These themes, applied to the care of the Hispanic diabetic client, extend the therapeutic relationship not only to a client, but to a larger, family group. Nursing care of the diabetic client must include a sensitivity to family roles based on kinship, where the means of involving family members in caring behaviors improves both the physical and psychological well-being of the diabetic patient.

Another important component includes the use of non-traditional health care rituals and practices (Stasiak, 1991). In a recent survey of herbal shops in Mexico, an average of four herbs per shop were found for use by diabetics (Garcia, 1995). In each of the shops the herbs were different, with no apparent commonalities. However, all these herbal therapies involved the use of "tea" to decrease blood sugar. Informants in the shops volunteered information on the value of these teas in maintaining diabetic family members' blood glucose levels at improved levels—such influences are being exported to Hispanic communities throughout the United States by diabetics and their families. Not including these influences results in skewed or ineffective assessments. At the very least, the therapeutic values of these nontraditional regimes must be seen in light of their placebo effect. Lack of hard scientific data regarding herbal remedies should come as no surprise given our past reliance on quantitative research. However, the emerging acceptance of qualitative research promises to open the doors to a more complete review of the beneficial results of nontraditional therapies by documenting healing due to caring relationships and neuro-immunological interactions.

Stasiak (1991) discusses the perceptions by Hispanics of health care providers as extensions of God and "good," thereby promoting a level of trust necessary for a therapeutic relationship. This generally positive view of nurses can be used to implement a positive health care delivery system, accepting of the families' values concerning care and health, however varied they may be.

Economic Factors

According to Joshu (1992), health care costs have increased at a rapid pace due to chronic illnesses such as diabetes mellitus. In 1981, the medical bills for the elderly population were three times that of other adults.

Patients who are insulin dependent receive 70% Medicare coverage (Joshu, 1992). The estimated costs of inpatient and outpatient care for diabetes mellitus in 1987 totaled $916 billion. Expenditures for diabetes medical care per person was 50% higher for those over 65 compared to those without diabetes mellitus. The total expenditure on nursing home care for people with diabetes mellitus in 1987 was $941.4 billion (Joshu, 1992). It is estimated that diabetes mellitus costs Americans $25 billion annually (American Diabetes Association, 1993). In Texas alone, the estimated direct and indirect costs of treating diabetes mellitus and its complications is $6 billion (American Diabetes Association, 1993). These figures provide the basis for the discussion of the larger economic impact of chronic illnesses such as diabetes mellitus and validate the need for improved health care models which focus on care in communities. The economics of health care and the era of reform would dictate that community health care delivery for early diagnosis of diabetes and wellness programs would be cost effective. The Operation Defeat Diabetes in Texas, Corpus Christi (1995) effort, a partnership of the American Diabetes Association, the Texas Diabetes Council of the Texas Department of Health, the Nueces County Health Department, and private industry, is an excellent example of a model program of rethinking health care delivery. Efforts such as this, implemented in socially competent ways, will result in a higher acceptance by the Hispanic population.

The daily expense for diabetic care is also important in planning patient care. Joshu (1992) estimates the cost of medication, monitoring supplies, laboratory tests, and doctor visits to be about $4,265 yearly. Rubin (1993) states that a higher control protocol that uses glucose monitoring four times a day would result in higher costs. Hispanic elderly women who live below the poverty line and are living alone have a higher rate of diabetes mellitus and, as such, are even less able financially to care for themselves. This is supported by clinical research by Garcia (1984) where chronic diabetic clients reported noncompliance was due not from lack of understanding, but rather from a lack of financial resources for glucose monitoring. These patients expected that the nurse should be responsible for glucose monitoring. Finding financial resources for clients and improving the nurses' understanding of the real problems are important links in providing care for Hispanics with diabetes mellitus.

Legal Factors

According to Ratner and El-Gamassey (1990), the diabetic nurse's certification is critically important because it helps to establish a standard of care promoting professional expertise and health care responsibility. At the same time, adherence to certification standards will decrease the likelihood of malpractice allegations. Joshu recommends all nurses, dieticians, and other care givers should be certified to provide better service and avoid litigations (1992). Ratner and El-Gamassey (1990) suggest that the Diabetes Program be recognized by the American Diabetes Association and the National Diabetes Advisory Board. The responsibilities of team members should be viewed as legal requirements. If the program is recognized by the above mentioned boards, procedure and content of instruction is centrally developed and categorically implemented. The diabetes nurse also ensures sufficient patient comprehension of instruction to carry out the therapy safely and effectively. In addition, a follow-up procedure should be established to reassess the effectiveness of instruction. Documentation in the clients' medical record is vital to avoid future legal problems. However, due to language barriers, the health care system has frequently been unable to correctly access or provide care. Anglo-Americans, in general, have not embraced the idea of broadening their language skills. Culturally competent nursing of the diabetes mellitus patient should include a nurse who not only speaks the language but also understands the culture of Hispanic clients.

APPLICATION OF FACTORS TO DIABETES MELLITUS PROTOCOLS

Communication in Hispanic Diabetic Care

Communicating Respect. Respect is a vital issue in the beginning of any therapeutic relationship; in the Hispanic patient, the nonverbal elements of respect include eye-to-eye contact but not to the extent that the eye contact can be perceived as piercing or staring. The verbal component directs health care individuals to the use of proper titles such as Mr., Mrs., Ms., or the Spanish counterparts of Don or Senor, Dona or Senora, or Senorita. It is not acceptable to call someone by a familiar name such as *Primo* (cousin), *Tía* (aunt), or *Abulita* (grandmother). The rules of using first names requires the client to give permission, rather than assume that calling them by their first name is acceptable. In general, the need for titles is more formalized and necessary than in the Anglo-American culture, especially in addressing or referring to an elderly person.

Assessment. Adequate communication between nurse and patient will build trust and rapport. An extensive open interview in an area that promotes confidentiality assists the nurse's understanding of the clients' perceptions concerning diabetes mellitus and how it will affect their lives. Burckhardt (1986) states that respecting the patient means talking to the patient as a person, and not talking down to him or her as an authoritarian figure. This is particularly important when assessing and interviewing the Hispanic client about diabetes. Keeping the intake interview open to the patient and his or her family is important in providing a system of family support. Furthermore, allowing the family to participate in the patient's care builds trust, respect, and encourages compliance. It has been the authors' experience that many Hispanic patients, especially males, will not return for follow-up appointments if they feel offended or perceive they have been belittled during the initial interview. The first encounter is a very important step toward ensuring continuous rapport (Yzaguirre, 1994a, 1994b).

Increased Knowledge of Diabetes. Every diabetic should attend a basic course on diabetes (Estey, Tan, & Mann, 1989). The classes should cover basic explanation of Type I and Type II diabetes, the signs/symptoms, and the complications. Other basics are food portions, self-monitoring of blood glucose, exercise, foot care, and how to manage hypoglycemia and hyperglycemia. Every Hispanic client and at least one other family member should be encouraged to attend and complete a full course on diabetes mellitus. Hendricks and Haas (1991) urge including the family when teaching the Hispanic patient due to their strong family ties. The Hispanic patient and his or her family should be encouraged to return for follow-up. Nurses should keep the instruction brief, simple, and clear to decrease confusion since the volume of information is overwhelming (Boswell, 1990). When teaching the Hispanic client, be sure of the level of comprehension of content. The diabetes nurse should demonstrate any psychomotor skills and ask for a return demonstration from the client and family members. The evaluation should include a written or verbal test to assess understanding. This should be done on a one-to-one basis.

Identification of Problems and Interventions. The diabetes nurse needs to pay particular attention to specific fears and anxieties when conducting health assessment on Hispanic patients. Identifying potential problem areas will help mobilize resources that can assist the Hispanic client to achieve compliance in self-care. In addition, if negative cues are detected, a family consultation may be necessary to assist the diabetic client to come to terms with the diabetes diagnosis. For many Hispanic clients, emphasis on short-term problems may be more beneficial than long-term issues due to the client's time orientation. However, younger Hispanic generations may be more futuristic and assist the older diabetic client in long-term orientations (Yzaguirre, 1994). Many Hispanics will do lifestyle changes or sacrifices for the family rather than for themselves.

After evaluating the patient's needs, ask if they are using any herbs or folklore medicines to treat their diabetes. Use social service referral to seek assistance from agencies in the community, especially in areas where the financial resources will be the key to compliance with the diabetic regime. This effort will increase cohesiveness to a more permanent relationship between the diabetes nurse and the Hispanic patient. Thorne (1990) feels that nurses cannot pass moral judgment on patients and then expect them to learn to take care of themselves. Teaching should be a positive exchange of ideas and information between the nurse and the Hispanic patient. Joslin (1985) explores the idea of writing up a contract between the nurse and patient to establish boundaries and expectations. This allows the nurse to teach, reinforce, and encourage the patient to follow treatment plans.

Teaching-Learning

Importance of Nurse-Client Relationship. The diabetes nurse should begin teaching after building a foundation of a one-to-one relationship with the client, particularly for those who have low self-esteem. Once the patient is ready, progression to group teaching should be encouraged. However, the client should determine if a Spanish- or English-speaking group would be most beneficial. A Spanish-speaking diabetes nurse should do the teaching to assist in bringing out cultural patterns and in assisting the diabetic client and family in problem solving. Hispanic patients do not feel comfortable answering questions through an interpreter. A Spanish-speaking nurse will more readily promote the interaction and culturally relevant milieu necessary. In addition, having clients become involved in a process of inclusion communicates respect. Yzaguirre (1985) actively encouraged her diabetes support group of Hispanic women to keep self-care diaries for twelve weeks. Patients reported a high level of satisfaction with their participation in self-care and compliance to the recommended diabetes mellitus regime. Hispanics are also more sensitive about getting the right answers to questions asked (Hendricks & Haas, 1991). Using broad or medical jargon makes it more difficult for Hispanics to understand the medical regimen. Keeping the focus simple and directed on learning increases cohesiveness between the nurse and the client and promotes client satisfaction. Becker (1985) points out that this kind of relationship helps the Hispanic patient to accept the diagnosis of diabetes;

acceptance is the first step toward accepting health care recommendations for wellness.

Assessing Learning. Regarding procedures such as insulin or blood glucose monitoring, the Hispanic patient and a family member should be encouraged to do return demonstrations to ensure accuracy of technique. It is usually better to do this on a one-to-one basis or in a family group to communicate respect (Stasiak, 1991). At the same time, maintaining a positive relationship with the Hispanic client is crucial to ensure the client will continue follow-up (Yzaguirre, 1994). Nurses' support for Hispanic patients making life-style changes will increase the patient's success. However, ultimately it is the client's choice that must be respected regarding health care behavior. Patients get tired of self-care activities and nurses should understand that noncompliance is not a nursing failure (Hentinen & Kyngas, 1992). The support to maintain compliance to the demands of the diabetes medical regimen (Thorne & Robinson, 1988) will require constant nursing attention.

It is important for the nurse to be positive and avoid discouraging patients who feel overwhelmed regarding their ability to absorb the mass of data required. Joslin (1985) encourages a personal approach with written material so that a patient can review it at home. Another approach is to include family members, such as a spouse or daughter/son, so that the knowledge is collectively acquired and family kinship caring strengthened (Stasiak, 1991).

Dietary Issues. The importance of communicating clearly is critical in dietary matters with the diabetic client. In Hispanics, the use of pictures of commonly used food to learn the exchange system is a simple method of improving success (Yzaguirre, 1985). Such use will improve communication and decrease confusion on the geographic variations of food names. For example, an enchilada in one area may include meat and cheese, while in another it will include only cheese and sauce; in one area sauce may be green while in another red. A picture may simplify and clarify food exchange recommendations or promote a discussion of variabilities otherwise not discovered. Dietary information should be provided in English or Spanish and include foods appropriate to the Hispanic diet. The diabetes nurse should do a continuous evaluation of learning by questioning the client and by modifying the diet to accommodate the dietary values of the Hispanic patient. Plastic food models can also be used to reinforce different food exchanges, portion size, etc. Inexpensive foods should be taken into consideration when presenting food exchanges. Ethnic food models should be used interchangeably for patients to see portion size. A one-to-one approach to ensure understanding (Ross, 1991) and a foundation of good communication are emphasized to promote compliance (Anderson, 1985).

A GUIDE FOR NURSES WORKING WITH HISPANIC DIABETICS

An Action Plan

1. Plan the Diabetic Curriculum following American Diabetes Association guidelines (1981, 1986, 1993). This plan needs to include translation into Spanish and identifying certified individuals who can teach in Spanish. The specific class schedule used for a county hospital (Yzaguirre, 1994) included the following schedule:

   Day I: Introduction
   What is diabetes?
   How does diabetes affect the body?
   Demonstration of blood glucose monitoring

   Day II: Dietary Information
   Diet selection and planning
   Handouts of exchange lists

   Day III: Review
   Demonstration of blood glucose monitoring
   Demonstration of insulin preparation/administration
   Demonstration of diet planning and selection
   General health principles
   Complications: hypoglycemia/hyperglycemia
   Skin/foot care/exercise
   Summary
   Evaluation

2. Network with other individuals involved in diabetic teaching in the community to establish a support group for diabetic education nurses. Promote involvement in the local chapter of the American Diabetes Association. List all classes that are provided by hospitals or community health groups and identify which of these are given in Spanish. Print this list through the local chapter of the American Diabetes Association and provide it to clients in the community. It is suggested that nurses network between hospitals and community health agencies to assist any client in promoting wellness.

3. Provide inservice programs to nursing staff in hospitals to publicize the education activity available. This should include successful techniques when working with Hispanic patients.
4. Obtain a complete list of community resources including addresses and telephone numbers. Translate this list into Spanish and print the list through the American Diabetes Association chapter. Nurses should have the list handy for clients who need these services.
5. Establish a linkage with community groups able to provide financial assistance to clients who would otherwise be unable to afford self-care requirements. Referrals to other community resources may also be necessary.
6. Establish a documentation of diabetic contact and compile statistical data regarding compliance, progress, or complications.
7. Systematically plan review of services and methods of improving interventions. The focus on effectiveness and efficiency with quality as a requirement will assist in promoting positive outcomes.

Information Sources for Diabetes

In many areas, the American Diabetes Association will be the sole source of information regarding diabetes (P.O. Box 930850, Atlanta, GA 31193-0850). For a small fee, they provide pamphlets in Spanish for use with clients.

In addition, exchange lists adapted to diets of Hispanics are available through local agencies such as the Health Department or local hospitals. An example of a teaching manual and the Mexican-American exchange lists developed by a local hospital are available by contacting Maryann Yzaguirre, Department of Registered Nurse Education, Del Mar College, Corpus Christi, TX 78404-3897. Since geographic variability in food preferences occurs, the best approach is to work through a local chapter of the American Diabetes Association or a dietician. However, establishing a source and having it available will decrease the frustration of the diabetic client who needs the information.

REFERENCES

American Diabetes Association. (1981). *Guidelines for diabetes care.* New York: American Diabetes Association.

American Diabetes Association. (1986). National standards for diabetes patients education and American Diabetes Association review criteria. *Diabetes Care, 9,* 36.

American Diabetes Association. (1993). *Diabetes Facts.* New York: American Diabetes Association.

Anderson, R. (1985). Is the problem of noncompliance all in our heads? *Diabetes Educator, 14*(4), 31-34.

Anderson, R., Nowacek, G., & Richards, F. (1985). Influencing the personal meaning of diabetes: Research and practice. *Diabetes Educator, 14*(4), 297-302.

Becker, M. (1985). Patient adherence to prescribed therapies. *Medical Care, 23*(5), 539-552.

Becker, M., & Janz, N. (1985). The health belief model applied to understanding diabetes regimen compliance. *The Diabetes Educator, 13*(3), 41-47.

Boswell, E. J. (1990). Selecting teaching strategies to promote patient adherence. *The Diabetes Educator, 13*(4), 410-412.

Burckhardt, C. (1986). Ethical issues in compliance. *Topics in Clinical Nursing, 7*(4), 9-16.

Estey, A., Tan, M., & Mann, K. (1989). Follow up interventions: Its effect on compliance behavior to a diabetes regimen. *Diabetes Educator, 16*(4), 291-295.

Garcia, B. R. (1984). Improvement of nursing care for diabetes mellitus through research. Unpublished manuscript, Corpus Christi State University, Nursing Department, Corpus Christi, Texas.

Garcia, B. R. (1995). Herbs for diabetes mellitus: A survey of Mexican remedies. Unpublished raw data.

Hendricks, R., & Haas, L. (1991). Diabetes in minority populations. *Nurse Practitioner Forum, 2*(3), 199-202.

Hentinen, M., & Kyngas, H. (1992). Compliance of young diabetics with health regimens. *Journal of Advanced Nursing, 7*(1), 530-536.

Huff, C. (1994, June 23). Forum's message: Diabetes can be controlled. *Corpus Christi Caller-Times.*

Joshu, D. H. (1992). *Management of diabetes mellitus: Perspectives of care across life span.* St. Louis: C. V. Mosby.

Marble, A., Krall, L., Bradley, R., & Stuart, J. (1985). *Joslin's Diabetes Mellitus.* (12th ed.) Philadelphia: Lea & Febiger.

Operation: Defeat Diabetes in Texas, Corpus Christi. (1995). (Available from American Diabetes Association, Texas Affiliate, Inc., c/o American Diabetes Association, Order Fulfillment Department, P. O. Box 930850, Atlanta, GA 31193-0850.)

Ratner, R., & El-Gamassey, E. (1990). Legal aspects of the team approach to diabetes treatment. *Diabetes Educator, 16*(2), 113-116.

Ross, F. (1991). Patient compliance—whose responsibility? *Social Science Medicine, 32*(1), 89-94.

Rubin, R. (1993). A tighter rein on diabetes. *U.S. News & World Report, 114*(25), 68.

Stasiak, D. B. (1991). Culture care theory with Mexican-Americans in urban context. In M. M. Leininger (Ed.), *Culture care diversity and universality: A theory of nursing* (pp. 179-201). New York: National League for Nursing Press.

Thomas, C. (1974). *Counseling and rehabilitating the diabetic.* St. Louis: C. V. Mosby.

Thorne, S. (1990). Constructive noncompliance in chronic illness. *Holistic Nursing Practice, 5*(1), 62-69.

Thorne, S., & Robinson, C. (1988). Health care relationships: The chronic illness perspective. *Research in Nursing & Health, 11,* 293-300.

Yzaguirre, M. (1994a) How does utilzing a certified diabetes nurse affect the patient's compliance to the diabetes medical regime? Unpublished manuscript, Corpus Christi State University, Division of Nursing, Corpus Christi, Texas.

Yzaguirre, M. (1994b) Proposal: The development of a diabetes education module. Unpublished manuscript, Texas A&M—Corpus Christi, Division of Nursing, Corpus Christi, Texas.

CHAPTER NINE

HIV/AIDS: Risk Factors, Incidence and Interventions among Latinos in the United States

Nilda P. Peragallo, PhD, RN

Melinda L. Alba, MS Candidate

The following vignettes are from actual interviews conducted by the author in Latin America. Each woman had a diagnosis of AIDS. Each has since died.

Olga

Olga was a 40-year-old woman with two years of high school education. She was married but separated from her husband for the past eight years. She had two daughters age 20 and 22. Olga lived with her parents, one brother, one daughter, and her grandson. The oldest daughter lived in Brazil with her husband.

Olga lived in Brazil with her former husband from 1979 to 1991. She separated from her husband in 1983. She stayed in Brazil where she met her partner, who was her only partner. He was married and told Olga he had sex only with his wife. Olga and this partner had vaginal, anal, and oral intercourse approximately two to three times per week for eight years. They never used condoms. Her partner became sick and died of AIDS in 1991. When her partner became sick, Olga discovered he had been frequenting prostitutes for years without using protection. Olga said, "I only had three partners in my whole life, I didn't drink, and I have never tried drugs, and now I have AIDS. What am I supposed to do?"

Edith

Edith was a 23-year-old single woman. She had a 5-year-old daughter and was 5 months pregnant. She had a history of substance abuse since she was 15 years old when she started using alcohol. At 16 she started using marijuana and inhaling "Neopren" (sniffing glue). When she was 20 years old, she began injecting drugs with a group of friends in her neighborhood. She started sharing syringes and needles; she denied having sex on these occasions because drugs decreased her libido; she stated she would rather steal than have sex for drugs.

She had a total of three sexual partners. At 17 years of age, she met her first partner and father of her 5-year-old daughter with whom she lived for four years. Her second partner was an alcohol and drug user with whom she consumed both. This relationship lasted for two months, and this partner was later diagnosed as HIV+ and is currently in prison for robbery to obtain drug money. A year later, she met her third partner who was from Brazil and the father of the baby she was pregnant with when I met her. She lived with this partner, who didn't drink or use drugs, for three months. She practiced anal sex for the first time with this partner. Edith never used condoms with any of her partners. Her last partner tested HIV negative.

Edith believed she became infected by sharing the drug apparatus with her best friend, Jessica. She asked, "What is going to happen to me and my baby? Is there anything I can do to get better?"

Maria Elena "Nena"

Nena was a 32-year-old woman, married but separated for the past ten years from the father of her two children, Katherine, 17, and Cristian, 15. Nena lived with Ivan, her common-law husband, for the past ten years. He is presently in jail charged with robbery.

Nena started using IV drugs four years ago. At first she used only oral amphetamines, but she frequented her sister's house where everybody got together to use IV drugs. There her sister's common-law husband injected her with IV drugs for the first time. She recalls being extremely careful at the beginning of her drug use not to share equipment. However, as time passed and her drug use increased to daily injections, she became "careless and started sharing the works" with her sisters, brother, brother-in-law, and friends who came to the house. Her partner, Ivan, had used drugs before but had discontinued using until Nena introduced him again. He was tested for HIV after Nena was diagnosed, and the results were positive.

Nena had a total of four sexual partners with whom she never used condoms. Two of her partners were drug users with whom she shared equipment. She practiced anal sex with her last partner, Ivan, for the first time. Nena described her feelings when told that she was HIV+ as "desperate"; she felt she could have avoided becoming infected if she would have had support to discontinue her drug use. She had planned to have a child with her partner, but realized that it was not possible. Both of Nena's sisters are also HIV+; her brother who is also an IVDU refuses to undergo testing.

Lidia

Lidia was a 34-year-old woman, separated from her partner, and with a third-grade education. She was unemployed and worked sporadically as a peddler. She had three sexual partners in her life. She had five children; three daughters from her first partner; two from the second partner; and was pregnant by her third partner when I met her. She never used a condom with any of her partners. Her last partner, "Patricio," was the only one with whom she practiced anal sex; he also was HIV+.

Lidia felt that she knew "nothing" on how or when to take precautions before becoming infected. Her greatest concern was with her pregnancy and the chances for the child to be HIV+; and whether there was any treatments available for her.

These women for the most part had few partners. Two of the women were drug users, but the other two contracted HIV through sexual contact. They all had in common the lack of condom use and the perceived powerlessness in the relationship. Two of these women were pregnant; it is unknown whether the children were HIV positive. The women died quickly after being diagnosed, since the diagnosis was made late.

Acquired Immune Deficiency Syndrome (AIDS) has afflicted more than 17 million persons worldwide (Center for Disease Control [CDC], 1994). AIDS and HIV infection have spread across all geographical, social, economic, cultural, and political barriers throughout the world. Its impact on the Latino communities in the United States has been devastating.

Latinos in the United States are disproportionately affected by AIDS and HIV infection. While Latinos comprise 9% of the U.S. population (U.S. Census, 1990), 19% of U.S. AIDS cases reported since the beginning of the pandemic are Latino males, and 20% Latino females (CDC, 1994). Recent epidemiological studies reveal that the rate of AIDS cases among Latino men is 109.8 cases per 100,000, and 26.0 cases per 100,000 for Latino women (CDC, 1995). Furthermore, the AIDS epidemic among Latinos is representative of multiple epidemics of the same source, influenced by the variety in lifestyles of individuals from different Latino subgroups.

AIDS is unequally distributed among the Latino ethnic subgroups. Puerto Ricans and Cubans rank third and fifth in population size within the Latino ethnic subgroups in the United States. Yet, in 1991, Puerto Ricans and Cubans residing in the United States ranked first and second as the Latino subgroups with the most AIDS cases (Diaz, Buehler, Castro, & Ward, 1993; Marin & Gomez, 1994).

In metropolitan cities such as Chicago, New York, and Miami, Mexicans were reported to have the lowest reported incidence of AIDS among all Latino subgroups while Puerto Ricans have the highest (AIDS among Hispanics in Chicago, 1994; Diaz et al., 1993). However, several sources indicate the incidence rate among Mexicans may be inaccurate due to lack of documentation and fear of deportation (Diaz et al., 1993; Selik, Castro, Pappaionou, & Buehler, 1989).

Modes of transmission also vary greatly according to Latino ethnic subgroup, gender, and birthplace. Primary source of exposure to HIV infection among Mexican women is attributed to blood transfusions. Among Puerto Rican, Cuban, and Dominican Republic women, the principal mode of exposure is injected drug use, the same as for Puerto Rican men. However, among other Latino men including Mexicans, Cubans, and Central and South Americans residing in the United States, primary exposure is attributed to male to male sexual relations (Diaz et al., 1993).

FACTS ABOUT AIDS AND HIV INFECTION AMONG LATINOS

- AIDS is the 3rd leading cause of death among Latino women aged 25–44.
- AIDS is the leading cause of death among Latino men aged 25–44 and Latino children.
- Case rates for Latino adolescents/adults and children are 2.5 to 7.5 times higher than for non-Hispanic Whites.
- AIDS is the leading cause of death among Latino women in New York and New Jersey, ages 15–44.

CHILDREN

Latino children have been harshly affected by the AIDS epidemic. Latino children make up 11% of the infected population under the age of 15 years. Of children with AIDS, 21% were Latino children in 1991 (Carrillo

& Uranga-McKane, 1994). In AIDS cases attributed to infected blood products, percentages were much lower among Latino children compared to non-Latino children, at 9.4% and 30.94%, respectively. However, in perinatal transmission, this trend was reversed with Latino children at 87.7% versus non-Latinos at 67.8%.

Most perinatal transmission was related to maternal drug use or to maternal partner's drug use. In 1991, it was estimated that 84% of the children in the United States with AIDS acquired it perinatally. Twenty-six percent were Latino children. Twenty-eight percent of infected Latino children had mothers who were injection drug users or whose sex partners were injection drug users (Diaz et al., 1993). In New York City, 78% of perinatally transmitted cases of AIDS among Latino children were related to injection drug use (Giachello, 1994).

It is no surprise that AIDS is the leading cause of death among Latino children since there is approximately a 25% probability that children will be born HIV positive through perinatal transmission (Giachello, 1994). The implication for children in this transmission category is straightforward. As the number of women becoming infected with HIV and AIDS increases, the number of children who contract the virus will increase proportionally.

WOMEN

Women with AIDS in the United States represented 13% of the cumulative total of 58,448 cases reported during 1994. Latino women represented 20% of this total with an incidence rate of 26 per 100,000. This rate is six times higher than that of White women (3.8 per 100,000). The incidence of new cases continues to rise for both men and women, but the proportionate increase has been higher for women during the past few years. Good estimates of HIV seroprevalence among sexually active women, and specifically among Latino subgroups, are not available. Among the most important concerns is that the epidemic among women has increased dramatically in the past decade, and that little progress has been made in studying and intervening to prevent the spread of AIDS among women and children.

In New York and New Jersey, AIDS and HIV infection are the leading causes of death among women ages 25 to 44. For adult Chicago females diagnosed in 1993 and 1994, the main transmission mode is heterosexual contact: 69% for Mexican women; 54% for Puerto-Rican women; and 67% for other Hispanic women (AIDS Chicago, Fourth Quarter, 1994). The composition of the "other Hispanic" group is unknown. Anecdotally, it appears that there has been a recent migration of Central and South Americans into Chicago. There is very little information about this group.

A growing source of concern is the elevated incidence of heterosexually acquired HIV infection among non-intravenous drug user (NIVDU) Latino women. Between 1991 and 1992, the number of AIDS cases among heterosexual Latinos increased by 17% (CDC, 1993), and Latino females had the highest percentage increase of heterosexually acquired AIDS among all racial/ethnic categories (CDC, 1994). Of additional concern is the large number of Latino women of reproductive age infected with HIV/AIDS, and the implications for perinatal transmission.

Sexually active Latino women are believed to be at greatest risk for HIV infection and AIDS (Ellerbrock, Bush, & Chamberland, 1991; Singer et al., 1990) compared to non-Hispanic Whites. Behavioral, cultural, and environmental factors have been suggested as sources for the higher risk of heterosexual transmission of the disease among Latino women (Diaz et al., 1993; Singer et al., 1990). Among women with AIDS, 27% report intravenous drug use as a mode of transmission, yet at least 66% report heterosexual contact as the source of infection (CDC, 1995). Eighty percent of the AIDS cases in Latino women were either intravenous drug users or women whose male partners were intravenous drug users. The higher rate of IVDU among Latinos in general has also been observed (National Research Council [NRC], 1990). Substantial variation, however, in the pattern of infection has been found among the different Latino subpopulations and among U.S. and foreign-born Latinos (Diaz et al., 1993).

MEN

Approximately 90% of cumulative AIDS cases in the United States have been in adult/adolescent men. Between the years of 1981 and 1990, HIV infection was the second leading cause of death among all males aged 25 to 44 years in the United States. Among Latino men in this same age group, it was the leading cause of death (CDC, 1994).

Although there is evidence of declining incidence rates of male-male exposure of HIV infection, such information may not be accurate for the Latino male. Diaz reported the predominant exposure category among men of Central American, South American, Cuban, and Mexican descent were associated with male-male sex at 65%. In contrast, among Puerto Rican males, the primary exposure category was injection drug use (Diaz et al., 1993; Selik et al., 1989).

The role of the Latino male in preventing the spread of AIDS has not been assessed to date. Yet, several practices by these men such as low or no condom use, ignorance about the spread of HIV infection to their women and children, high-risk sexual practices (extramarital affairs, prostitutes, anal sex, and sex with other men) all play a major role in the spread of AIDS in this community.

ASSESSMENT

No effective HIV/AIDS treatments or vaccines have been developed yet, and none can be expected within the near future. At present, interventions must be directed at preventing transmission of HIV. Recent research has indicated that administration of Zidovudine to HIV-infected pregnant women and their newborns may reduce the risk of perinatal HIV transmission (Connor et al., 1994). Prevention is the only means available to avert the further rise of the AIDS epidemic in the United States. A more complete understanding of the social, cultural, and sexual environment that places some individuals from this population at particular risk is essential. It is also important to prevent tendencies toward stereotyping when discussing such issues.

Nonetheless, several aspects of Latino culture have been identified as potential barriers to the reduction of HIV transmission among this population. The concept of "machismo," for example, which exaggerates the importance of the male in Latino society, is viewed as increasing the Latino woman's HIV risk (Singer et al., 1990). Machismo is traditionally inculcated at an early age and stresses the dominant position of the male in Latino society to the point that, even within families with older female siblings, the boy is granted a position of dominance both in the eyes of the parents and among his female siblings. This cultural construct has been seen to impair the ability of Latino women to exert control over their own sexual behavior (Singer et al., 1990). In addition, males in Latino society are not culturally sanctioned from extramarital sexual activity, which has important repercussions for AIDS risk within the Latino family.

Among women, the concept of "marianismo" is equally prevalent. In this construct, the woman is expected to play a submissive, obedient, and subservient role to the man. Girls are educated at an early age to act as a "little woman" to their fathers, brothers, and husbands, while being self-sacrificing, chaste, dependent, and respectful to the male, and restricted to the home environment. A "good woman" traditionally centers her life around her husband and children and is expected to avoid self-indulgence and sensuality, while always remaining available to the sexual desires of her man (Singer et al., 1990). This role expectation has direct effects on the Latino woman's level of self-esteem (Marin, 1989), which in turn is related to powerlessness to control factors that place her at risk for HIV infection and AIDS (NRC, 1990; Singer et al., 1990). The lack of control Latino women have in sexual relations and contraceptive use increases their risk considerably.

The religiosity of Latino culture, in which approximately 85% of Latinos in the United States identify themselves as practicing Catholics (Medina, 1987), reinforces these gender roles and has a direct influence on Latino attitudes toward contraception in general and condom use in particular. Condoms are viewed among Latinos as associated with prostitution, sexually transmitted disease, uncleanliness, diminished sensation, and discomfort. These factors, as well as the expected submissive role of Latino women and the tendency toward modesty within Latino culture, act as important barriers to condom use among Latinos (Marin, 1989; NRC, 1990; Singer et al., 1990).

A lack of knowledge about HIV/AIDS and misconceptions about modes of transmission of the virus are prevalent among Latinos, with studies showing that Latinos score among the least knowledgeable of ethnic/racial groups (Aruffo, Coverdale, & Vallbona, 1991; Singer et al., 1990). The low levels of education and literacy among Latinos in general and the lack of culturally and linguistically appropriate educational and informational AIDS materials also contribute to the high infection risk among Latinos (NRC, 1990; Singer et al., 1990). Lower educational levels may also influence an individual's ability to use information to change behavior (Aruffo, Coverdale, & Vallbona, 1991).

The relationship between acculturation level and risk for certain diseases, as well as the effects of poverty on a population, have become apparent. In a study of Puerto Rican women, acculturation was a predictor of disease knowledge and risk for HIV. These results imply a future transmission among Puerto Rican women to mirror the transmission patterns of the non-Hispanic White females where drug use or contact with a user is the primary mode of exposure. Acculturation as a variable in disease prevention efforts among ethnic minorities has come under increasing study, accompanied by acculturation scales designed for the Latino population (Cuellar, Harris, & Jasso, 1980; Deyo, Diehl, Hazuda, & Stern, 1985; Szapocznik, Scopetta, Kurtines, & Aranalde, 1978). The positive association between acculturation and social mobility has serious implications for Latinos, many of whom remain among the lowest socioeconomic levels in the United States. Low acculturation levels have also been related to family conflicts, psychological problems, sex role conflicts, and drug use.

Studies have shown that traditional cultural views defined by religious, family, and social values reflect a protective effect in Latino women. However, low acculturated Latinos may be at a greater risk than their safe behavior suggests because perceived knowledge is low, knowledge about their body is limited, and they may not be able to negotiate condom usage with their husbands or sexual partners. Less acculturated Latino women also have greater misconceptions about the transmission of AIDS and are less aware that healthy people could be infected. In addition, perceived risk of contracting AIDS was found to be moderately underestimated among these women (Marin, 1989; Nyamathi et al., 1993; Peragallo, 1995).

The added pressures of poverty, including high male unemployment rates and the necessity for the female to seek employment outside of the home, which may create added stress by creating shifts in cultural norms, have further implications for placing Latinos at risk for HIV infection, particularly as they are related to the increase of IVDU among Latinos, and the accompanying unsafe sexual and needle-sharing practices (Diaz et al., 1993; Ellerbrock et al., 1991; Marin, 1989; NRC, 1990; Singer et al., 1990).

Aspects of Latino sexual behavior related to cultural norms place the Latino female at risk for HIV infection. Because homosexuality is highly stigmatized among Latinos, bisexual practices are not uncommon. It has been documented that some Latino men who engage in male-to-male sex do not regard themselves as homosexual, or even bisexual, as long as they assume the dominant role (insertive as opposed to receptive) and/or engage at the same time in heterosexual sex (Carrier, 1989; Holmes & Fernandez, 1988; Parker, 1988; Peragallo, 1992; Singer et al., 1990). Nor is there a stigma attached to this behavior, as long as the male fulfills his "masculine"—heterosexual—role.

There is some evidence that Hispanic men who engage in bisexual practices do not perceive themselves to be at risk of contracting AIDS because they do not define themselves as "gay" and AIDS is viewed as a "gay disease" (Marin, 1989; Medina, 1987). Their perception of risk for AIDS is underestimated with false interpretations of the disease and personal practices. As long as they assume the insertive versus receptive role in anal intercourse or continue to have sexual relations with women, Latino men believe they are not at risk for the disease (Carrier, 1989; Holmes & Fernandez, 1988; Parker, 1988). Economic considerations may also influence the frequency of liaisons with (receptive) homosexual men as an alternative to heterosexual sex (Carrier, 1989).

The reluctance to view homosexual activity as such has important implications for the perception of HIV/AIDS risk, given misconceptions of AIDS as a "gay" disease (NRC, 1990; Singer et al., 1990). At the same time, reports indicate that Latino men and women, as well as adolescents, engage in anal intercourse in order to avoid unwanted pregnancy and/or to maintain the woman's virginity, a status highly valued in this society (Carrier, 1989; Holmes & Fernandez, 1988; Parker, 1988; Singer et al., 1990).

Latino male contact with females may include women with "spoiled reputations," who fill the roles of prostitute, lover, or common-law wife. Extramarital sex is considered culturally acceptable for men. Results from a study by Choi, Catania, and Dolcini (1994) demonstrated Latino men were 7.5 times more likely than Latino women to have extramarital affairs. Degree of religiosity was a predictor of extramarital coitus among Latino females. However, this was not valid among Latino males (Choi, Catania, & Dolcini, 1994). There are also indications that homosexual extramarital relations are considered preferable, in that they represent less of a threat to the stability of the family (Singer et al., 1990).

Visiting prostitutes has also been seen as an accepted part of the sexual life of Latino males. In these relations, condom use is often avoided for fear that the prostitute may assume that the man is infected with a sexually transmitted disease (Carrier, 1989). Studies also indicate that many prostitutes are IVDUs and/or infected with HIV/AIDS (NRC, 1990). Men engaged in these practices are important vectors for transmission of the disease to Latino women. The likelihood of HIV/AIDS transmission is further increased by the reported reluctance of HIV-infected Latino men to inform their sexual partners of their infection risk (Marks, Richardson, Ruiz, & Maldonado, 1992).

Some studies of AIDS interventions that included women have shown that high risk behaviors were resistant to the intervention (Wiebel et al., 1993). Some found male-female differences in intervention outcomes; for example, condom use increased for men but not for women (Caslyn, Saxon, Wells, & Greenberg, 1992). One possible strong incentive for behavioral change among Latino females might be the opportunity to decrease the chance of giving birth to an infected child (Heagarty & Abrams, 1992). This could prove to be very important for Latino women, who place a high value on children.

Since women, particularly in Latino cultures, often have less control over sexual relationships than men, it is extremely important to investigate the dynamics of sexual relationships for Latino females, particularly with respect to communication, negotiation, gender roles, and power. Among Latinos, the concept of "machismo" fosters exaggerated male importance and dominance. Together with the concept of "marianismo," this leads to the socialization of girls and women as self-sacrificing, chaste, submissive, respectful, and obedient to men. These role expectations have been associated with low self-esteem and depression among Hispanic women—conditions that have been found to be associated with HIV risk behaviors (Emmons et al., 1987; Klein et al., 1987; Ostrow et al., 1987). The combination of submissive role expectations and low self-esteem may make Latino women more likely to agree to high-risk sexual practices, including anal intercourse, to defer to male refusal to use condoms, and to be reluctant to question husbands' extramarital sexual practices (Marin, 1989; Medina, 1987). In addition, the high value placed on female virginity before marriage has been found to encourage anal sex between unmarried heterosexual young people (Carrier, 1989; Parker, 1988).

Intervention efforts that rely on Latino women to introduce condoms into a sexual relationship ask that women assume new roles that may be construed as controlling men's sexuality and may lead to domestic conflict (Schneider, 1988, p. 99). The National Academy of Sciences (1990), in its most recent report on the prevention of HIV, recommended support of research to develop protective measures other than condoms for preventing HIV transmission during sexual contact—specifically, methods that can be used unilaterally by women. Until such an option is available, however, other strategies must be pursued.

Most earlier AIDS intervention research and many current studies have focused on homosexual men and IV drug users (Calsyn et al., 1992; Coates et al., 1988; Coates et al., 1989; D'Emaro et al., 1988; Des Jarlais & Friedman, 1988; Friedman et al., 1988; Hays, Kegeles, & Coates, 1993; Institute of Medicine, 1988, 1994; Kaplan & O'Keefe, 1993; Kelly et al., 1991; Kelly et al., 1992; Kelly, St. Lawrence, & Hood, 1989; Office of Technology Assessment, 1988; Valdiserri et al., 1989). Intervention studies of women usually concern IV drug users and do not consider Latino women (Caslyn et al., 1992; Colon, Rivera-Robels, Sahai, & Matos, 1992; El-Bassel & Schilling, 1992; Feucht, Stephens, & Gibbs, 1991; Friedman et al., 1991; Kaplan & O'Keefe, 1993; Magura et al., 1993; McCusker et al., 1992; Schilling et al., 1991; Stephens, Feucht, & Roman, 1991; Watters et al., 1994; Wiebel et al., 1993). It has been well established that it is of utmost importance to develop effective behavioral interventions to reduce risk of HIV infection, especially among women (Ickovics & Rodin, 1992; Mays & Cochran, 1988). We know now that male-to-female transmission is 12 times more effective than female-to-male transmission (Padian, Shiboski, & Jewel, 1990), and that minority populations, women of color, and inner city women are at greater risk.

The ability of individuals within the social and cultural context of their communities to recognize their problematic behaviors or to change them once recognized is influenced by community values that shape behaviors, perceptions of risk, and options for risk reduction. In the Hispanic culture, gender roles are important determinants of perceptions of risk, actual risk, and alternatives for risk reduction. However, the Latino's perception of risk for AIDS is faulty and attributable to a lack of both disease knowledge as well as knowledge of partners' activities. Although men and women alike are aware of the practices that increase risk for contracting the disease, many overlook their personal sexual practices and lifestyles, believing their risk for AIDS is minimal or nonexistent.

Helping this group to recognize risks in their own lives would aid in developing an effective intervention plan for this community.

Behavior change in one culture is not adequate to presume similar results will occur in different cultures. The preferred strategies being employed for risk reduction are not always those advocated by the larger society, and different cultures vary in their definitions of acceptability. The Catholic religion is deeply embedded in Hispanic culture, affecting sexual attitudes and practices. For example, condom use is low among Hispanic males. In addition to religious prohibitions against the use of contraceptives, condoms are associated in Hispanic culture with prostitution and uncleanliness as well as diminished sensation and discomfort (Marin, 1989). Celibacy or avoidance of homosexual relations is the preferred risk reduction strategy. However, results from a number of studies suggest that homosexual/bisexual men are reducing their risks not by celibacy but by reducing the number of sexual contacts outside of a primary relationship and/or eliminating or modifying anal intercourse by use of condoms (National Academy of Sciences, 1990). This creates difficulties in obtaining social support of prevention programs, since the most frequently used methods for reducing risk are commonly disapproved of. Clearly, AIDS prevention depends on identifying strategies that are accepted by those at risk and at least tolerated by the larger society, whose cooperation is essential for providing access to prevention alternatives.

The need for interventive and educational programs among the Latino population is evident. Low levels of AIDS knowledge and awareness, reluctance to abandon risky behavior, and more frequent misconceptions about AIDS and HIV transmission have made the Latino population extremely vulnerable.

Identification and understanding of the specific factors that place a population at risk are necessary steps toward designing effective educational and preventive programs. Failure to recognize women as a separate entity, rather than merely a vector for transmission, and to understand the cultural and socioeconomic diversity of target populations, as well as the lack of community involvement in necessary health services have placed this population at greater risk for the disease.

Any design for preventive and educational programs must take these risk behaviors into consideration, as well as understand them from within an appropriate cultural context. It is therefore imperative to formulate an accurate description of this population and the factors that contribute to their risk of AIDS/HIV.

Nursing is at the entry point of the health care system, thus placing nurses as gatekeepers in screening for risk for HIV infection, providing health services, education, information, and referral to those at risk in a culturally competent manner.

REFERENCES

AIDS among Hispanics in Chicago. (1994, Third Quarter). *AIDS Chicago: AIDS Surveillance Report,* 1-13.

Amaro, H. (1995). Love, sex, and power: Considering women's realities in HIV prevention. *American Psychologist, 50,* 437-447.

Aruffo, J. F., Coverdale, J. H., & Vallbona, C. (1991). AIDS knowledge in low-income and minority populations. *Public Health Reports, 106*(2), 115-119.

Bandura, A. (1977). Self-efficacy: Toward a unifying theory of behavioral change. *Psychology Review, 84,* 191-215.

Becker, M. H. (1974). The health belief model and personal health behavior. *Health Education Monograph, 2,* 220-243.

Calsyn, D., Saxon, A., Freeman, G., et al. (1992). Ineffectiveness of AIDS education and HIV antibody testing in reducing high-risk behaviors among injection drug users. *American Journal of Public Health, 82,* 573-757.

Calsyn, D., Saxon, A., Wells, E., & Greenberg, D. (1992). Longitudinal sexual behavior changes in injecting drug users. *AIDS, 6,* 1207-1211.

Carrier, J. M. (1989). Sexual behavior and spread of AIDS in Mexico. *Medical Anthropology, 10,* 129-142.

Carrillo, E., & Uranga-McKane, S. (1994). *HIV/AIDS.* In C. Molina & M. Aguirre-Molina (Eds.), *Latino health in the U.S.: A growing challenge* (pp. 313-337). Washington, DC: American Public Health Association.

Catania, J. A., Kegeles, S. M., & Coates, T. J. (1990). Toward an understanding of risk behavior: An AIDS risk education model (AREM). *Health Education Quarterly, 17*(1), 53-72.

CDC. (1993, November 19). Update: Mortality attributable to HIV infection among persons aged 25-44 years—United States, 1991 and 1992. *MMRW, 42*(45), 869-872.

CDC. (1994, April 29). Zidovudine for the prevention of HIV transmission from mother to infant. *MMRW, 43*(16), 285.

CDC. (1994, August 5). Recommendations of the U.S. Public Health Service Task Force on the use of Zidovudine to reduce perinatal transmission of human immunodeficiency virus. *MMRW, 43,* RR-11.

CDC. (1994, November 18). Update: Trends in AIDS diagnosis and reporting under the expanded surveillance definition for adolescents and adults—United States, 1993. *MMRW, 43*(45), 826-835.

CDC. (1995, February 10). Update: AIDS among women—United States, 1994. *MMRW, 44*(5), 81-83.

Choi, K. H., Catania, J. A., & Dolcini, M. M. (1994). Extramarital sex and HIV risk behavior among U.S. adults: Results from the National AIDS Behavior Survey. *American Journal of Public Health, 84,* 2003-2007.

Coates, R. A., Calzavara, L. M., Soskolne, C. L., Read, S. E., Flanning, M. M., Sheperd, F. A., Klein, M. H., & Johnson, J. K. (1988). Validity of sexual histories in a prospective study of male sexual contacts of men with AIDS or an AIDS-related condition. *American Journal of Epidemiology, 128,* 719-728.

Coates, T. J., McKusick, L., Kuno, R., & Stites, D. P. (1989). Stress management training changed number of sexual partners but not immune function in men infected with HIV. *American Journal of Public Health, 79,* 885-887.

Colon, H. M., Rivera-Robels, R., Sahai, H., & Matos, T. (1992). Changes in HIV risk behaviors among intravenous drug users in San Juan, Puerto Rico. *British Journal of Addiction, 87*(4), 585-590.

Connor, E. M., Sperling, R. S., Gelber, R., Kisseley, P., Scott, G., Osullivian, M. J., Vandyke, M., Bey, W., Shearrer, R. L., Jacobson, E., Jimenez, E., Oneill, B., & Brazin, J. F. (1994). Reduction of maternal-infant transmission of human immunodeficiency virus type 1 with Zidovudine treatment. *The New England Journal of Medicine, 331*(8), 1173.

Cuellar, I., Harris, L. C., & Jasso, R. (1980). An acculturation scale for Mexican-Americans: Normal and clinical populations. *Hispanic Journal of Behavioral Sciences, 75,* 51-55.

D'Emaro, J., Quadland, M., Shattls, W., Schuman, R., & Jacobs, R. (1988). *The "800 men" project: A systematic evaluation of AIDS prevention programs demonstrating the efficacy of erotic, sexually explicit safer sex education on gay and bisexual men at risk for AIDS.* Paper presented at the IVth International Conference on AIDS. Stockholm, Sweden.

Des Jarlais, D. C., & Friedman, S. R. (1988). The psychology of preventing AIDS among intravenous drug users. *American Psychologist, 43*(11), 865-870.

Deyo, R. A., Diehl, A. K., Hazuda, H., & Stern, M. P. (1985). A simple language-based acculturation scale for Mexican-Americans: Validation and application to health care research. *American Journal of Public Health, 75,* 51-55.

Diaz, T., Buehler, J. W., Castro, K. G., & Ward, J. W. (1993). AIDS trends among Hispanics in the United States. *American Journal of Public Health, 83*(4), 504-509.

Ekstrand, M., & Coates, T. (1988, June). *Prevalence and change of AIDS high-risk behaviors among gay and bisexual men.* Paper presented at the IV International Conference on AIDS. Stockholm, Sweden.

El-Bassel, N., & Schilling, R. (1992). Fifteen-month follow up of women methadone patients taught to reduce heterosexual HIV transmission. *Public Health Reports, 107,* 500-504.

Ellerbrock, T. V., Bush, T. J., & Chamberland, M. J. (1991). Epidemiology of women with AIDS in the United States, 1981 through 1990. *Journal of the American Medical Association, 265*(22), 2971-2975.

Emmons, C. A., Joseph, J. G., Kessler, R. C., Watman, C. B., Montgonery, S. B., & Ostrow, P. G. (1987). Psychosocial predictors of reported behavior in homosexual men at risk for AIDS. *Health Education Quarterly, 13*(4), 331-345.

Feucht, T. E., Stephens, R. C., & Gibbs, B. H. (1991). Knowledge about AIDS among intravenous drug users: An evaluation of an education program. *AIDS Education Prevention, 3*(1), 10-20.

Friedman, S. R., Des Jarlais, D. C., Sotheray, J., Garber, J., Cohen, H., & Smith, D. (1988). AIDS and self-organization among intravenous drug users. *International Journal of Addictions, 23*(3), 201-219.

Friedman, S. R., Jose, B., Neaigus, A., et al. (1991). *Peer mobilization and widespread condom use by drug injectors.* Paper presented at the VI International Conference on AIDS. Florence, Italy.

Giachello, A. (1994). *Maternal/perinatal health.* In C. Molina & M. Aguirre-Molina (Eds.), *Latino health in the U.S.: A growing challenge* (pp. 313-337). Washington, DC: American Public Health Association.

Hays, R., Kegeles, S., & Coates, T. (1993). *Community mobilization promotes safer sex among gay and bisexual men.* Paper presented at the IX International Conference on AIDS. Berlin, Germany.

Heagarty, M., & Abrams, E. (1992). Caring for HIV-infected women and children. *The New England Journal of Medicine, 2,* 887.

HIV/AIDS Surveillance Report (1994). *U.S. HIV and AIDS cases reported through June 1994, 6*(1), 1-27.

Holmes, V., & Fernandez, R. (1988). HIV in women: Current impact and future implications. *The Female Patient, 13,* 47-54.

Icovics, J., & Rodin, R. (1992). Women and AIDS in the United States: Epidemiology, natural history and mediation mechanisms. *Health Psychology, 11,* 1-16.

Institute of Medicine. (1988). *Confronting AIDS.* Washington, DC: National Academy Press.

Institute of Medicine (1994). *Development of anti-addiction medications: Issues for the government and private sector.* Washington, DC: National Academy Press.

Kaplan, E., & O'Keefe, E. (1993). Let the needles do the talking! Evaluation of the New Haven needle exchange. *Interfaces, 23,* 7-26.

Kelly, J., St. Lawrence, J., Diaz, Y., Stevenson, L., Hauth, A., Brasfield, L., Kalichman, S., Smith, J., & Andrew, M. E. (1991). HIV risk behavior reduction following intervention with key opinion leaders of population: An experimental analysis. *American Journal of Public Health, 81,* 168-171.

Kelly, J., St. Lawrence, J., & Hood, H. (1989). Behavioral interventions to reduce AIDS risk activities. *Journal of Consulting and Clinical Psychology, 57,* 60-67.

Kelly, J., St. Lawrence, J., Stevenson, Y., Hauth, A., Brasfield, T., Kalichman, S., Smith, J., & Andrew, M. (1992). Community AIDS/HIV risk reduction: The effects of endorsements by popular people in three cities. *American Journal of Public Health, 82,* 1483-1489.

Kelly, J. A., Murphy, D. A., Washington, C. D., Wilson, T. S., Koob, J. J., Davis, D. R., Ledezman, G., & Davantes, B. (1994). The effects of HIV/ AIDS intervention groups for high risk women in urban clinics. *American Journal of Public Health, 84*(12), 1918-1922.

Klein, D. E., Sullivan, G., Wolcott, D. D., Landsverk, J., Namir, S., & Fawzy, F. (1987). Changes in AIDS risk behaviors among homosexual male physicians and university students. *American Journal of Psychiatry, 144*(6), 742-747.

Leventhal, H., Hochbaum, G., & Rosenstock, I. (1973). *The impact of Asian influenza on community life: A study in five cities.* (Pub. No. 766). U.S. Department Health Education and Welfare, Public Health Service: Washington, DC.

Magura, S., Siddiqi, Q., Shapiro, J., Grossman, J., & Lipton, D. (1991). Outcomes of an AIDS prevention program for methadone patients. *The International Journal of Addictions, 26,* 629-655.

Marin, B., & Gomez, C. (1994). Latinos, HIV disease and cultural strategies for HIV. *Prevention and Education,* 1-13.

Marin, B., Gomez, B., & Hearst, N. (1993). Multiple heterosexual partners and condom use among Hispanics and non-Hispanic Whites. *Family Plan Perspect, 25,* 170-174.

Marin, B., & Marin, G. (1990). Effects of acculturation on knowledge of AIDS and HIV among Hispanics. *Hispanic Journal of Behavioral Science, 12,* 110-121.

Marin, G. (1989). AIDS prevention among Hispanics: Needs, risk behaviors, and cultural values. *Public Health Reports, 104,* 411-415.

Marin, G., Sabogal, F., Marin, B., Otero-Sabogal, R., & Perez-Stable, E. (1987). Development of a short acculturation scale for Hispanics. *Hispanic Journal of Behavioral Sciences, 9*(2), 183-205.

Marin, G., Tschann, J., Gomez, C., et al. (1993). Acculturation and gender differences in sexual attitudes and behaviors: A comparison of Hispanic and non-Hispanic White unmarried adults. *American Journal of Public Health, 83,* 1759-1761.

Marks, G., Richardson, J. L., Ruiz, M. S., & Maldonado, N. (1992). HIV-infected men's practices in notifying past sexual partners of infection risk. *Public Health Reports, 107*(1), 100-104.

Mays, V. M., & Cochran, S. D. (1988). Issues in the perception of AIDS risk and risk reduction by Black and Hispanic/Latino women. *American Psychologist, 43,* 949-957.

McCusker, J., Stoddard, A., Zapka, J., Morrison, C., Zorn, M., & Lewis, B. (1992). AIDS education for drug abusers: Evaluation of short-term effectiveness. *American Journal of Public Health, 82,* 533-540.

Medina, C. (1987). Latino culture and sex education. *Siecus Report, 15*(3), 2-4.

National Academy of Sciences. (1990). *AIDS: The second decade.* Washington, DC: National Academy Press.

National Research Council. (1990). *AIDS: The second decade.* National Academy Press/National Research Council, Washington, DC.

Nyamathi, A., Bennett, C., Leake, B., Lewis, C., & Flaskerud, J. (1993). AIDS—Related knowledge, perceptions, and behaviors among impoverished minority women. *American Journal of Public Health, 83,* 65-71.

Nyamathi, A. M., Leake, B., Flaskerud, J., Lewis, C., & Bennett, C. (1993). Outcomes of specialized and traditional AIDS counseling programs for impoverished women of color. *Research in Nursing and Health Care, 16*(1), 11-21.

Office of Technology Assessment. (1988). *How effective is AIDS education?* Washington, DC: U.S. Congress Office of Technology Assessment.

Olmedo, E., Marinez, J. L., & Martinez, S. R. (1978). Measure of acculturation for Chicano adolescents. *Psychology Reports, 42,* 159, 170.

Ostrow, D. G., Joseph, J. G., Morgan, A., Kessler, R., Emmons, C., Phair, J., Fox, R., Kingsley, L., Dudley, J., Chmiel, J., & Van Raden, M. (1987). Psychosocial aspects of AIDS risk. *Psychopharmacological Bulletin, 22,* 678-683.

Padian, N., Shiboski, S., & Jewell, N. (1990). The effect of number of exposures on the risk of heterosexual HIV transmission. *Journal of Infectious Diseases, 161,* 883-887.

Parker, R. (1988). Acquired immunodeficiency syndrome in urban Brazil. *Medical Anthropology Quarterly, 1*(2), 155-175.

Peragallo, N. (1992). *A nursing intervention to prevent AIDS in Chile.* Unpublished raw data.

Peragallo, N. (1995). Latino women and AIDS risk. Submitted to *Journal of Public Health Nursing.*

Race and Hispanic origin. (1991). *1990 Census Profile.* Washington, DC: U.S. Department of Commerce, Bureau of the Census.

Rotheram-Borus, M. J., & Koopman, C. (1991). Sexual risk behaviors, AIDS knowledge, and beliefs about AIDS among runaways. *American Journal of Public Health, 81*(2), 208-210.

Schilling, R., el-Bassel, N., Schinke, S., Gordon, K., & Nichols, S. (1991). Building skills of recovering women drug users to reduce heterosexual AIDS transmission. *Public Health Reports, 106,* 297-304.

Schneider, B. E. (1988). Gender and AIDS. In R. Kulstak (Ed.), *AIDS 1988: AAAS Symposia Papers.* Washington, DC: American Association for the Advancement of Science.

Selik, R., Castro, K., Pappaionou, M., & Buehler, J. (1989). Birthplace and the risk of AIDS among Hispanics in the United States. *American Journal of Public Health, 79,* 836-839.

Singer, M., Flores, C., Davison, L., Burke, G., Castillo, Z., Scanlon, K., & Rivera, M. (1990). SIDA: The economic, social and cultural context of AIDS among Latinos. *Medical Anthropology Quarterly, 4*(1), 72-113.

Stephens, R., Feucht, T., & Roman, S. (1991). Effects of an intervention program of AIDS related drug and needle behavior among intravenous drug users. *American Journal of Public Health, 81,* 568-571.

Szapocznik, J., Scopetta, M. A., Kurtines, W., & Aranalde, M. A. (1978). Theory and measurement of acculturation. *Interamerican Journal of Psychology, 12,* 113-130.

Ten thousand cumulative AIDS cases. (1994, Fourth Quarter). *AIDS Chicago: AIDS Surveillance Report,* 1-12.

Valdiserri, R., Lyter, D., & Leviton, L. (1989). AIDS prevention in homosexual and bisexual men: Results of a randomized trial evaluating two risk reduction interventions. *AIDS, 3,* 21-26.

Watters, J., Estilo, M., Clark, G., & Lorrich, J. (1994). Syringe and needle exchange as HIV/AIDS prevention for injection drug users. *Journal of the American Medical Association, 271,* 115-120.

Wiebel, W., Jimenez, A., Johnson, W., Ouellet, L., Lampinen, T., Murray, J., Javanovic, B., & O'Brien, M. (1993). *Positive effect on HIV seroconversion of street outreach intervention with IUDs in Chicago: 1988-1992.* Paper presented at the IXth International Conference on AIDS. Berlin, Germany.

CHAPTER TEN

The Sociocultural Context of Stress and Depression in Hispanics

Ester Ruiz Rodriguez, PhD, RN, CS

I recall my mother telling me as I was growing up that Anglo women did not take good care of their young children. She saw Anglo mothers as encouraging their children to emulate inappropriate adult ways, such as asking questions and demanding to be heard. As I went on to college and interacted more with Anglos, I learned that Anglo mothers valued independence and assertiveness and sought to impart these traits to their children. To my traditional Mexican mother this appeared somewhat odd—as not allowing children to be children. Her perception about what was problematic clashed with the Anglos' perception about what was appropriate socialization behavior. Culture influences our perceptions, what we see and hear and how we organize information (Antai-Otong, 1995). The meaning attributed to being ill, for example, is distinct from the objective progression of a disease and is largely directed by cultural perception (Kleinman, 1987). What is labeled as a symptom, and the expectations for how the symptom is treated, also varies cross-culturally (McGoldrick, Pearce, & Giordano, 1985).

Changes in culture either as a consequence of time or migration reveal the damaging as well as the protective health aspects of a particular cultural group. However, it is not the cultural change per se that affects health, but the extent to which cultural values, rules of behavior, and traditional ways of coping are affected (Corin, 1994). Cultural change from both time (exposure to the dominant culture) and migration (continued immigration and farmworker migration) exerts an effect on Hispanics living in the United States today. It is thus not surprising that perceptions of conflict, stress, or behavioral/psychological disorders are dependent on the cultural context within which such phenomena appear. Different cultures reinforce, support, and tolerate different behaviors and provide acceptable ways for their expression. Cultural context defines what is normal and healthy, yet what is normal and healthy is not universal across cultures nor across gender (Hughes, 1978).

In this chapter, then, I will focus my discussion on the sociocultural context of stress and depression in Hispanics, including suggestions for making culturally sensitive assessments. The following case study illustrates, as well, the relevance of sociocultural context on clinical presentation of issues involving stress and depression.

The Case of Señora C

Señora C was a monolingual (Spanish only) migrant farm worker who was born and raised in Mexico and as an adult came to the United States with her six children to be with her husband. Seeking help, she saw her family nurse practitioner who then referred her to a psychiatric clinical nurse specialist (CNS).The nurse practitioner wondered if Señora C should be medicated for her depressive symptomatology. Señora C's presenting complaint was wanting to understand why she could not stop thinking of a young woman whose murder she had witnessed three months before. She did not perceive herself as depressed although for the past three weeks she had been experiencing early morning awakening and decreased appetite, energy, and sexual interest. She also reported an overwhelming urge to cry without any logical reason. Her husband was upset with her for disturbing his sleep. According to him, Señora C was getting up in the middle of the night and looking out the windows as if searching for something. Señora C had no memory of being out of bed.

Although from a professional's perspective, witnessing a murder would qualify as ample trauma to explain the subsequent symptomatology, Señora C disagreed with the referring nurse practitioner's assessment. Her reasoning was that she hardly knew the murdered woman, the woman had died three months before, while her symptoms had started only three weeks ago.

Señora C was an employee of a packing plant where she worked twelve-hour days six days per week and could not afford to take another day to seek medical attention. It was evident that the CNS would get only one opportunity to help Señora C. The CNS asked Señora C what she thought was going on. She was silent and scrutinized the CNS for a few moments and then replied that she thought that the "dead woman's spirit" was wandering around the packing plant. After dark she and her coworkers became frightened and refused to use the restroom facilities for fear of encountering the dead woman's spirit. The CNS asked her to say more. She proceeded to reveal in detail the murder she had witnessed.

The young woman and her boyfriend were having an argument at work. At one point, the young woman turned to Señora C and asked her to call the foreman and the police. When Señora C returned to her work station after having informed the foreman, the boyfriend shot the young woman and a man who had come to the young woman's aid. The boyfriend fired at Señora C but missed. The boyfriend was eventually subdued. As she was dying, the young woman implored her work colleagues to please take care of her children. Señora C reports that after the funeral she and her colleagues agonized regarding what to do about the children since they wanted to honor the dying woman's request. They collected money and sent it to the children who were all in Mexico.

Señora C then stated that the young woman's spirit was wandering around the plant because she and her colleagues had failed to have a mass for the young woman at the plant as they had desired. The owner, who was not Catholic, did not allow it. The CNS asked what could be done now. Señora C stated that she and a few of her friends could say a few prayers at the plant and perhaps rid themselves of the young woman's spirit, and the owner need never know. Although she experienced some relief with this decision, the CNS reflected that she still seemed burdened. Señora C replied, "Why can't I forget her? She was nothing to me. I hardly knew her." The CNS pointed out that she still seemed to have some unfinished business with the dead young woman, and Señora C shook her head affirmatively. The CNS wondered aloud if there was a message involved and Señora C again shook her head affirmatively and stated, "Yes, but what is it?"

The CNS decided to use the empty chair gestalt technique to help Señora C attempt to decipher the message. After carefully explaining that an exercise involving the imagination might be helpful in helping to decipher "the message," Señora C agreed to try. With direction, Señora C was able to imagine the dead young woman sitting in the empty chair across from her. She described her appearance including the clothing the young woman was wearing. The CNS suggested and Señora C complied by asking the young woman if she had a message for her. Señora C said, "She says yes." Again the CNS suggested and Señora C complied by asking, "What is your message?" At this point, Señora C's face contorted and her abdominal muscles contracted in an undulating motion so that she appeared as if she might vomit. What came out of her mouth, however, was agonizing grief and she wept for several minutes during which the CNS sat by her and quietly waited. When she quieted down, the CNS asked what the young woman had replied. Señora C simply said, "my daughter."

Señora C proceeded to talk about her own eighteen-year-old daughter who had eloped the year before and married someone of whom her husband disapproved. He had subsequently disowned the daughter and forbade Señora C to contact her. About four weeks earlier, Señora C had inadvertently heard that her daughter was having problems and was scheduled for uterine surgery. She was extremely worried about her daughter but did not know how to contact her without incurring her husband's wrath. Upon hearing herself verbalize this, Señora C decided that contacting her daughter was more important than following her husband's edict. She was significantly relieved by her decision. Her face softened and she visibly appeared less burdened. The CNS discussed the ramifications of her decision, especially the consequences upon her relationship with her husband. Señora C was adamant, however, that her daughter needed her and nothing was more important than that. Who knew what the future held, look what had happened to the poor dead woman who never got to see her children again. Señora C was very thankful for the CNS's time, but no she could not take more time off of work to return to talk.

Two months after this episode, the CNS saw Señora C at a local school where the CNS was to give a presentation on the mental health of adolescents. Señora C walked up to the CNS and said that she had come especially to tell the CNS how helpful she had been. Señora C related that she and some fellow workers held a small mass at the plant, and the dead woman's spirit was no longer plaguing them. She had recontacted her daughter and her husband had relented, adjusted to, and forgiven her and the daughter. More importantly, her maternal bond and role were reestablished with her daughter and she now wanted to refer her daughter for counseling with the CNS.

STRESS IN HISPANICS

There are several broad categories of predisposing factors to stress. First, there are the biological factors, which include genetic background, nutritional status, biological sensitivities, and general health. Second, there are psychological factors, which include intelligence, verbal skills, personality, and self-esteem. Lastly, and more germane to our discussion, are sociocultural factors, which include age, gender, education, socioeconomic level, religious upbringing, and cultural background. This last category is what constitutes the sociocultural context of an individual's experience, and significantly affects how an individual appraises, responds to, and is affected by stress. The sociocultural context provides the individual with the symbols and meaning of particular events, and provides a frame of reference through which the environment is perceived, stressors appraised, and coping skills developed.

One of Leininger's (1978) primary beliefs was that a nurse needs to examine cultural beliefs and practices to establish the sociocultural context of the client (whether individual, family, group, or community). Such a systematic appraisal allows the nurse to intervene within the cultural context of the client. Andrews and Boyle (1995) also suggest that a cultural assessment consists of both process and content. The process consists of the nurse's approach while content is related to the actual information collected about the client.

The information (content) Señora C offered indicated that she was a mother of six, lived in a patriarchal marital relationship, had clear ideas about her problems (symbols and meanings were culturally bound), and had a strong belief in prayer and the power of the Catholic mass (solutions). The process involved eliciting from the client in her own language her perception of the problem and her solutions. Process also involved reflecting on her nonverbal behavior. The empty chair intervention was couched as an exercise of the imagination, a framework she could understand. This is particularly important for a client who believes in the supernatural. Without an adequate explanation, a client such as Señora C could resist the intervention, or attribute malicious intent to the provider. Both result in lessened provider credibility and a weakened nurse-client relationship. Permission to proceed with the exercise was also solicited, thus respecting the client's right of refusal and engaging the client in the intervention. The process also involved discussing the ramifications of decisions chosen by the client.

Various studies have revealed relevant findings about the mitigating influence of culture on stress and disease. Berkman and Syme (1979) reported that social connectedness offers a buffer against disease and mortality. Marmor (1981) concluded that aspects of culture can act as buffers against stress. In Hispanics, social connectedness/social support was also found relevant. De la Rosa (1988) reported that social support enabled Puerto Rican subjects to cope with stressful situations and, consequently, were less likely to become ill. Briones et al. (1990) found direct associations between level of stress and depression and between support networks and depression. Individuals with more life stresses had higher rates of depression; however, support networks mitigated the influence of stress on depression, thus decreasing rates of depression. Prior knowledge of the particular camp in which Señora C resided allowed the CNS an insider's view of Señora C's social network as well. Migrant farm workers may stay at the same place from a few weeks to several months. Señora C's coworkers, although supportive, did not form a consistent social network. In Mexico, a disruption in family ties might have been mitigated by the extended family. Other members most likely would have kept track of Señora C's daughter and conveyed messages and information back and forth without violating her husband's command. Additionally, family pressure might have softened Mr. C's attitude. However, since the C's had no extended family in the United States and their social network consisted of work colleagues, such an option was not possible. Because the CNS was aware of the traditional aspects of Señora C's culture, which places a greater emphasis on relationships, relationship needs took precedence over individual needs.

Every Hispanic, like individuals from other ethnic minority groups, functions simultaneously in two systems: the immediate nurturing environment and the larger societal system (Norton, 1978). This dual affiliation places a burden on Hispanic parents who must attempt to build their own and their children's self-esteem within their own culture yet socialize them into the dominant society (Julian, McKenry, & McKelvey, 1994). Building self-esteem within their own culture is important and has been found to be one of the best predictors of stress resilience (Padilla, Wagatsuma, & Lindholm, 1985). Señora C functioned in two systems: her immediate family served as her nurturing system while her work and the health care system belonged to the dominant society. Increased stress is experienced by first generation individuals like Señora C when dealing with dominant society institutions.

Acculturative stress is the stress experienced by individuals as they accommodate and adjust to the culture of the United States. For Hispanics, acculturative stress has received increasing attention in the literature as a risk factor for affective disorders. Smart and Smart (1995) defined acculturative stress as "the psychological impact of adaptation to a new culture" (p. 25). The integral nature of the family in daily life, strong kinship bonds, and the family as a problem-solving unit make Hispanic families especially susceptible to the stresses of acculturation. Such stresses can lead to disrupted social ties when the extended family and the nuclear family are separated by distance, greater risk for physical illness, and role entrapment due to sociopolitical factors which relegate low acculturated individuals to service or menial labor (Smart & Smart, 1995). Furthermore, the disruptive nature of acculturative stress adversely affects the family's decision-making process (Smart & Smart, 1994).

Señora C was a victim of acculturative stress. Being monolingual Spanish affected her ability to affectively and effectively interact with the dominant English-speaking world. Her inability to speak English and adjust to the dominant society values kept her trapped in farm labor positions where her work colleagues and immediate supervisors all spoke Spanish.

One of several findings reported by Padilla, Wagatsuma, and Lindholm (1985) suggests that each generation experiences acculturative stress differently. Their research concluded that the most stress was experienced by first-generation Mexican-Americans (those who were born in Mexico and migrated to the United States), followed by third-generation Mexican-Americans (those who were born in the United States, and their parents were born in the United States, but all their grandparents were born in Mexico).

It is not surprising that first-generation immigrants experience stress in adapting to the United States. Leaving one's country of origin and migrating to a country with different values, customs, and language would induce stress. It is, however, interesting that third-generation Mexican-Americans, who along with their parents lived their entire lives in the United States, experience more acculturative stress than second-generation Mexican-Americans.

This finding may be related to the phenomena that Hayes-Bautista found in third-generation Hispanics (1994). By the third generation, whatever psychological and physiological immunity Latino immigrants possess when they migrate to the United States is lost. An increased vulnerability to disease accompanies increased acculturation for Latinos and increased tendency for lower birth weight babies. Furthermore, as acculturation increases, increased smoking and drinking patterns in women approximate mainstream society's levels (Black & Markides, 1993), and rates of depression among Hispanics increase as well (Golding, Karno, & Rutter, 1990).

However, Fernandez and Sanchez's (1992, 1993) results support that Hispanic identification is independent from American identification. Weak identification with the American mainstream society (low acculturation) was associated with increased acculturative stress and perceptions of discrimination. More importantly, when low identification with the mainstream was accompanied with strong ethnic identification, adjustment was hampered even more. In a meta-analytic study of 49 reports, Moyerman and Forman (1992) reported that in the relationship between acculturation and adjustment, socioeconomic status was a significant intervening variable. Higher socioeconomic level participants demonstrated greater increases in adjustment with acculturation. This finding supports earlier comparisons between upper middle and lower socioeconomic Cuban immigrants and their adjustment to the United States (Pedraza-Bailey, 1985).

Señora C is an example of an individual with weak mainstream identification and strong ethnic identification, whose life circumstances are likely to keep her in this mode. Her lack of language proficiency, low socioeconomic status, traditional Hispanic gender ascription, and low education restrict her environment and networks to those that are more similar to her than not. Increased variability in environment and networks provide a contrast or stimulation which could facilitate increased acculturation.

A study which focused on stress and coping strategies among early immigrants (migration before 12 years of age), late immigrants (migration after 12 years of age), second-generation Hispanics (parents born outside of the United States), and third-generation Hispanics (grandparents born outside of the United States) was conducted by Mena, Padilla, and Maldonado (1987). Late immigrants experienced greater acculturative stress than the other groups, and coped by taking a direct, planned action (individualistic approach). Second- and third-generation groups coped by talking to others about the problem (social network). Early immigrants employed both coping strategies. This study suggests a shift of how stress is perceived in groups who come from a majority and move into a minority position. Señora C came to the United States as an adult and she came from a country where she was part of the majority. She responded in a fashion consistent with the Mena, Padilla, and Maldonado first-generation research participants. Her response to her problem was to seek an individual solution by going to the local health clinic.

DEPRESSION IN HISPANICS

With her depressive symptomatology, Señora C is a good example of what the research on depression in Hispanics has revealed: she was a woman, an ethnic minority group member, undereducated, and poor. Consistently, the literature on depression has indicated that regardless of ethnicity, women tend to have more depressive symptoms than men (Kaplan, 1986; Russo, Amaro, & Winter, 1987). Frequent correlates of depression are female gender, lower socioeconomic level, and lower educational level (Belle, 1984; Gibson, 1983; Golding & Burman, 1990; Hall, Williams, & Greenburg, 1985). Salgado de Synder, Cervantes, and Padilla (1990) suggest that Hispanic females are more likely to suffer from affective disorders because of biological vulnerability, sex role conflicts, lack of adequate social support networks, and lack of control over their environment. Other risk factors correlated with depression for Hispanic women are an overrepresentation of younger ages and living arrangements incongruent with gender stereotypes of the Hispanic women. One in seven Hispanic women over the age of 15 is separated or divorced, and many have no husband present (Amaro, 1987).

Golding, Karno, and Rutter (1990) reported that two-week rates of dysphoria were common in non-Hispanic Whites and Hispanics. For Hispanics born in the United States, the rates of depressive symptoms were similar to those of non-Hispanic Whites. Rates of depressive symptoms were higher for the U.S.-born Mexicans than for Mexicans born in Mexico.

On the other hand, Salgado de Synder (1987) reports that female Mexican immigrants as a group are at risk for the development of psychological problems. Salgado de Snyder examined depressive symptomatology in Hispanic subjects. Subjects who experienced discrimination, gender-role conflicts, and concerns about raising a family in the United States had significantly higher depressive symptomatology scores. Señora C's conflicts with her husband regarding interaction with their daughter were gender-role conflicts and certainly familial concerns were evident.

Traditional cultural expectations may predispose Hispanic women to depression according to Hernandez (1986). Specifically, Hernandez cites several cultural beliefs and behaviors as conducive to depression. Among them are passivity or an unassertiveness toward father, husband, and other male authority figures; manipulation; seduction or cultural intolerance for differences, distrust, and confusion about sexuality; and obligation or an overinvolvement with children. Señora C certainly was unassertive with her husband and was strongly connected with her children. Her children provided her with motivation to assert herself with her husband. Other than decreased interest in sexual intimacy, no other information was solicited about Señora C's sexuality.

Multiplicity of stressful situations has also been implicated in depression for Hispanic women. With increasing life stresses, Puerto Rican women experience powerlessness, low self-esteem, loss of identity, and depression (Comas-Diaz, 1981). Multiple life stresses were evident in Señora C's life—marital and family issues, work concerns, and situational issues related to poverty.

What is considered normal or abnormal is based on one's cultural perspective. Culture influences the expression, presentation, recognition, labeling, explanations for, and distribution of illness. How symptoms are expressed and how they are perceived and treated vary widely, however. According to Escobar (1987), Hispanics are high somaticizers. They may deny depression but complain of headaches, backaches, stomach aches, and other physical phenomena prompted (sometimes consciously associated) with sorrow and suffering. Although Señora C acknowledged somatic symptoms, in contrast to high somaticizers, she did not present them as her reason for seeking treatment. Her main concern was ridding herself of unwanted thoughts of the dead woman.

Golding, Burnam, Benjamin, and Wells (1993) cite alcohol use and abuse as factors related to primary and secondary depression among Mexican-Americans and White non-Hispanic Americans. In their study, results indicate that alcohol dependency or abuse increased the risk of major depression 2 to 7 times. Drinking to forget increased the risk for Mexican-American alcoholics but not non-Hispanic Whites and abstinence was associated with greater risk for depression among lifetime alcoholics born in Mexico but not native-born Mexican-Americans (Golding et al., 1993). Low-income, female gender, and low acculturation were associated with increased risk for secondary depression. Alcohol or drug use was not a contributing risk factor to Señora C's dysphoria as she did not drink alcohol or use drugs.

Access to mental health services has been an issue for many years when utilization patterns between Hispanic and non-Hispanics are reviewed. However, Hispanic women more than Hispanic men are underrepresented in mental health facilities, and this difference appears related to marital status according to McGrath, Keita, Strickland, and Russo (1990). However, the path analysis research conducted by Briones et al. (1990) suggests that other factors are involved with mental health treatment readiness. Their research suggests that socioeconomic status is more indicative of utilization readiness than ethnicity.

Señora C exhibited many of the risk factors for depression that have been mentioned. She was female and poor with low acculturation and low education. Her peer and culturally supported belief in the supernatural could have been misinterpreted if she had offered this information through an interpreter to a health provider not sensitive to the nuances of Señora C's culture.

Several factors have been identified in the above discussion relating to affective functioning in Hispanics. Acculturative stress, female gender, socioeconomic level, and alcohol consumption are risk factors which increase Hispanic susceptibility to stress disorders and depression. Acculturative stress is disruptive to families, and in some studies has been related to increased overall stress and psychological functioning. Some studies suggest that higher acculturation is associated with increased stress, while other studies suggest the opposite. Gender differences have been implicated with acculturative stress and depressive symptomatology, as has low socioeconomic level. Associations between acculturative stress and ethnic loyalty, and family pride may be tapping into an ethnic identity component of acculturation. In spite of the uncertainty of the relationship, it is clear that acculturative stress is related in some fashion to affective symptomatology. It is necessary for nurses who wish to provide ethnically competent care to understand the impact of acculturative stress on affective disorders. Furthermore, how gender and poverty contribute to and color the presentation of affective disorders among Hispanics is also essential knowledge. Frequently gender role orientation bears the blame in depression when the real culprit is socioeconomic level.

POVERTY AS A RISK FACTOR

At least one out every three Hispanic children and 56% of the Hispanic elderly live in poverty (Moccia & Mason, 1986). The number of Hispanic female-headed households is increasing and approximately 56% of these families live below the federal poverty level compared with approximately 22 to 25% of Hispanic married couple families (Firestone & Harris, 1994). Increasing poverty among Hispanics continues in spite of increasing labor force participation, time at work, and educational levels. Underemployment, which includes working below one's capability or part-time employment (with no health benefits), abounds in the Hispanic population. There are two times as many underemployed Mexican males compared to White males and 1.6 times as many underemployed Mexican females compared to White females (de Anda, 1994).

Poverty reduces access to adequate nutrition, shelter, transportation, clothing, employment, education, and health care. All these factors are essential for good physical and psychological health. Freeman (1994) states that culture is a prism through which the effects of poverty are expressed. Those effects include inadequate physical and social environment; inadequate information and knowledge; increased risk-promoting lifestyles, attitudes, and behaviors; and diminished access to health care. These effects, which are the direct result of poverty but manifested primarily in ethnic minority groups, lead to decreased survival.

The poor have to adjust and adapt to continuing oppressive life conditions which lead to feelings of powerlessness, helplessness, or resignation (Pesznecker, 1984). Such life conditions lead to a higher prevalence of psychologic distress among people living in poverty. Poverty and stresses regarding money are directly associated with depression, anxiety, and feelings of powerlessness (Malosky, 1982).

Frequently, health providers limit their assessment to the individual and do not evaluate the environmental factors that have led to the individual's current state. The implications of the Hispanic poor and Hispanic women being more vulnerable to affective disorders necessitates that nurses thoroughly analyze their approach to these two groups.

Because of the emphasis on individualized care in nursing, there is a tendency to address poverty as an individual issue where the nurse teaches the client how to adapt to poverty, and educational institutions teach nursing students about interventions with the individual client, but not how to intervene to change poverty (Martin & Henry, 1989; Moccia & Mason, 1986). Butterfield (1990) refers to this approach as placing the emphasis on downstream endeavors. Downstream endeavors are especially attractive during this time of increased attention to health care costs. Defining poverty as an individual issue shifts the focus away from environmental factors that maintain current poverty levels, and ultimately prevent individuals from initiating and sustaining health changes (Crawford, 1990). Focusing on upstream endeavors would involve grappling with environmental factors. Nurses would learn how to influence economic and political factors that contribute to the current poverty in all ethnic minority populations in the United States. Delving into such factors would address, for example, why Hispanics do not receive the same economic benefits associated with increasing education when compared with non-Hispanic Whites. A societal versus individual perspective would address the impact of changes in the labor market on women, Hispanics, and other ethnic minority groups.

SUMMARY

The case study of Señora C provided an example of how tuning in to the client's sociocultural context allowed an intervention to be tailored to the client which resulted in successful resolution of the presenting complaint and accompanying symptoms. Furthermore, Señora C's implementation of an impromptu mass serves as a group intervention as well. A patient such as this may be thought as a good candidate for treatment with antidepressants; however, Señora C's income was such as to prohibit medication and it was unlikely she would have complied, given that she did not believe herself depressed. Medication, if used, might have led to abatement of the depressive symptoms because medication would treat the "disease" of depression. However, medication is unlikely to have led to resolution of Señora C's sociopsychological issues, her "illness."

Differential diagnosis of this client as suffering from post-traumatic stress disorder is warranted. By using the DSM-IV as well (American Psychiatric Association [APA], 1994), signs and symptoms of post-traumatic stress disorder, such as occur after an unusually distressing event, become clearer: intruding thoughts of the dead woman with efforts to avoid these thoughts and the difficulty in staying asleep. A provider could also speculate that she was using the mechanism of denial. She denied the dangers of the situation to herself in order to stay functional in the environment to which her circumstances restricted her. The important diagnostic issue for treatment becomes how the total sociocultural picture is integrated to provide effective services for this client.

An attempt has been made in this chapter to stress the importance of sociocultural context when dealing with stress and depression in Hispanics. Some aspects of sociocultural context are not manipulable, such as gender or socioeconomic level. Being aware of how these factors contribute to a client's risk for stress or depressive illness helps the nurse to understand and place client motivation and compliance into perspective. A nurses's interventions may be directed at the individual client level when the needed change is required at the societal level. By understanding a client's sociocultural context, a nurse can design interventions that bridge the client's world and the health care system, and thus enhance the client's health and self-esteem and promote collaboration for the client's well-being.

REFERENCES

Amaro, H., & Russo, N. F. (1987). Hispanic women and mental health: An overview of contemporary issues in research and practice. *Psychology of Women Quarterly, 11*(4), 393-407.

American Psychiatric Association. (1994). *Diagnostic and Statistical Manual of Mental Disorders, DSM-IV.* Washington, DC: American Psychiatric Association.

Andrews, M. M., & Boyle, J. S. (1995). *Transcultural concepts in nursing care.* Philadelphia: Lippincott.

Antai-Otong, D. (1995). *Psychiatric nursing.* Philadelphia: Saunders.

Belle, G. (1984). Inequality in mental health: Low-income and minority women. In L. Walker (Ed.), *Women and mental health policy* (pp. 135-150). Beverly Hills: Sage.

Berkman, L. F., & Syme, L. (1979). Social networks, host resistance and mortality: A nine-year follow-up study of Alameda County Residents. *American Journal of Epidemiology, 109*(2), 186-204.

Black, S. A., & Markides, K. S. (1993). Acculturation and alcohol consumption in Puerto Rican, Cuban-American, and Mexican-American women in the United States. *American Journal of Public Health, 83*(6), 890-893.

Briones, D. F., Heller, P. L., Chalfant, H. P., Roberts, A. E., Aguirre-Hauchbaum, S. F., & Farr, W. F. (1990). Socioeconomic status, ethnicity, psychological distress, and readiness to utilize a mental health facility. *American Journal of Psychiatry, 147*(10), 1333-1340.

Butterfield, P. (1990). Thinking upstream: Nurturing a conceptual understanding of the societal context of human behavior. *Advances in Nursing Science, 12,* 1-8.

Comas-Diaz, L. (1981). Effects of cognitive and behavioral group treatment in the depressive symptomology of Puerto Rican women. *Journal of Consulting and Clinical Psychology, 19,* 627-632.

Corin, E. (1994). The social and cultural matrix of health and disease. In R. G. Evans, M. L. Barer, & T. R. Marmor (Eds.), *Why are some people healthy and others not? The determinant of health of populations* (pp. 93-133). New York: Aldine de Gruyter.

Crawford, R. (1990). Individual responsibility and health policy. In P. Conrad & R. Klein (Eds.), *The sociology of health and illness: Critical perspectives.* New York: St. Martin's Press.

de Anda, R. M. (1994). Unemployment and underemployment among Mexican-origin workers. *Hispanic Journal of Behavioral Sciences, 16*(2), 163-175.

de la Rosa, M. (1988). Natural support systems of Puerto Ricans: A key dimension for well-being. *Health and Social Work, 13*(3), 181-190.

Escobar, J. I. (1987). Cross-cultural aspects of the somatization trait. *Hospital & Community Psychiatry, 38*(2), 174-180.

Fernandez, D. M., & Sanchez, J. I. (1993). Acculturative stress among Hispanics: A bidimensional model of ethnic identification. *Journal of Applied Social Psychology, 23*(8), 654-668.

Fernandez, D. M., & Sanchez, J. I. (1992). Multidimensional measurement of ethnic identification: Hispanic versus American or Hispanic-American? Paper presented at the Annual Meeting of the American Psychological Association, Washington, DC, August 1992.

Firestone, J. M., & Harris, R. J. (1994). Hispanic women in Texas: An increasing portion of the underclass. *Hispanic Journal of Behavioral Sciences, 16*(2), 176-185.

Freeman, H. (1994). Luncheon Address. Presentation at the Implications of Cultural Values, Beliefs, and Norms for Health Research Conference, Milwaukee, Wisconsin, September 1994. Sponsored by the University of Wisconsin-Milwaukee School of Nursing.

Gibson, G. (1983). Hispanic women: Stress and mental health issues. *Women and Therapy, 2,* 113-133.

Golding, J. M., & Burman, M. A. (1990). Immigration, stress and depressive symptom in a Mexican-American community. *Journal of Nervous and Mental Disease, 178*(3), 161-171.

Golding, J. M., Burman, M. A., Benjamin, B., & Wells, K. B. (1993). Risk factors for secondary depression among Mexican-Americans and non-Hispanic Whites: Alcohol use, alcohol dependence, and reasons for drinking. *Journal of Nervous and Mental Diseases, 181*(3), 166-175.

Golding, J. M., Karno, M., & Rutter, C. M. (1990). Symptoms of major depression among Mexican-Americans and Non-Hispanic Whites. *American Journal of Psychiatry, 147,* 861-866.

Hall, A. H., Williams, C. A., & Greenberg, R. S. (1985). Support stressors and depressive symptoms in low-income mothers of young children. *American Journal of Public Health, 75*(5), 518-522.

Hayes-Bautista, D. E. (1994). Luncheon address. Paper presented at the annual meeting of the National Association of Hispanic Nurses, Costa Mesa, CA.

Hernandez, M. (1986). Depression among Mexican women: A transgenerational perspective. Paper presented at the biannual meeting of the National Coalition of Hispanic Health and Human Services Organization, New York.

Hughes, C. (1978). Medical care: Ethnomedicine. In M. Logan & E. Hunt (Eds.), *Health and the human condition* (pp. 150-157).

Julian, T. W., McKenry, P. C., & McKelvey, M. W. (1994). Cultural variations in parenting: Perceptions of Caucasian, African-American, Hispanic, and Asian-American parents. *Family Relations, 43,* 30-37.

Kaplan, A. (1986). The self-in-relation: Implications for depression in women. *Psychotherapy, 23*(2), 234-242.

Kleinman, A. (1987). Anthropology and psychiatry: The role of culture in cross-cultural research on illness. *British Journal of Psychiatry, 151,* 447-454.

Leininger, M. (1978). *Transcultural nursing: Concepts, theories and practices.* New York: Wiley.

Malosky, V. P. (1982). Sources of stress: Events or conditions. In D. Belle (Ed.), *Lives in stress: Women and depression* (pp. 35-53). Beverly Hills: Sage.

Marmor, M. G. (1981). Culture and illness: Epidemiological evidence. In M. J. Christie & P. G. Mellet (Eds.), *Foundations of psychosomatics* (pp. 323-340). Chichester: Wiley.

Martin, M. E., & Henry, M. (1989). Cultural relativity and poverty. *Public Health Nursing, 6*(1), 28-34.

McGoldrick, M., Pearce, J. K., & Giordano, J. (1985). *Ethnicity and family therapy.* New York: Guilford Press.

McGrath, E., Keita, G. P., Strickland, B. R., & Russo, N. F. (1990). *Women and depression.* Washington, DC: American Psychological Association.

Mena, F. J., Padilla, A. M., & Maldonado, M. (1987). Acculturative stress and specific coping strategies among immigrant and later generation college students. *Hispanic Journal of Behavioral Sciences, 9*(2), 207-225.

Moccia, P., & Mason, D. J. (1986). Poverty trends: Implications for nursing. *Nursing Outlook, 34*(1), 20-24.

Moyerman, D. R., & Forman, B. D. (1992). Acculturation and adjustment: A meta-analytic study. *Hispanic Journal of Behavioral Sciences, 14*(2), 163-200.

Norton, D. (1978). Black family life patterns, the development of self and cognitive development of Black children. In G. Powell (Ed.), *The psychosocial development of minority group children.* New York: Brunner/Mazel.

Padilla, A. M., Wagatsuma, Y., & Lindholm, K. J. (1985). Generational and personality differences in acculturative stress among Mexican-Americans and Japanese Americans. *Spanish Speaking Mental Health Research Center Occasional Papers, 20,* 15-38.

Pedraza-Bailey, S. (1985). *Political and economic migrants in America.* Austin: University of Texas Press.

Pesznecker, B. L. (1984). The poor: A population at risk. *Public Health Nursing, 1*(4), 237-249.

Russo, N. F., Amaro, H., & Winter, M. (1987). The use of inpatient mental health services by Hispanic women. *Psychology of Women Quarterly, 11,* 427-442.

Salgado de Snyder, V. N. (1987). Factors associated with acculturative stress and depressive symptomatology among married Mexican immigrant women. *Psychology of Women Quarterly, 11*(4), 475-488.

Salgado de Snyder, V. N., Cervantes, R. C., & Padilla, A. M. (1990). Gender and ethnic differences in psychosocial stress and generalized distress among Hispanics. *Sex Roles, 22,* (7-8), 441-453.

Smart, J. F., & Smart, D. W. (1995). Acculturative stress: The experience of the Hispanic immigrant. *The Counseling Psychologist, 23*(1), 25-42.

Smart, J. F., & Smart, D. W. (1994). The rehabilitation of Hispanics experiencing acculturative stress: Implications for practice. *Journal of Rehabilitation, 60,* 8-12.

CHAPTER ELEVEN

Special Populations: The Homeless in Puerto Rico

Catalina Quesada, PhD, RN

Evelyn Crouch-Ruiz, PhD, RN

The homeless are in all areas of Puerto Rico: in the rural and urban areas, in parks, in private and public housing. They sleep under a newspaper, on the benches of the city plaza, under bridges, around the garbage they collected in the streets. They walk without direction looking for something to eat or sell. We try to ignore them; try not to see their ugly, painful reality, seeing only what we want to see.

It is hard for those who have food on the table, the love of a family, and a job to think about a group of people who have none of these commodities. But we need to look at the reality to be able to improve the quality of life for all and to stop this growing problem.

On January 6, 1992, the newspaper *El Neuvo Día* featured a cover story on the homeless in Puerto Rico, depicting the extraordinary differences between the haves and the have-nots. Modern Puerto Rico, which boasts the highest per capita income of any Caribbean country, and which supports almost 40 universities and dozens of technical schools, also has a least 12,000 individuals who live in the streets.

In 1987, the federal government approved the McKinney Bill for assistance for the homeless. In this bill, a homeless person is defined as an individual who does not have a fixed adequate night residence; whose night residence is a public or private shelter, a temporary home, a public or private place not designed as a night residence for human beings. This definition includes victims of domestic violence, runaways, castaways, or aging individuals.

What are the causes of homelessness? There are several direct causes, such as alcohol and drug abuse, AIDS, and other serious physical and mental illness. Of the 12,000 homeless estimated in Puerto Rico, there are at least 6,142 with severe mental illness.

Puerto Rican culture values family life and intimacy. When we examined a recent profile of the homeless in the southern area of Puerto Rico, we found that 79% were male over 55 years old, 63% had no family, 49% had never married, 14% were divorced, and 80% had an alcohol or drug addiction.

In treating the homeless, coordination of services between agencies is a must. In Puerto Rico, the state government, represented by the Department of Social Services, receives funding that they in turn distribute to public and private entities. According to De León (1989), the McKinney Bill has benefited 21 organizations on the island. These funds are used to remodel or expand facilities that assist the homeless as well as for operational expenses and professional services.

In some cities in Puerto Rico, services are offered using a model of interaction between public and private programs. This model proposes meeting the needs of the homeless in order of priority and according to the resources available within allocated centers.

Intervention takes place on several levels. Initially, there is the need to satisfy basic food and personal hygiene requirements. In these centers, too, the person is received as they are without rejecting their appearance or mental status. They receive counseling and assistance in their hygiene and an interpersonal relationship is initiated, which is also considered a strategy for primary intervention.

A second level of services includes the creation of emergency temporary shelters. Although there are several shelters in Puerto Rico, more are needed to cope with the needs of the homeless population. Some shelters currently provide interdisciplinary services with a team including medical doctors, psychiatrists, nurses, psychologists, and social workers. These teams are responsible for assessing the needs of the homeless person, and recommending and carrying out interventions. They also are responsible for integrating the homeless into the service network available in the community.

A third level includes mental health and addiction services. There are 23 case managers in 12 Mental Health Centers that are distributed around the island. Their services are broad and cover identification of homeless persons to assist in securing a safe home.

A fourth level concerns the provision of permanent housing for homeless people. The lack of housing and the resistance of the homeless to live in the housing provided pose formidable obstacles here, however. For the homeless who have been living in the streets for some or most of their lives, living in a house/apartment is a challenge. It is hard to adjust to rules and regulations.

The needs of the homeless are many, and the resources are always too few. Often the homeless do not want the kind of help that is available. Often the help that is available is insufficiant or inappropriate to that particular individual. Often, too, their behavior makes it impossible to help them.

CONCLUSION

The problems of the homeless are serious; many are mentally ill or suffer addictions that prevent them from seeking help. Efforts to change their customs and have them live in acceptable dwellings are nearly impossible. It would be more useful to develop programs that can *prevent* homelessness. Addictions and mental illness contribute to homelessness; we must invest in the prevention of these illnesses. Providing children with homes and families that value them and promote their well being is also essential as is preventing child and spouse abuse, and providing good education and accessible recreation to low-income families.

With these strategies and enhancing the several mentioned previously, we can help deal more proactively with the current crisis and hopefully help prevent future homelessness while promoting mental health.

REFERENCES

De León, S. (1989). *Los Deambulantes en Puerto Rico.* Unpublished paper.

Guzman, Milagros. (1994). *Puerto Rico: The meeting of the Hispanic and Anglo-Saxon cultures in the world of work.* San Juan, Puerto Rico: Boriquen.

CHAPTER TWELVE

Special Populations: Hispanic Migrant Workers

Josephine A. (Ulibarri) Hibbeln, RN, MSN

The majority of Hispanic Americans are native born. The first Hispanics colonized the western United States in 1548, 72 years before the first English settlers founded the Plymouth Colony. For this study, Hispanics are largely descendants of Mexican families who owned and lived on the land in the Southwestern United States. In 1848, Mexico agreed to cede the territory that is now Texas, California, Utah, Nevada, parts of New Mexico, Arizona, Colorado, and Wyoming to the United States in the Treaty of Guadalupe Hidalgo. According to the treaty, the Mexican people who chose to remain in the Southwest were guaranteed rights to their land. However, the U.S. government treated the people as illegal immigrants, disregarding their rights according to this treaty (Kirkman-Liff & Mondragon, 1991).

The legal importation of Mexican farm laborers took place in the early stages of World War II with the passage of the Bracero Act, a response to the United States' need to stabilize its agricultural production due to the largely Anglo migrant farm labor force being called into military service (Ryder, 1995).

Despite this history and the contributions made, the majority of Hispanic Americans tend to live on the fringes of American society (Ryder, 1995). No group lies farther from the center of America's social structure than the migratory farmworker.

Position in any social structure is the major determiner of the availability and distribution of resources (Ginsberg, 1991). Health care analysts have long understood that the quality of health care available to different groups is influenced by their socioeconomic status. The availability and distribution of resources to meet the needs of the migrant farmworker are found at the furthest end of the socioeconomic spectrum. Dever's (1991) study concluded that the demographic patterns, socioeconomic conditions, lifestyle characteristics, and disease categories of the migrant and seasonal

The new Migrant Health Center logo will identify all the centers. Graphic artist Andrew Soldana, whose family were migrant farmworkers in Texas, designed it to honor all migrant farmworker families.

farmworkers in the United States reflect agrarian third-world conditions rather than those of the most powerful and affluent nation in the world.

U.S. MIGRANT HEALTH CARE: AN HISTORICAL PERSPECTIVE

I do not believe the human body and the human mind were made to sustain the stresses migrants must face, worse stresses than I have seen anywhere in the world, and utterly unrecognized by most of us; nor do I believe that a rich and powerful nation in the second half of the twentieth century ought to tolerate what was an outrage even centuries ago: child labor, forms of peonage, large scale migrancy. . . . (Dr. Robert Coles, Physician and Child Psychiatrist, quoted by R. Rosenthal, 1993)

Seasonal or migratory farmworkers are a highly mobile population that moves from the south to the north and back again to follow the fruit and vegetable growing season (Ryder, 1995). Migrant farmworkers are not homeless as many believe. They move from home bases mainly in Florida, Texas, and California. Migrant streams move up each coast and up the center of the country, working their way as far north as the states of Washington, Michigan, and Maine, then working their way back to their home bases (Ryder, 1995).

Agricultural regions in the United States have traditionally been dependent on minority farm labor. During the Great Depression, the national conscience was awakened to the plight of migrant farmworkers. Due to the combined effects of natural and manmade disasters in the late 1930s, 85% of the migratory farmworkers were White Americans who, as a means of survival, joined the three existing streams of migrant labor (Grey, 1993).

Herculean efforts by the Farm Security Administration (FSA) to improve the living conditions for the nation's migrants and to create a migrant medical care program existed into the 1940s. Part of the FSA's interdisciplinary approach to health care was the expanded role given to nurses. With nurses functioning as initial providers with supervisory or consultative physician input, thousands of migrant workers and their families experienced their first regular source of medical care, receiving immunizations, nutritional advice, physical nurture, and mass adult education (Grey, 1993).

With the apparent success of the FSA's migrant medical program, the medical community feared that health care was moving toward a national health care system and stressed that the care of indigents was a local concern that required no extensive government interference. The strength of the medical profession's desire to control the practice of medicine led to the eventual demise of the federal migrant health programs in 1946 (Grey, 1993).

Federal support for the health needs of migrant and seasonal farmworkers did not begin again until the late 1950s when Congress established a committee to investigate the lack of sanitary conditions and inadequate immunizations for migrants and residents of farming areas (Executive Summary, 1985). The Migrant Health Act, which established authorization for delivery of primary and supplemental health services to migrant and other seasonal farmworkers, was signed into law on September 25, 1962, by President Kennedy. The Migrant Health Act is funded under Section 329 of the Public Health Service Act and is administered by the Bureau of Primary Health Care in the Health Resources and Services Administration, U.S. Department of Health and Human Services (Dailey, 1994). The Migrant Health Act laid the foundation for the Migrant Health Program (MHP) which allocates federal grant money to stimulate state and local health programs to provide health care to migrants and seasonal farmworkers and to assist the states in implementing and enforcing applicable and acceptable environmental health standards.

The Migrant Health Program allocates federal grant money for migrant health centers in areas where 4,000 or more migrants live. In areas without centers, or with fewer than 4,000 workers, the program provides for granting funds to public and nonprofit agencies to provide health services to migrant and seasonal workers (Watkins, Larson, Harlan, & Young, 1990). There are approximately 136 migrant health centers in 39 states and Puerto Rico. Four hundred to six hundred clinic sites are staffed and maintained along the migrant streams during the peak season each year.

Federal funding through the Migrant Health Program is allocated as grant money. Grantees must compete with each other for the scarce dollars (Stilp, 1994). Whether or not a health center gets funding is frequently dependent on exhaustive lobbying skills.

In recent years, limitations on the amount of federal funding available and the allocation of funds on the basis of provider-patient encounters have led to a reduction of staffing. Priority is now given to secondary instead of primary level health care and health promotion, as was originally intended (Watkins et al., 1990). The Migrant Health Program is due for reauthorization by Congress in 1995. The recent passage of the Balanced Budget Amendment by the House of Representatives could result in entire public health programs being eliminated in order to adhere to the requirement of the amendment (de Vries, 1995). The present danger is clear: the Migrant Health Program may be eliminated (Ryder, 1995).

MIGRANT DEMOGRAPHIC PATTERNS AND HEALTH STATE

The Office of Migrant Health estimates that there are three million migrant and seasonal farmworkers and their dependents distributed across almost every state in the United States, with the greatest concentration in California (Dever, 1991; Rust, 1990). At least 80% are U.S. citizens (Goldsmith, 1989) and more than one-fourth are women (Farmworker Justice Fund, 1995).

Although the migrant farmworker population is highly diverse (Blacks, Southeast Asians, Native Americans, and Haitians), farm work not done by farm owners and their families is largely performed by Hispanics of Mexican origin (Moses, 1989). Even in the East Coast stream there has been a change of demographics from a large number of Black to a predominately Hispanic population (Watkins et al., 1990). The Wisconsin study (Slesinger

& Cautley, 1981) found that Hispanics represented 92% of migrant farmworkers in that area. A study by Horton (1988) reported that Mexicans make up 97% of Colorado's migrant population.

On average, Hispanic farmworkers are younger family men who, because of a lack of education, work as seasonal migrant farmworkers (Ginsberg, 1991). They enter into a cycle in which they become chronically, seasonally unemployed for a number of months a year and seriously underemployed even during peak working seasons, with resulting low annual earnings (Kissam, 1993). At peak harvest, workers are still at the mercy of climate, market, and short-term contract conditions, which usually lead to loss of wages between contracts. Short-term contracts also result in ineligibility for unemployment insurance benefits and the possible losses of social security benefits. Consequently, the migrant and seasonal farmworkers are among the poorest people in the United States. Even when all able bodies in a family work, very few families are able to emerge from poverty (Kissam, 1993).

There are no population-wide health status data available on migrant farmworkers. Because of the farmworkers' migratory lifestyle, it has been difficult to do research and to report on their health status as a group (Dever, 1991; Galarneau, 1992). Studies have been conducted by individual clinics within their geographic locations, but no information has been collected across migratory streams or across the farmworker population as a whole (Dever, 1991). Rust's (1990) literature review from 1966 through 1989 concluded that progress has been made in assessing the dental and nutritional status of migrant farmworker families, but that basic indicators of migrant health and disease remain unknown. Dever's (1991) study reported that the quality of life and health status of farmworkers at their home bases is worse than that for farmworkers working upstream. Access to health care tends to be more limited at their home base because migrant families live in some of the poorest rural areas where they compete for health care with a concentration of other impoverished people living under the same conditions.

Due to their impoverished state, poor education (3 of 10 have completed fewer than five years of school), their lack of proficiency in the English language (Spanish is the primary language for 90% with just over half able to speak both English and Spanish), and their constant mobility, migrant farmworkers lack any power to affect economic and political changes in policy, at any level (Slesinger & Cautley, 1981). Even at their home bases, migrant farmworkers are sequestered from mainstream America by distance, economic status, language, and cultural factors (Foulk, Lafferty, & Ryan, 1991).

The average age of migrant farmworkers is 49 years in a country where average life expectancy is 75 years (Health Care, 1990). The migrant farmworkers' work, which begins before daybreak, consists of backbreaking hoeing, planting, weeding, thinning, irrigating, or harvesting. They work steadily until sunset, sometimes seven days a week, at fast-paced repetitive tasks with short breaks to eat what little food they bring to the fields. They're constantly exposed to the sun, dust, wind, rain, pesticides, and wide extremes of temperature. Death from heat stroke is not uncommon. Unsafe transportation, pesticides exposure, and other dangers commonly account for hundreds of deaths and injuries each year. Migrant farmworker families have higher rates of parasitic and infectious diseases, skin diseases, and chronic diseases than other populations in the United States and are more likely to experience significant maternal and newborn health problems (Fisher, 1993; Gaston, 1993). Adult farmworkers, who have often been in the stream since childhood suffer from debilitating back pain and arthritis (O'Brien, 1983). Migrant farmworkers, who are approximately six times more likely to develop tuberculosis than the general population because of their substandard and overcrowded living conditions, are also constantly exposed to unsafe water supplies and other unsanitary conditions (Duran, 1993; Gaston, 1993).

Migrant farmworkers are paid minimum wages by the hour (Watkins et al., 1990), lack medical insurance or information about low-cost or free health care or social services in communities they migrate to, and lack access to most medical facilities (Farmworker Justice Fund, 1995; Marentes, 1993). Fewer than half of migrant children under age 16 receive the recommended annual physical checkup. Only one-third of migrant children under age 16 receive an annual dental checkup. The incidence of chronic conditions is several times greater among migrant children, and childhood mortality in migrant children appears to be 1.6 times higher than in the rest of the U.S. population (Slesinger, Christenson, & Cautley, 1986).

Farmworkers are excluded completely or partially from federal laws that protect other workers, including the National Labor Relations Act (which guarantees the right to join a union and bargain collectively), the Fair Labor Standards Act (which governs minimum wage and child labor), and the Occupational Safety and Health Act (which governs standards of health and safety in the workplace). Furthermore, most migrant farmworkers are excluded from state laws, such as workers compensation and unemployment insurance (Moses, 1989).

The greatest tragedy is the labor that is extracted from children. The Fair Labor Standards Act (FLSA) under the Department of Labor restricts the employment of young workers in agriculture who are 15 years of age and younger. However, farmworkers' children are excluded from the protection provided in the 1938 Child Labor Act. Children as young as 10 years old can legally work in the fields in this country. Three hundred children die annually in work-related injuries and 25,000 are injured in farm accidents (Zuroweste, 1993).

Delays in seeking care, the unavailability or lack of access to care, working and housing conditions, the nomadic lifestyle due to the transitory nature of their work, the perception of illness, and their need to work in order to survive are critical reasons for the poor health status of the migrant farmworker population (Dever, 1991).

DELETERIOUS EFFECTS TO MIGRANT HEALTH

The harsh lifestyle and socially marginal occupation place migrant farmworkers in a hierarchical society with few prospects for social mobility or protection (Vega, Warheit, & Palacio, 1985). With exposure to environmental stressors, other populations with greater social integration, material resources, and residential stability do not manifest the psychiatric symptomatology which is evident among migrant farmworkers (Vega et al., 1985). The environmental stressors (poverty, inadequate housing, malnutrition, hazardous working conditions, pesticide exposure, and infectious and chronic diseases) they are frequently exposed to have deleterious effects on the health of migrant farmworkers and their families.

Poverty

Migrant and seasonal farmworkers make it possible for people to buy inexpensive fruits and vegetables all year round. Yet, nearly all migrant farmworkers live in poverty and do not have enough money to buy the same fruits and vegetables for their own families (Duran, 1993). Migrant home bases are characterized by a socioeconomic status in which 58% of all households fall below nationally defined poverty levels (Dever, 1991).

A family is classified as poor if pretax cash income falls below the minimum standard established by the official federal government poverty measure. The minimum standard is presently set at $14,334 for a family of four (Allen, 1993). Part-time or part-year employment, which may be the only option for many families, does not ensure financial stability, and one full-time minimum wage job is not sufficient to lift a family out of poverty (Allen, 1993). According to the National Agricultural Workers Survey, the average earning for farmworkers is $6,500 per year from farmwork. Including farmwork and nonfarmwork earnings, the typical migrant nuclear family of four has an annual income of $6,823 (Kissam, 1993). Due to low earnings, many migrant farmworkers are forced to take their children to the fields where the children are exposed to all types of risks, hazards, and indignities (Marentes, 1993). Migrant women, who do every kind of farm labor, routinely earn less than men for the same work (Farmworker Justice Fund, 1995).

In 1938, the Department of Labor passed the Fair Labor Standards Act (FLSA), which provided minimum wage and child labor protection to everyone *except* agriculture workers. It was another 30 years before FLSA included agriculture workers and even now two-thirds of migrant farmworkers are not covered by the law (Rosenthal, 1993). The minimum wage law requires a threshold of 500 person days of employment before the Fair Labor Standards Act applies (Fraser, 1993). According to the National Agricultural Workers Survey, the annual average number of farmworking days for migrant farmworkers is 141 days (Kissam, 1993). Not only are migrant and seasonal farmworkers unprotected by the minimum wage law, but FLSA standards also have an overtime exemption for most agricultural employment (Fraser, 1993).

The National Labor Relations Act allows for collective bargaining rights for more than 40 million workers across the country *except* farmworkers (Rosenthal, 1993). Any successful labor contracts, between farmworkers and huge corporate interests in agriculture, have been achieved against overwhelming odds (Rosenthal, 1993). In April 1995, the Farm Labor Organizing Committee (FLOC) reached an agreement with the Vlasic Pickle Growers Association in Ohio which called for a 23% hourly increase, applied through the 1998 harvest season. Under this agreement, the farmworkers, who do hoeing and vine-training, will receive an increase up to $4.70 per hour (Farm, 1995).

Agricultural employers, who employ 10 or more farmworkers during a 20-week period or who pay out at least $20,000 per quarter in agricultural wages, are required to pay unemployment insurance taxes (Fraser, 1993). However, most of the migrant farmworkers' unemployed time is not covered by unemployment insurance (Kissam, 1993). In order to be able to make valid unemployment insurance claims, individuals have to be employed for 20 consecutive weeks. Most migrant farmworkers do not work for 20 consecutive weeks nor do they have options regarding their length of employment. Even for those farmworkers with valid claims, there is a one-week waiting period before they are able to collect. Migrant families do not have the resources to wait a week, as they must continue to move on to find work during the growing season (Kissam, 1993).

Migrant farmworkers lack financial support following work-related injuries because, in most instances, they are not covered by Workers Compensation (Rosenthal, 1993; Zuroweste, 1993). Workers Compensation falls under state jurisdiction and coverage varies considerably from state to state.

Poverty has a deleterious effect on migrant farmworkers' health. Because of low wages, every productive moment must be spent working. Even pregnant women, nursing mothers, and children work in the fields to help support the family (Health care, 1990). Spontaneous abortions are not uncommon among young pregnant women who work long hours (O'Brien, 1983). Poverty contributes to the occurrence of accidental and assaultive injury. The death rate from unintentional injury as a whole is twice as high in low-income areas as in high-income areas and the use and abuse of alcoholic beverages influence the likelihood of virtually all types of injury (McDermott & Lee, 1990).

Inadequate Housing and Transportation

Migrant farmworkers and their families suffer from health problems related to poor sanitation and overcrowded living conditions. Contaminated water, close living quarters, and the sharing of everything from dishes to towels contribute to their poor state of health. Unsafe housing is an ongoing problem even though the Migrant and Seasonal Agricultural Worker Protection Act (enacted in 1983) requires farm labor contractors to provide safe housing.

Housing may consist of cheap apartments, motels, mobile homes, or farm buildings. Most housing made available to migrant families by employers consists of shacks in labor camps, located on dusty and muddy roads and in need of both exterior and interior repairs. The doors on the shacks may have ripped screens or no screens at all and the floors (some have no floors at all) are inadequate. Furnishings are sparse. Refrigeration and cooking appliances may or may not be available or functional. Rosenthal (1993) describes a one-room shack standing unattached and unanchored on stone piling, lifting off the pilings and tilting from side to side as the family moved from one end of the room to the other. Playgrounds for children consist of dirt yards and fields.

Houses in labor camps are often located in the middle of fields. When the fields are sprayed with pesticides and herbicides, the houses and occupants are also sprayed (Wilk, 1993). Drinking water is generally in short supply and the only source of water may be from irrigation ditches contaminated with pesticides and fertilizers (O'Brien, 1983; Wilk, 1993). Water supplies, when tested by public health authorities for bacterial safety, are often found to have unacceptable contamination levels, one reason for the often occurring diarrhea among infants and young children (O'Brien, 1983). Toilet facilities often consist of community outhouses or of nothing more than a hole in the ground (Health care, 1990).

Crowded conditions are the norm—17 people sharing a two-room shack or a couple with a young baby sharing a small trailer with several teenagers. Separate sleeping arrangements can mean separation by a blanket or sleeping out in the fields or orange groves (Kissam, 1993). In 1994, a farmworker was found dead in a field in northwest Ohio. Law enforcement concluded that the farmworker was run over while he slept.

Privacy is a rare commodity. After trying to give a 14-year-old virginal girl instructions on how to use a vaginal cream dispenser at bedtime, the author discovered that the girl's only access to toilet facilities was an outhouse several hundred yards away from the room where she slept with the rest of her family.

Water may be supplied by a central well pump and may not be available for washing and cleaning.

Migrant farmworkers travel with extended families in whatever conveyance they may have. A vehicle may be their home for an undetermined period of time. The time traveled may be extended by days or weeks because of breakdowns. Work may have to be found before their final destination in order to pay for gasoline or automobile parts. With eventual work, housing, and luck, the vehicle continues to run and provide the means to get from camp to the work site, to the grocery store, and to the nearest available health clinic. However, there may only be one driver and in order to get to the grocery market or to the health clinic the driver, who may also be the main wage earner, has to be available.

Malnutrition

Migrant families are highly vulnerable for nutrition-related disorders because of their poverty, migratory lifestyle, and cultural practices. Cardiovascular disease, diabetes, and anemia can all be attributed to malnutrition in this population (Goldsmith, 1989). Most clinic visits for migrant children ages one to four are related to infectious and nutritional health problems. Malnutrition makes children especially vulnerable to such infectious diseases as dysentery, hepatitis B, typhoid fever, and other intestinal and respiratory ailments (Goldsmith, 1989). Other nutrition-related health problems are dental disease and obesity.

Obesity is a problem at all age levels in migrant families and although none may look malnourished, they in fact are (Goldsmith, 1989). Like other people with little money, migrant families tend to buy foods high in starches and fats. Common staples in a Mexican migrant family's diet are foods (beans, rice, potatoes, chili, and tortillas) high in carbohydrates and low in vitamins, iron, and protein (Wheeler, 1991). While the amount of food consumed is usually adequate, the quality lacks essential nutrients and contributes to obesity in a population already vulnerable to cardiovascular disease and diabetes.

Nutritional studies on migrant populations by Dewey, Strode, and Fitch (1984) and by Watkins et al. (1990) found that the consumption of protein and grain products by migrant families were generally adequate. The consumption of dairy products and fruits and vegetables, however, was below the recommended nutritional standards. Low hematocrit levels were common among pregnant women and to a lesser extent among children. Mexican-American migrant girls who frequently marry in their early teens and/or bear children beginning at ages 13 to 17 years have poor diets and are also often anemic. Migrant family babies, 8 to 36 months of age whose diets are almost totally reliant on milk, are also found to be anemic (Schneider, 1986).

The Dewey and Watkins studies also found that migrant children tend to consume cereals high in sugar, eat sweet rolls instead of bread (whole wheat bread is seldom eaten), and mostly drink high sugar content non-carbonated and carbonated drinks (low fat milk was seldom consumed), all foods which contribute both to dental caries and obesity. The Dewey study also found the main source of meat to be frankfurters.

The role of migrant children seems to influence the purchase of foods high in sugar content. Migrant families tend to shop as a family group and the parents depend on the children, who are more likely to speak and read English, to read labels and make choices. Most mothers interviewed by Dewey et al. (1984) stated that they usually bought the foods their children requested. The conclusion drawn from this information is that nutritional education should best be directed at bilingual children, as they may have more influence in fostering dietary changes within their families.

Neither the Dewey nor the Watkins studies addressed other issues that may influence the dietary intake in migrant families, such as the necessity to buy foods which do not require refrigeration. While in transition, migrant families have to carry the food they eat or they have to be able to buy it. When work is found, the migrant families live in substandard housing with few amenities. Again, cooking facilities and refrigeration are luxuries not necessarily available to them. As a result, intestinal parasitic infections afflict up to one-half of the migrant population. The physical impact of the infection varies with the type of parasite, but in all cases intestinal parasites increase nutritional losses (Goldsmith, 1989).

Tuberculosis is another disease attributed to malnutrition in migrant families. Because of the poor nutritional status, poverty, and overcrowded housing conditions, farmworkers are about six times more likely to develop tuberculosis (TB) than the general population of employed adults (Goldsmith, 1989). While the TB problem among migrants is not necessarily linked with AIDS, there is a growing concern that their poor nutritional status, bad sanitation, and pesticide exposure will compromise their immune systems and make the migrant families more vulnerable to disorders and infections resulting from a depleted immune system (Goldsmith, 1989).

Most migrant families qualify for and would benefit from food stamps. However, they find accessibility too complex. The lack of understanding of the bureaucratic jargon, and the hassles required to obtain food stamps discourage most families. Migrant families are also more likely to require food stamps during relocation periods. But, it is often at those times that they are refused emergency services because they cannot follow the usual administrative steps required for eligibility (Goldsmith, 1989). Those families who are successful in obtaining food stamps find limited choices in what they can buy with the food stamps in the small country stores where they shop (Goldsmith, 1989).

Hazardous Working Conditions

In 1987, agriculture surpassed mining as the nation's most hazardous occupation with 1,700 work-related deaths (Rust, 1990). Farmworkers are constantly exposed to dangers posed by farm machinery, knives, and machetes used to harvest crops; to orthopedic injuries from lifting, carrying loads, or falls; to debris, toxic pesticides, and temperature excesses; and to burns from fire and explosion of combustible materials. McDermott and Lee (1990) reported that 60% of migrant farmworkers' visits to a local emergency room and 13% to a rural migrant clinic were due to injuries. Seventy percent of the injuries involved either the back and spine, arms, or legs; and 28% of the accidents were related to overexertion (McDermott & Lee, 1990). Farmworkers tend to suffer from carpal tunnel syndrome and other tenosynovitis, secondary to friction or repetitive movements, and they have the highest incidence of osteoarthritis of any occupation in the United States. Other occupational risks farmworkers are exposed to are dermatoses caused by contact with irritating or sensitizing substances, infections, photoallergy to the sun, heat stress, bee stings, snake bites, and dusts and airborne allergens (Moses, 1989).

Migrant female farmworkers, who are exposed to all the indignities and risks experienced by male migrant farmworkers, also suffer the indignity of sexual harassment (Farmworker Justice Fund, 1995; Rosenthal, 1993).

Recurring reasons for medical visits to migrant health clinics and emergency departments are very much tied to poor environmental conditions and workplace hazards (Wilk, 1993). In 1992, working conditions for migrant and seasonal farmworkers were the same as those described by farmworkers in 1952 and 1962 when the House and Senate held hearings authorizing the Migrant Health Program (Duran, 1993). Unfortunately, migrant health centers do not have the necessary manpower or technical assistance required to be able to deal with these environmental and occupational health issues.

Industries who employ full-time workers are required by the Occupational Safety and Health Administration (OSHA) to have adequate toilets, drinking water, and handwashing facilities. Lack of these amenities are tolerated in agriculture where compliance by growers has been a serious problem and where sanitation standards have not been uniformly maintained. Seldom is water available in the fields for either drinking or washing. Toilets are not available and workers have to relieve themselves where they can, usually right in the fields. To avoid this indignity, women frequently abstain from liquids before going to work and suffer from dehydration and urinary tract infection (Goldsmith, 1989; Meister, 1991). Dehydration in pregnant migrant women is also believed to decrease the effectiveness of the placental barrier and increase fetal exposure to contaminants (Meister, 1991).

Misrepresentations with respect to working arrangements and living conditions often take place when migrants are recruited for work. Once recruited, the lives of migrant farmworkers are endangered when they are transported in vans without seat belts, driven by unlicensed and uninsured drivers. The seats are sometimes removed so that more people can be crammed into the vans (Wilk, 1993). Once transported to the contracted work site, the migrant farmworkers are at the mercy of the crew leaders and growers who recruited them (Rosenthal, 1993).

The Migrant and Seasonal Agricultural Worker Protection Act (MSPA) (AWPA), under the U.S. Department of Labor, was enacted in 1983 to protect farmworkers from unscrupulous recruitment practices and to set labor standards for the provision of housing, transportation safety, disclosure of wages, and working conditions. The enforcement of the statute has been poorly upheld. Migrant Legal Services Programs suffered massive cuts during the Reagan administration and have been severely underfunded since then (Rosenthal, 1993). More recently, growers and employers have made attempts to change the law to reverse a unanimous Supreme Court decision affirming a worker's right to file suit for injuries sustained as a consequence of being transported in vehicles that are in violation of the MSPA statute (Rosenthal, 1993). In Ohio, an amendment to the State Budget Bill has been written in an effort to reduce lawsuits against farmers who hire migrant farmworkers (Carle, 1995).

Approaches to work-related injuries have tended to emphasize programs to make workers more careful, rather than to the reduction of exposure to job hazards (McDermott & Lee, 1990). Even with increased public sector enforcement of regulatory activities and better funding for programs oriented toward serving farmworkers, the improvement of working conditions for migrant and seasonal farmworkers cannot succeed without collaboration between the public and private sectors (Rosenthal, 1993).

Pesticides

Until his death in 1993, Cesar Chavez campaigned to end the use of the toxic pesticides routinely sprayed on crops. Almost all commercial crops in the United States are heavily and repeatedly sprayed with chemical pesticides, most of which can neither be washed off produce nor degraded by cooking (Moses, 1989). "Pesticides" is a term which includes insecticides, rodenticides, herbicides, fungicides, and defoliants. Migrant farmworkers receive multiple exposures to many different pesticides and inert ingredients (ingredients which are not required to be tested for acute and chronic health effects or listed by name on the pesticide label) over a working lifetime. Toxic exposures start at a very young age, because agriculture is the only industry in which children comprise a significant part of the work force, and because infants and very young children are often taken to the fields with their parents (Moses, 1989).

The U.S. Environmental Protection Agency and the International Agency for Research on Cancer reported on the findings of 53 agricultural chemicals tested. Two have been found to be definitely carcinogenic (arsenic and vinyl chloride), 13 were found to be probably carcinogenic, and 16 have been categorized as possibly carcinogenic (Rust, 1990).

The results of exposure to pesticides may be cancer, severe nerve disorders, reproductive problems, infertility, skin disorders, and liver and kidney disease (Goldsmith, 1989). Breast milk can be contaminated with a variety of pesticides and many pesticides cross the placental barrier, resulting in newborn infants already contaminated at birth. Many pesticides have been shown to be teratogenic, embryotoxic, or fetotoxic, resulting in spontaneous abortion, fetal deaths, or a broad range of developmental, behavioral, or growth problems (Moses, 1989).

Exposure to pesticides occurs by direct spraying of crops while farmworkers are working, by wind drift from sprayed fields (estimates are that pesticides can drift as far as 50 miles, dependent on particle size and wind conditions), by direct dermal contact with residues on crops, by the transfer of residue while eating, smoking, or defecating, by bathing in or drinking pesticide contaminated water and from the soil in which the crops are grown (Goldsmith, 1989; Moses, 1989; Wilk, 1993).

Pesticides can cause immediate or acute effects or long-term chronic effects (Wilk, 1993). The acute health effects of pesticide exposure range from contact dermatitis to eye and upper respiratory tract irritations and to systemic poisoning, which can lead to death (Moses, 1989). Short-term mild to moderate pesticide poisoning can cause nausea, vomiting, headaches, dizziness, muscle cramps, and blurred vision (Wilk, 1993). Pesticide-related skin problems include contact dermatitis to chronic allergic dermatitis and, in some instances, disabling conditions (Moses, 1989). Without patch testing to confirm the diagnosis, it is difficult for health care providers in migrant health clinics to differentiate between a dermatitis due to pesticide exposure and an allergic contact dermatitis. In either case, sunlight frequently aggravates the skin condition (Moses, 1989).

The majority of migrant farmworkers do not know the names of the pesticides to which they are exposed or the risks to their health. This has contributed, along with the frequency of exposure to different pesticides at multiple employment locations, to the failure in documentation of exposures and illness and to poorly kept records (only the state of California requires mandatory reporting of pesticide-related illness). The result has been little worker population-based scientific data. Because appropriate studies have not been done, little is known about the magnitude of chronic health problems related to pesticide exposure (Moses, 1989).

Chronic effects can occur even without indications of acute health effects and can occur although exposure ceased years before. The development of chronic disease can range anywhere from 15 to 30 years from the time of last exposure (Moses, 1989).

Safeguards, such as the use of protective clothing, posting warning signs on treated fields, delayed entry into the fields until the pesticides have dissipated, frequent washing of hands and face, and the regular washing of clothes with soap and water reduce exposure to pesticides. Unfortunately, there is seldom clean water for drinking or for washing of hands and face. Safeguards are generally ignored, impossible to implement, or ineffective (Goldsmith, 1989). Amendments to federal and state pesticide laws and regulations that would protect farmworkers and better their working conditions are strongly resisted by the agricultural and agrichemical industries (Moses, 1989).

In August 1992, new regulations were added in the Worker Protection Standards under the Environmental Protection Agency. Also added was a *right to know* provision. Employers must provide information about safety and the hazards of pesticides (True, 1993). Wilk (1993) contends that the information provided must be understandable by the workers so that they can protect themselves and that farmworkers must have the right to sue the employer if there is a failure to comply with the regulations and law. The Environmental Protection Agency (EPA) right-to-know regulations are only as good as their enforcement (Wilk, 1993).

Prevalent Infectious and Chronic Diseases

Tuberculosis. A report from the Centers for Disease Control (CDC) indicates that migrant farmworkers are approximately six times more likely to develop tuberculosis than the general population because of their substandard and overcrowded living conditions (Fisher, 1993).

The treatment of tuberculosis in the migrant population is very difficult. Follow-up on treatment is found to be one of the biggest problems facing both the migrant population and clinic health care providers (Brothers & Zimmerman, 1993).

Sexually Transmitted Diseases. As with tuberculosis, the incidence and prevalence of sexually transmitted disease (STD) among migrant families are difficult to establish because the population at risk is constantly changing and because neither the Centers for Disease Control (CDC) nor other health services collect epidemiologic data on STD by ethnicity (Smith, 1988). Inadequate health knowledge, poor accessibility to health care, migratory lifestyle with limited follow-up care, and language and cultural barriers contribute to the vulnerability of the migrant population to STDs.

Smith's 1988 study on sexually transmitted diseases reported that Mexican-American males and females have little knowledge of the classic symptoms of STDs and that Mexican-American migrant females have less knowledge about STD prevention and transmission than any of the groups studied.

Because the majority of Mexican-American migrants are Catholic and believe that STD affliction is sinful and shameful, the subject is not talked about freely. About half of the Mexican-American males and females in Smith's study thought that STDs can be caused by supernatural events.

Hispanics statistically account for 15% of the cases of HIV/AIDS in the United States. Results of surveys of HIV positive cases among migrant farmworkers (Foulk et al., 1991) have shown that the majority of HIV positive cases have been Haitians and Hispanics from the Eastern migratory stream. The respondents in the survey revealed little knowledge about HIV/AIDS and its transmission. Only 2.9% of the respondents reported self-injection of recreational drugs; however, 82% reported self-injecting therapeutic drugs, for medicinal purposes with little concern about needle use. The Foulk et al. (1991) study points out the urgent need for Hispanic-specific HIV/AIDS education with variations for Hispanic subgroups and the importance of targeting the injection of therapeutics.

Dental Disease. Dental caries has decreased by 35% in America due to the availability of fluoride, the decrease in sugar consumption, better dental health education, and the increase in dental resources. Decay rates for children in low socioeconomic families, however, have increased four times (Dental Care Needs and Services, 1988). Dental care resources available to migrant families outside of community and migrant health centers range from extremely limited to nonexistent. Even if migrant families had Medicaid dental insurance, the low reimbursement rate discourages dentists from accepting them as patients for preventative or curative treatment (Good, 1992).

Most migrant children have some degree of dental disease (Koday, Rosenstein, & Lopez, 1990). Without health insurance benefits, many migrant children are left without dental care and continue to suffer the pain and irreversible progression of dental disease (Good, 1992).

Eye Disease. Migrant families have a two to three times greater incidence of retinopathy, the leading cause of blindness in the United States. Even Mexican-Americans previously undiagnosed with diabetes have presented with retinopathy at the time of examination.

Another prevalent eye condition in the migrant population, which has been observed by the author and not found addressed in the literature, is pterygium. At least three or four migrant workers present during the seasonal clinics and others during the off-season with "eye irritation" and loss of visual acuity. Pterygium is a triangular connective tissue overgrowth of the conjunctiva which can extend over the cornea, leading to visual loss and discomfort. It is thought to be an irritative and degenerative phenomenon caused by ultraviolet light (Smeltzer & Bare, 1992). Pterygium can be surgically removed, but access to this type of intervention is seldom an option for migrant workers.

Diabetes and Hypertension. Diabetes in the migrant family is 338% above the U.S. average (Dever, 1991). Among the elderly, over 60% of clinic visits by males and 80% by females are for diabetes and hypertension (Dever, 1991).

As with other Hispanic populations, especially within the Mexican-American population, diabetes is prevalent in the migrant farmworker.

Mexican-Americans are believed to have characteristics that increase their risk for diabetes. Lean Mexican-Americans exhibit hyperglycemia in greater percentages than non-Hispanic Whites and hyperinsulinemia is more prevalent, suggesting that the Mexican-American ethnicity has a greater tendency to be insulin resistive (Martinez, 1993). According to the San Antonio Heart Study, discussed by Martinez (1993), hyperinsulinemia is found to be more prevalent in the nondiabetic offspring of Mexican-American parents. This supports an inherited genetic defect as a possible component in the development of non-insulin dependent diabetes mellitus (NIDDM). The San Antonio Heart Study also concluded that the incidence of end-stage renal disease (ESRD) is six times higher in Mexican-Americans than in non-Hispanic Whites and the rates of nephropathy are similar to those seen in insulin-dependent diabetes mellitus (IDDM) patients.

Screening for early detection of diabetes in the Mexican-American population is inadequate at best. The stresses of the migratory lifestyle, working conditions, poverty, malnutrition, and poor accessibility to health care compound the vulnerability of the migrant to the complications of diabetes.

There is much reference in the literature to the prevalence of hypertension in the migrant farmworker population, but little specific data related to the cause of hypertension other than its relationship to diabetes. Hypertension is more prevalent among Hispanic Americans than among non-Hispanic Whites, although the condition mostly goes unrecognized and untreated (Novello, Wise, & Kleinman, 1991). Poverty, diet and eating habits, the stress of a migratory life, deplorable working and housing conditions, constant exposure to the elements, inadequate health care, and feelings of powerlessness are contributors to the hypertensive condition and the increased risk for cardiovascular and cerebrovascular disease in migrant families. Diagnostic studies are rarely performed on migrants because of time, costs, and relocation issues.

Incidence rates for hypertension are higher in migrant women than in men. This may be stress-caused disease resulting from responsibilities and relocation pressures (Monrroy, 1983). Migration causes social and physical isolation of farmworkers and their families, especially wives who may have no ongoing social network to provide emotional, social, or financial support (Meister, 1991).

As with other conditions discussed, the continuity of care following the diagnosis of hypertension in migrants is very poor and may in itself aggravate the condition. Prescriptions often run out or are lost long before health care is available as families move from one location to another. Follow-up care is often sought only when the condition interferes with work.

Psychological Distress. Stresses related to limited social mobility, transience, poverty, discrimination, and incidence of traumatic life events put migrant families at risk for mental disorders (Vega et al., 1985). The highest mean scores for psychophysiological distress in the Health Opinion Survey (HOS) used by Vega et al. (1985) were found among very young adult Mexican males (between 18 to 20 years) and among the middle-aged respondents of both Mexican sexes. At greatest risk were females between the ages of 50 to 59 (circumstances which contribute to psychological stress in the migrant female may well relate to the same circumstances which result in hypertension). The survey by Vega et al. demonstrated that migrant farmworkers are at greater risk for psychological disorders than the general population, including other ethnic groups and better educated Mexican-Americans.

In clinical literature, the working class Mexican-American population is especially noted for its tendency toward somatization (Vega et al., 1985). Because mental health and physical health are difficult to disentangle, especially with limited medical resources available for the migrant population, Vega et al. (1985) surmise that a large segment of the migrant population is being treated for somatic problems that are of a psychiatric nature.

BARRIERS TO MIGRANT HEALTH CARE

Hispanic-Americans, in general, suffer from diseases of neglect and limited access to health services (Munoz, 1988). Novello et al. (1991) report that differences in health behaviors and health status exist between U.S.-born Hispanics and the rest of the U.S. population, including other ethnic minorities. Even foreign-born Hispanics, on arriving to the United States, tend to be in better health then U.S.-born Hispanics.

Lack of Available Services

The capacity of the Migrant Health Program to meet the tremendous needs of the migrant population is as limited as its funding (Duran, 1993).

As there is no legal right to health care in the United States for the general population, there is no legal right to health care for migrant farmworkers (Duran, 1993). Migrant and seasonal farmworkers are barred from traditional health care services by differences in language, culture, lack of local transportation, poverty, poor access to referral sources, and the absence of continuity of medical care and follow-up (Zuroweste, 1993).

Funded with $58.6 million, the Migrant Health Program provides care to a half million patients a year, allowing 4% coverage per person or approximately $118.00 (20% of which goes for administrative costs) (Stilp, 1994). This compares with the $2,800 average per capita health care bill in the United States (Stilp, 1994).

Since 1962, when the Migrant Health Act was passed, migrant health centers have struggled to serve the migrant and seasonal farmworker population. Even though the high rate of mobility of farmworkers makes it difficult for the Migrant Health Program to provide continuous comprehensive care, access to health care is better upstream than in migrant home bases (Dever, 1991). Migrant health centers function as islands of care for an undervalued population in underserved communities where local residents themselves do not have adequate access to health care (Zuroweste, 1993). At its best, however, it is believed that the Migrant Health Program serves less than 20% of the population (Duran, 1993).

Migrant health centers are isolated from one another as well as from the larger mainstream health care communities. Consequently, many of the health services that are needed the most, such as referrals, clear explanation of diagnosis and treatment, reinforcement of compliance, health education, and preventive health services are not being delivered (Goldsmith, 1989).

Due to budget cuts in health care, it becomes more and more difficult to refer migrants to private physicians or regional hospitals (Stilp, 1994). Attempts at referrals are some of the most frustrating, time consuming, frequently futile, and demoralizing exercises which staff in seasonal clinics and migrant health centers experience. More distressing are referrals for children who require the services of specialists such as a cardiologist, otologist, or dermatologist. Often the available physician is an hour away and the family can't afford to miss a day of work or doesn't have transportation for getting the child there. Migrant health providers are constantly in the position of having to beg for care for their clients (Stilp, 1994). "Because of our position as a grantee and having to beg for care, I have to be nice to everyone—the Feds, the state, the legislators, the doctors, the pharmacists, and the hospitals." "Yet, because of our powerless position, no one has to be nice to me" (Stilp, 1994).

Transportation can be a major barrier to the availability of health care. Clinics are generally located far from the migrant camps. Some of the farmworkers, especially those who are single, are bused to their work locations and may not be able to arrange individual transportation from the field or labor camps. Large groups arrive together for evening clinics, and they all have to stay until the last person has been seen. It is not unusual to have a mother with a sick infant have to wait for several hours after the infant has been seen for transportation to a pharmacy or home. Often the pharmacy has closed before the last member in the group is seen. Arrangements have to be made to return for prescriptions and treatment is delayed.

Health care providers feel the frustration with the lack of opportunity for continuity of care and follow-up (O'Brien, 1983). Long-term health teaching is nearly impossible. Even short-term teaching can be a challenge because one must try to provide information during limited clinic hours to a physically depleted clientele with language and cultural barriers. Continuity of care and commitment are areas of concern with seasonal clinic staff. Seasonal clinics are often staffed with resident physicians from nearby medical centers on a rotation basis. During a period of 12 weeks, we have had eight different residents providing care. Although attempts are made to provide follow-up care with the same resident, it is not often possible and the patient may see three or even four doctors for the same problem during the course of a summer.

Seasonal clinics are handicapped by limitations in space (location), time, and staffing. Our particular seasonal clinic operates in a university student health center where space becomes available for approximately 12 weeks. With two of those weeks used to set up and repack clinic supplies, availability to migrant clients is reduced to 10 weeks. The hour limitations imposed by the student health center are also not necessarily the most accessible to the farmworkers.

Federal funding for the migrant health centers under the Migrant Health Program are grants which do not allow for inpatient hospital services. For this reason, rural hospitals, with their own economic concerns, do not welcome migrant families. With no financial access for inpatient services, migrant families undergo delays in treatment that result in increased mortality and morbidity, loss of work, and increased uncompensated costs to the hospitals. Consequently, migrant families are more likely to attempt to utilize emergency services, which in turn may result in denial of services or in the provision of inferior health services because of their inability to pay (Stilp, 1994).

Migrant Health Program grant money was initially made available to private nonprofit corporations for the provision of primary outpatient care. However, because of reductions in the amount of funding in recent years, migrant health centers have had to refocus priorities from primary care, health promotion, and disease prevention to secondary level care (Watkins et al., 1990). This has had serious consequences in areas of maternal and child health because of the importance of outreach and health education in prenatal and well-child care. Pregnancy is the most frequent presenting health condition for migrant females aged 15 to 19 (Dever,

1991) and migrant women are more likely to enter prenatal care later in their pregnancy and to receive fewer prenatal visits than are recommended (Watkins et al., 1990). Of the migrant mothers surveyed by Slesinger et al. (1986), 40% experienced at least one out-of-hospital birth, and over 23% gave birth to at least half of their children outside a hospital.

Access to health care is even worse for migrant workers in areas where the number of farmworkers is dispersed over a large geographic area. In these areas, a voucher program is utilized since a migrant health center is not justified. Voucher programs were devised to provide services for farmworkers through contracts with local physicians. Funding for these programs has been significantly reduced by the Department of Health and Human Services and migrants who happen to be employed in these outlying areas frequently have no available health care services (Stilp, 1994).

Staffing decline is a continuous problem for migrant health centers. In 1989, the National Service Corps, a program under the Public Health Service designed to supply physicians, dentists, and nurse practitioners for migrant clinics, was allowed to expire by the Reagan administration. It was reauthorized by Congress in 1990. The turnover of physicians, who have received funding through medical school in exchange for their service to medically underserved areas, has been rapid as they are lured into the private sector by larger salaries. This has led to the closure of many migrant health centers (Stilp, 1994).

Nurse practitioners, on the other hand, can play a major role in the provision of health care to migrant and other underserved populations. A family nurse practitioner can provide primary health care services to individuals and families (Pickwell & Warnock, 1994). Nurse practitioners are highly effective, less costly, and are well accepted by patients. Because some states do not recognize nurse practitioners, however, without federal legislation allowing nurse practitioners however, independent practice, migrant families and other poor Americans will continue to be underserved.

Lack of Health Insurance

Almost universally, migrant farmworkers are without insurance. Although it is estimated that 90% of farmworkers qualify for Medicaid, fewer than 10% sporadically receive any type of benefits. Those who qualify are discouraged from applying by the turn around times and the enormous barriers in enrollment procedures and administrative requirements (Gaston, 1993; Zuroweste, 1993). The few migrants who are on Medicaid in their home state find that it is not accepted in other states when they migrate, because there is no reciprocity between states. In instances when they do apply for Medicaid in another state, migrant families find that there may be several weeks between the application and the interview. In many instances, the family is ready to leave the area before receiving any benefits (Poss & Meeks, 1994). Because income qualification guidelines are based on recent paychecks and not on overall yearly income, migrant farmworkers find themselves in a Catch-22 situation (Poss & Meeks, 1994). If they begin to earn a salary before they apply for Medicaid, they will make too much money to qualify.

Medicaid, jointly funded by federal and state funds, is a program which was created in 1965 under Title XIX of the Social Security Act. Its purpose is to provide health care services to low-income families and long-term care to low-income elderly and disabled people. However, it is designed to provide coverage only to categorically defined groups, and not universal coverage to the poor. Medicaid benefits are received by fewer than 50% of the country's poor, as the remainder fail to meet the categorical requirements.

Medicaid is an open-ended, means-tested, entitlement program that ensures a basic package of federally mandated benefits to all who qualify. This means that states may add services other than those mandated by the federal government, but may also limit the scope of coverage by variations in the welfare eligibility rules to which Medicaid eligibility is linked. For example, to be covered by Medicaid, families with children must qualify for AFDC (Aid to Families with Dependent Children) benefits and AFDC eligibility is determined by the states. States may establish the *need standard* that defines AFDC eligibility as they wish. Many states' need standards are far from equivalent with subsistence-level incomes and most states fail to update their need standards based on cost-of-living increases. In 35 states, income eligibility levels for AFDC families are below 50% of the poverty level. Medicaid can also become a revolving door for migrant families as their financial circumstances fluctuate; by the time they become old enough for Medicare, migrants have long since dropped out of the migrant stream (Stilp, 1994).

To further complicate the Medicaid bureaucracy, eligibility is determined at the county level and state policies are implemented differently by each county. Most migrants remain in one state for no more than four months during their migratory season, at which time they earn their major income for the entire year (Slesinger & Cautley, 1981). Yet, some counties continue to estimate the farmworkers annual income by multiplying the workers' current monthly income by 12.

County agencies are not adequately staffed during the migrant season to handle applications for Medicaid from Spanish-speaking workers and office hours are not adjusted to accommodate people who usually work six to seven days a week (Slesinger & Cautley, 1981). Even those migrant families with occasional Medicaid coverage find themselves with little access to health care because private physicians exhibit low levels of participation in Medicaid, leaving recipients dependent on public clinics and hospital emergency rooms for health care.

Language and Culture

Hispanic migrant farmworkers retain their basic Hispanic culture and for 90% of them Spanish is their primary language. Although farmworkers share the Spanish language and many of the same social scripts with other Hispanics, they are considered to be socially and culturally different from Hispanic people in urban areas of the United States because of their migratory lifestyle (Foulk et al., 1991).

Migrant farmworkers retain their first language even though the second and subsequent generations may be fluent in English (just over half of Hispanic farmworkers are able to speak both English and Spanish with younger workers more able to speak English than those 50 years or older (Slesinger & Cautley, 1981)). Because the Spanish language best serves to express emotions, feelings, and beliefs within the affective domain, under stress, migrant families tend to revert to their first language (Smith, 1988).

The ability of health care providers to communicate with migrant patients in their own language enables them to have a more complete understanding of patients' needs and to provide more complete case management services (Watkins et al., 1990). Those patients who are not fluent in English must use a translator when seeking health care services. Valuable information may be withheld as the client may be reluctant to divulge private information through a translator who may be a stranger, youngster, or another family member. The information conveyed back and forth from the client to the health care provider through an interpreter may result in misunderstanding or misinformation which can lead to the client's lack of trust in the provider and in the health system (O'Brien, 1983). Our seasonal clinics are staffed with family practice residents from surrounding teaching hospitals. A great number of these residents are themselves foreign-born with English as a second language. This results in greater language and cultural differences, even for our English-speaking migrants.

The importance of trust (confianza) in providers is the prime determinant for the migrant family to seek not only health care, but also to comply with treatment and recommendations. Most health care providers are ignorant of migrant culture, have little if any knowledge of the Spanish language, and may be viewed with suspicion by migrant workers seeking health care. Mistrust in the providers of health care can cause delays in seeking care and can result in the patient waiting until the symptoms become severe and medical attention can no longer be delayed.

Horton (1988) found that the initial attitude of migrant people toward doctors is consistently one of distrust. Until demonstrated otherwise, migrants fear that doctors are interested only in the money they can get from their clients and that doctors do not really care about them. Migrant families interviewed by Horton (1988) reported that doctors who take time to talk about the patient's home and family generate a sense of caring. It is not unusual for home-based families living on the U.S. side of the border to seek health care in Mexico because their trust in Spanish-speaking physicians in Mexico is generally greater than their trust in non-Spanish-speaking health care providers in clinics or health departments in the United States (Horton, 1988).

Culture awareness will enhance the development of trust. To achieve success with Mexican-American migrants, health care providers must be attentive to the client's socialization to health and illness as well as to constraints posed by their occupational mobility (O'Brien, 1983). Mexican-American migrant workers' understanding of the cause and treatment of certain illness is guided by folk beliefs (O'Brien, 1983). Nearly all families accept the existence of traditional ailments such as mal ojo, empacho, susto, and mollera caida (Horton, 1988). When ill, most Mexican-American migrants turn first to their indigenous folk beliefs and practices. If treatment is unsuccessful, the professional health care system is approached. Occasionally, folk beliefs regarding the etiology of illness may block acceptance of modern medical treatment and some patients may discard prescribed medication if a preferred folk remedy is available; however, most often both systems are used simultaneously (O'Brien, 1983).

The use of Mexican folk remedies or alternative treatment regimens should be explored rather than being dismissed as cultural weaknesses. Health care providers may be able to build on these folk remedies by giving permission for their use, if not medically contraindicated, thus enhancing the client's trust in the process (Goldsmith, 1989). For example, herbal teas are used by migrant families for the treatment of various ailments. With an understanding of their value, health care providers can encourage migrant mothers to give a sick child tea to maintain proper hydration. It benefits both the child and the mother by allowing the mother to maintain control over the child's care (Wheeler, 1991).

However, there are practices that are not harmless. In Mexico, migrant families have access to and may seek advice regarding diagnosis, treatment, and medications, directly from persons working in pharmacies (Horton, 1988). Considerably more medications are available through Mexican pharmacies without prescription than in the United States, and persons working in Mexican pharmacies (not necessarily pharmacists) are more apt to give clinical advice and offer treatment (Horton, 1988). The use of nonprescription antibiotics obtained from Mexican pharmacies is common for the treatment of diarrhea or uncomplicated respiratory infections. The prevalence of drug allergies is high because of this practice (Horton, 1988). Injectable antibiotics and vitamins are also easily obtained. This practice increases the migrants' risk for blood-borne pathogens such as hepatitis and HIV. Not infrequently, migrant families arrive at health care centers in the United States asking for renewal of unlabeled drugs which they have been taking.

Health care has low priority as migrant families struggle to survive. As is prevalent in Hispanic culture, migrant families' criteria for health are: a sturdy body, the ability to maintain a high level of normal physical activity, and the absence of persistent pain and discomfort. Migrant farmworkers tend to perceive themselves to be healthier than they really are upon clinical examination and do not consider a condition an illness unless it becomes so debilitating that they are unable to work (Smith, 1988).

If a disorder is experienced frequently, it may be perceived as minor, harmless, normal, and treatable with home remedies (Smith, 1988). By the time migrant farmworkers seek health care, the condition has often become acute, and severe symptoms from long untreated illnesses are often present (O'Brien, 1983).

The majority of migrant families seeks care for acute problems rather than for preventative services, such as periodic physical examinations that focus on health education and patient risk status. Preventative education for the migrant family cannot be effective solely on what is provided in a health care facility. The migrant workers' social and work environment necessitates out-reach education programs. It is wise to solicit assistance from migrant families themselves when developing educational programs to assure the message will be pertinent and accepted. The use of camp health aides with leadership skills, who are members of the migrant community, can help both the patients and health care providers by bridging the gaps that may develop due to language or culture differences (Brothers & Zimmerman, 1993).

The family is the most important Hispanic institution. In that tradition, migrant farmworkers form close family bonds and migrate in extended family groups (McDermott & Lee, 1990; Smith, 1988). Family groups work as a team with older women cooking and watching infants and toddlers as older children, many as young as nine or ten, work alongside their parents (O'Brien, 1983). The family is the primary source of emotional support, advice, and counsel. When ill or feeling distress, the Mexican-American migrant is used to being surrounded by family. The hospital is viewed as a place where one goes to die or a place where one is isolated from family and friends. Hospitalization for the migrant, where visitors are limited, can be a devastating experience (O'Brien, 1983).

The male is the head of the household, the dominant decision maker in the family unit, and the female is the primary health care provider. Important family decisions are made by men. Consequently, male input is often solicited by the female caregiver during health care evaluation and even in the selection of professional health care providers (Smith, 1988).

Migrant women are less likely to use family planning methods than other populations. However, when birth control is utilized, the female is responsible for the method used. For this reason, condom presentations, aimed primarily at male migrants are ineffective (Foulk et al., 1991; Watkins et al., 1990). Issues related to sex are not openly discussed in mixed company and coeducational presentations on condom use and demonstration are considered to be inappropriate (Foulk et al., 1991). Because children are highly valued, rather than focusing on contraception, condom campaigns should promote condom use as a means of maintaining the health of family providers.

Respect and privacy are key Hispanic values. Addressing an adult by his or her surname is a sign of respect. If the patient does not feel that respect, he or she is less likely to trust and value another's opinion and may choose not to follow recommendations given. Mexican-American patients, regardless of their social circumstances, prefer to be addressed by their last name (Smith, 1988).

Modesty is pervasive and same-gender health care providers increase migrant patients' comfort. Male patients prefer to see male providers. Women are embarrassed by any pelvic examination and most feel uncomfortable being examined by a male physician. Their sense of modesty often interferes with their need to comply with routine examinations and many will refuse treatment if such an examination is necessary (O'Brien, 1983). Respect for migrant patients can be demonstrated by adequate draping (Smith, 1988).

CONCLUSION

In spite of many hearings and studies regarding the plight of the farmworker, the changes which have taken place in the past 33 years have been insignificant (Marentes, 1993).

We must continue efforts to help bring migrant farmworkers from the darkness and into American consciousness. Health care providers must strongly advocate for decent wages, housing, and working conditions, and for pesticide controls and the effective enforcement of those controls.

Even tremendously increased investments in public sector enforcement activities, regulatory activities, and service programs oriented toward serving migrant farmworkers will not be effective unless there are new methods of collaboration between the public and private sectors in terms of coming to a solution that is not adversarial (Rosenthal, 1993).

We, as health care providers, must put forth greater efforts to develop a better understanding of all ethnic minority citizens and to recognize and serve their health care needs. We must also encourage better representation of minority groups in nursing and other health care professions. Most importantly, health care advocates must continue to push for equitable health care legislation for all U.S. citizens regardless of ethnicity, social status, or age.

REFERENCES

Allen, C. E. (1993, September). Families in poverty. *The Nursing Clinics of North America, 29*(3), 377-393.

Brothers, J., & Zimmerman, D. (1993). A camp health aide? *Nursing Management Letters, 24*(11), 12-13.

Carle, J. (1995, March 27). ABLE subsidy might get plowed under. *Sentinel-Tribune,* pp. 1, 2.

Ciesielski, S. D., Seed, J. R., Eposito, D. H., & Hunter, N. (1991). The epidemiology of tuberculosis among North Carolina migrant farm workers. *Journal of the American Medical Association, 265*(13), 1715-1719.

Dailey, C. Y. (Ed.). (1994). *1994 Migrant health centers referral directory.* U.S. Department of Health & Human Services, U.S. Public Health Service Health Resources, and Services Administration Bureau of Primary Health Care.

Dental care needs and services: Community and migrant health centers. (1988). Washington, DC: U.S. Department of Health & Human Services. Public Health Services, Health Resources and Services Administration, Bureau of Health Care Delivery and Assistance.

deVries, C. (1995, February). *What the contract with America means for nurses.* ANA informational report.

Dever, G. E. (1991). Migrant status: Profile of a population with complex health problems. *Migrant Health Newsline: Monograph Series, 8*(2), 1-16.

Dewey, K. G., Strode, M. A., & Fitch, Y. R. (1984). Dietary change among migrant and nonmigrant Mexican-American families in northern California. *Ecology of Food and Nutrition, 14,* 11-24.

Duran, D. (1993, May). *Migrant farmworkers in the United States implementation of the Helsinki accords briefings of the commission on security and cooperation in Europe.* Washington, DC, 46-48.

Executive Summary. (1985, June). *Methodology for designating high impact migrant and seasonal agricultural areas.* U.S. Department of Health & Human Services, Public Health Service Health Resources, and Services Administration, 1-7.

Farm. (1995, April 8). FlOC, Ohio Vlasic pickle growers reach agreement on 5-year contract. *Sentinel-Tribune,* p. 14.

Farmworker Justice Fund, Inc. (1995, January/February). Farmworker women speak out: Health policy recommendations. *MCN Clinical Supplement Migrant Clinicians Network,* 4.

Fisher, J. (1993, May). *Migrant farmworkers in the United States implementation of the Helsinki accords briefings of the commission on security and cooperation in Europe.* Washington, DC, 39-77.

Foulk, D., Lafferty, J., & Ryan, R. (1991, September/October). Developing culturally sensitive materials for AIDS education specifically targeted to migrant farmworkers. *Journal of Health Education, 22*(5), 283-286.

Fraser, J. (1993, May). *Migrant farmworkers in the United States implementation of the Helsinki accords briefings of the commission on security and cooperation in Europe.* Washington, DC, 3-9.

Galarneau, C. A. (1992). Farmworkers as "different" a matter of difference or indifference? *Migration World, 20*(1), 29-33.

Gaston, M. (1993, May). *Migrant farmworkers in the United States implementation of the Helsinki accords briefings of the commission on security and cooperation in Europe.* Washington, DC, 41-44.

Ginsberg, E. (1991). Access to health care for Hispanics. *Journal of the American Medcial Association, 265*(2), 238-241.

Goldsmith, M. F. (1989). As farmworkers help keep America healthy, illness may be their harvest. *Journal of the American Medical Association, 261*(22), 3207-3213.

Good, M. E. (1992). The clinical nurse specialist in the school setting: Case management of migrant children with dental disease. *Clinical Nurse Specialist, 6*(2), 72-76.

Grey, M. R. (1993). Dustbowls, disease, and the new deal: The farm security administration migrant health problems, 1935-1947. *The Journal of the History of Medicine and Allied Sciences, 48*(1), 3-39.

Health care for migrant workers: The shame of it. (1990, December). *The Journal of Practical Nursing,* 28-29.

Horton, D. G. (1988). Health care utilization by migrant farmworkers at their home base residence. *Migration World, 16*(3), 31-34.

Iorio, D. C. (1985). The agricultural worker: Occupational health's neglected client. *Occupational Health Nursing, 33*(11), 566-568.

Kirkman-Liff, B., & Mondragon, D. (1991). Language of interview: Relevance for research of southwest Hispanics. *American Journal of Public Health, 81*(11), 1399-1403.

Kissam, E. (1993, May). *Migrant farmworkers in the United States implementation of the Helsinki accords briefings of the commission on security and cooperation in Europe.* Washington, DC, 9-14.

Koday, M., Rosenstein, D. I., & Lopez, G. M. N. (1990). Dental decay rates among children of migrant workers in Yakima, WA. *Public Health Reports, 105*(5), 530-533.

Marentes, C. (1993, May). *Migrant farmworkers in the United States implementation of the Helsinki accords briefings of the commission on security and cooperation in Europe.* Washington, DC, 21-22.

Martinez, N. C. (1993). Diabetes and minority populations: Focus on Mexican-Americans. *The Nursing Clinics of North America, 28*(1), 87-95.

McDermott, S., & Lee, C. V. (1990). Injury among male migrant farm workers in South Carolina. *Journal of Community Health, 15*(5), 297-305.

Meister, J. S. (1991). The health care of migrant farm workers. *Occupational Medicine, 6*(3), 503-518.

Monaghan, T. (1995). Letter interview. Trust Care Home Health Services, Sandusky, Ohio.

Monrroy, L. S. A. (1983). Nursing care of raza/latina patients. In M. S. Orque, B. Bloch, & L. S. A. Monrroy (Eds.), *Ethnic nursing care a multicultural approach* (pp. 115-148). St. Louis: Mosby.

Moses, M. (1989, March). Pesticide-related health problems and farmworkers. *American Association of Occupational Health Nurses Journal, 37*(3), 115-130.

Mountain, K., & Hill, R. (1992). MCN outlines strategies for improving migrant health care. *Nurse Practitioner: American Journal of Primary Health Care, 17*(8), 8-9.

Munoz, E. (1988). Care for the Hispanic poor: A growing segment of American society. *Journal of the American Medical Association, 260*(18), 2711-2712.

Novello, A. C., Wise, P. H., & Kleinmann, D. V. (1991). Hispanic health: Time for data, time for action. *Journal of the American Medical Association, 265*(2), 253-255.

O'Brien, M. E. (1983, June). Reaching the migrant worker. *American Journal of Nursing,* 895-897.

Pickwell, S. M., & Warnock, F. (1994). Family nurse practitioner faculty clinical practice with undocumented migrants. *Family & Community Health, 16*(4), 32-38.

Poss, J. E., & Meeks, B. H. (1994). Meeting the health care needs of migrant farmworkers: The experience of the Niagara County migrant clinic. *Journal of Community Health Nursing, 11*(4), 219-228.

Preface. (1993, May). *Migrant farmworkers in the United States implementation of the Helsinki accords briefings of the commission on security and cooperation in Europe.* Washington, DC, iii-v.

Rosenthal, R. (1993, May). *Migrant farmworkers in the United States implementation of the Helsinki accords briefings of the commission on security and cooperation in Europe.* Washington, DC, 14-21.

Rust, G. S. (1990). Health status of migrant farmworkers: A literature review and commentary. *American Journal of Public Health, 80*(10), 1213-1217.

Ryder, E. R. (1995). What's wrong with this equation? *Migrant Health Newline, 1*(12), 1, 4.

Schneider, B. (1986, February). Providing for the health needs of migrant children. *Nurse Practitioner: American Journal of Primary Health Care, 11*(1), 54, 56, 58.

Slesinger, D. P., & Cautley, E. (1981). Medical utilization patterns of Hispanic migrant farmworkers in Wisconsin. *Public Health Reports, 96*(3), 255-263.

Slesinger, D. P., Christenson, B. A., & Cautley, E. (1986). Health and mortality of migrant farm children. *Social Science and Medicine, 23*(1), 65-74.

Smeltzer, S. C., & Bare, B. G. (1992). *Brunner and Suddarth's textbook of medical-surgical nursing* (7th ed.). Philadelphia: Lippincott.

Smith, L. S. (1988). Ethnic differences in knowledge of sexually transmitted diseases in North American Black and Mexican-American migrant farmworkers. *Research in Nursing and Health, 11,* 51-58.

Stilp, F. J. (1994). The migrant health program in the United States: A personal view from the front line. *Migration World, 22*(4), 13-21.

True, L. (1993, May). *Migrant farmworkers in the United States implementation of the Helsinki accords briefings of the commission on security and cooperation in Europe.* Washington, DC, 44-46.

Vega, W., Warheit, G., & Palacio, R. (1985). Psychiatric symptomatology among Mexican-American farmworkers. *Social Science and Medicine, 20*(1), 39-45.

Watkins, E. L., Larson, K., Harlan, C., & Young, S. (1990). A model program for providing health services for migrant farmworker mothers and children. *Public Health Reports, 105,* 567-575.

Wheeler, M. C. (1991). Nursing in a migrant setting. *Imprint, 38*(3), 70, 72, 127.

Wilk, V. (1993, May). *Migrant farmworkers in the United States implementation of the Helsinki accords briefings of the commission on security and cooperation in Europe.* Washington, DC, 51-56, 122.

Zuroweste, E. (1993, May). *Migrant farmworkers in the United States implementation of the Helsinki accords briefings of the commission on security and cooperation in Europe.* Washington, DC, 48-51.

CHAPTER THIRTEEN

Recruiting Hispanic Nursing Faculty

Evelyn Ruiz Calvillo, RN, DNSc

Increasing the number of ethnically diverse faculty into health occupation programs has been an issue for many years. However, recruiting ethnically diverse faculty into higher education has seen "minimal progress" (National Education Association [NEA], 1992). Hispanics, for one, are underrepresented among college faculty (2.2%) and administrators (2%) (Justz, 1995). African American, Hispanic, and Native American faculty and health care practitioners, taken together, are also underrepresented at all levels of education and practice (UCI Health Sciences and Office of Nursing and Allied Health, 1993). Of the 16,503 full-time nursing faculty, 91.2% were White, 5.8% African American, 1.6% Asian, 0.8% Hispanic, and 0.6% Native American (National League for Nursing [NLN], 1991). While there have been some changes reported since then, they have been very subtle—a 1% increase in the number of Hispanic faculty in 1993, for example (NLN, 1993).

CONTRIBUTING FACTORS

"Despite the cries of many opponents of affirmative action that too many minorities were being hired because of special programs and hiring quotas, African-Americans, American Indians, and Hispanics made minimal

Acknowledgement of Contributions by ethnically diverse nurse educators and leaders who participated in the workshop, "Matching a diverse student population: Recruiting ethnically diverse faculty into health occupations programs." Workshop funded and sponsored by Project Diversity, ID No. 92-0696, The Chancellor's Office, California Community Colleges. Implemented by Diane Sloane, RN, PhD, Director, Marsha Roberson, RN, MN, Coordinator, Regional Health Occupations Resource Center, Santa Barbara City College, Santa Barbara, CA.

progress during the 1980s in rectifying their underrepresentation in many areas of academic employment, particularly within faculty ranks" (American Council of Education, 1992). Three decades of affirmative action have still not changed the underrepresentation of Hispanics on college and university campuses nor in the composition of faculty.

Many factors have been identified as contributing to the low numbers of Hispanic nursing faculty. A crucial factor is the low number of Hispanic nurses who are prepared to teach at learning institutions at the associate degree, baccalaureate, and graduate levels. It is reported that only 2.1% of Hispanic nurses prepared at the masters level and only 0.1% of Hispanic nurses have earned doctorates (NLN, 1992).

Perhaps the most critical factor affecting the number of potential Hispanic faculty is the low enrollment of Hispanic students into nursing. Nursing enrollments for Hispanics were reported at 3.1% in 1991 (U.S. Department of Education, 1991). The "pool" for potential faculty members, which has not changed dramatically in recent years, is not large enough to impact academia. While an increase has been seen recently, the number of ethnically diverse students entering nursing continues to remain low (NLN, 1994), which essentially affects the number of students who continue into graduate education in preparation for teaching.

Studies have also shown that most Hispanic students receive their nursing degree at the associate level, only a small number of Hispanic students are entering graduate programs, and an even smaller number are graduating (NLN, 1993). "Hispanic students are particularly at risk of becoming lost in the academic world" (Dietz, 1992, p. 5). According to Dietz, the typical college or university campus by nature is an unfamiliar social and academic situation often comprised of predominately White undergraduates, faculty, and staff (NEA, 1991). The situation is complicated by the fact that many Hispanics enter college with poor language and reading skills, often due to inept preparation in high school. Continuation of their education is affected as well by economics. In 1992, the National Institute of Health (NIH) revealed that minority students often have difficulty with transition from the associate to the baccalaureate degree and from the masters to the doctorate degree. "Many bright minority students attend two-year colleges because of financial reasons" (NIH, 1995, p. 24).

Perhaps the most ubiquitous force leading to change now is the rapid growth rate of ethnic groups in some states (e.g., California) which have seen an increase in certain ethnic groups, especially Hispanics. The latest U.S. census reported that the number of people of Hispanic origin nationwide reached 22.3 million, representing a 53% increase from the previous 1980 census. It has been predicted that Hispanics, the fastest growing "minority" group, will comprise an estimated 20% of the U.S. population by the year 2030. Large numbers of Hispanics are located in the Western region of the country. In Los Angeles County, California, approximately 60% of the population is Hispanic (United Way Metropolitan Region, 1994). Healthcare providers and related organizations in areas where Hispanic populations are growing are ever more concerned with enabling nurses and other health care professionals to provide culturally sensitive care to this large group.

Culturally sensitive care is given when the provider considers and incorporates culture and ethnic beliefs into care, as well as health promotion based on diseases specific to racial and ethnic differences. Standardized and computerized medical and nursing interventions or pathways for various medical and nursing diagnoses cannot be adapted to fit a person's lifestyle and health beliefs that have been influenced by belonging to a specific cultural group. At times poor communication is due not just to language difference but, more importantly, lack of communication via value and belief differences between patient and health care providers. For such providers, this situation frequently leads to anger, frustration, and stereotyping. The same anger and frustrations may be experienced by the patient. Treating and educating patients about health promotion based on cultural considerations and beliefs can lead to a faster and better recovery. One solution here is to provide healthcare providers from the same ethnic or cultural group. Unfortunately, while health care organizations are currently recruiting Hispanic nurses intensely, the prospect of attractive benefits and security in an uncertain job market often leads to postponement of plans to continue further education.

Additionally, as many state and federally supported educational institutions are faced with potential cutbacks in dollars, serving the customer (i.e., the diverse student) has become important. As the numbers of ethnically diverse students entering college or universities increase, institutions are also concerned about serving and, most importantly, satisfying the customer—the earning of a degree. Attrition, another contributor to the low numbers of Hispanic nurses, is often seen by students as the responsibility of the teaching institute. In response, many colleges and universities have implemented retention programs which, if successful, among other strategies use role models from the underrepresented populations being served. Having access to successful role models, among other services provided by the institution, appears to motivate student success, leading to enhanced customer satisfaction.

MATCHING A DIVERSE STUDENT POPULATION

An important issue in any diversification issue is whether there is a real and meaningful rationale for changing the status quo of a teaching institution. Demand for change has been influenced by the ideals and values that an ethnic mix of students brings to educational institutions. In many institutions, demands by ethnic groups are made through involvement in governance or by demand for changes in the classroom. In less rare instances, demands are made by public protest.

Educational institutions are beginning to realize the impact a large, diverse student population has on the success of providing a meaningful and appropriate learning experience, including this essential ingredient: role models and mentors from the same ethnic group. Matching a diverse student population is now a key variable in recruiting diverse faculty into educational programs including health occupations programs.

Because their cultural traits and skills are different than mainstream U.S. culture, it has been proposed that cultural mismatch can lead to failure by "minorities" to achieve academic success (Rhyno, 1992). The interaction of many factors such as cultural traits and values, preparation for college course work, and other social forces such as inadequate financial aid and lack of student support services (e.g., child care) play a role in academic success. To assign responsibility to one factor for failure is certainly short-sighted. However, modification of a nursing program through the hiring of diverse faculty who can relate to students from the same culture does appear to offer one answer to a complex issue.

MODELS FOR CHANGE

Institutions continue to seek ways of increasing the number of ethnically diverse faculty. Many models or frameworks have been proposed or implemented at teaching institutions to address the issue of multiculturalism, either by changes in curricula to reflect diversity in society or to increase the numbers of ethnically diverse students into the different disciplines. Numerous "minority" recruitment programs, educational outreach, tuition assistance, retention models, and mentoring models have been suggested or implemented to increase the opportunities for the ethnically diverse student to enter the health professions (NEA, 1991; Werning, 1992). Federally supported models such as the Area Health Education Centers (AHEC) have concentrated on increasing the ethnically underrepresented health profession workforce who can provide primary health care. Funding from the division of nursing, health organizations, and private foundations has increased the number of graduates who can practice in various areas, although little impact has been made in increasing the number of Hispanics with a masters or doctorate degree.

Few, if any models, projects, or programs have addressed the recruitment and retention of ethnically diverse nurses who are prepared to consider faculty appointments. A systematic, comprehensive model for the recruitment and hiring of full-time underrepresented faculty into health occupations programs is proposed by this author. The model was developed following input by nursing professionals participating in an invitational workshop sponsored by a college located in the south central region in California (Calvillo, 1994). Invited participants included ethnically diverse educational and health institution leaders, as well as leaders from diverse professional nursing ethnic groups. The participants were invited based on their expertise and experience in recruiting diverse faculty and because of their past interest or work and commitment to making changes at institutions of learning.

The workshop provided a forum in which specific strategies could be identified to increase the pool of underrepresented master's prepared candidates for full-time positions in health occupations programs. It was expected that there would be an increase in the appreciation that current faculty have for incorporating diversity into full-time employee pools in health occupations programs. Additionally it was expected that these experts would develop hiring procedures that would aid in the employment of underrepresented full-time faculty in health occupations programs, as well as provide allied health directors, health occupations faculty, health institution and agency leaders, and ethnically diverse leaders the opportunity to develop a plan that could be used as a model for addressing the need to increase the number of underrepresented educators.

The workshop approach to identify strategies for recruitment, hiring, retention, and sensitizing current faculty was chosen with confidence that the invited participants would formulate ideas based on past experience with and expertise in the issues concerning the paucity of diverse faculty. Four work groups emerged from the individual participants' interest in a specific workshop objective. The significant benefits gained through the group process, composed of experts, insured that priority strategies would be identified. Guidelines were provided for direction on identification of strategies specific to the group objective. Each group was asked to identify strategies as well as methodologies, resources, outreach, and suggestions for successful implementation. Some of the strategies identified evolved from previous documents developed by ethnic professional nurse leaders (California Ethnic Minority Nurse Leadership Congress, 1993; Furata, 1992). Following discussion, the priority strategies were identified and then presented to all workshop participants. Feedback and recommendations from workshop participants were consolidated into a written format (Calvillo, 1994).

MODEL FOR RECRUITING ETHNICALLY DIVERSE NURSING FACULTY

A "Model for Recruiting Ethnically Diverse Faculty into Health Occupation Programs" (see Figure 13.1) evolved from the identification of strategies and methods by the four work groups. The major system elements of the model include supportive resources and the resources for recruitment of potential faculty, the strategies process, the increase in diverse faculty, and the role diverse faculty can play in identifying more resources.

All elements of the model are linked toward the goal of recruiting ethnically diverse faculty. The subsystems consist of four strategies to assure success: recruitment, hiring, retention, and sensitizing current faculty and staff to the advantages of a diverse faculty. An additional important subsystem is identified as the individual faculty candidate who is actively being recruited. The individual subsystem includes all values, beliefs, knowledge, attitudes, aspirations, and experiences both personal and professional that a faculty candidate brings with him or her which should be taken into consideration when hiring.

The subsystems are all impacted by the input components of the model which are the supportive resources and the sources for recruitment of potential faculty candidates, directed at success of the four strategies. Supportive resources include: (a) funding agencies, government agencies, and private enterprises that can provide financial aid for the development of recruitment programs targeting ethnically diverse faculty; (b) political and professional groups such as the American Nurses Association and the National League for Nursing, which can provide assistance with recruitment, information such as statistical data, and the development of a speakers bureau; (c) career centers at universities that have graduate programs; and (d) the Chamber of Commerce, Welcome Wagon, and other city/county agencies that provide information or resources to faculty new to a geographic area.

Multiple methods to recruit potential faculty candidates include: (a) career days; (b) ethnically sensitive printed materials which include role models; (c) invitations of ethnic practitioners to conferences and workshops as participants and attendees; (d) interrelationships with ethnic organizations, especially for assistance with mentor programs; (e) marketing of the teaching role as a specialty; and (f) bridging with health agencies and graduate programs to provide teaching internships and to develop adjunct faculty positions for involvement in curriculum development and participation as guest lecturers.

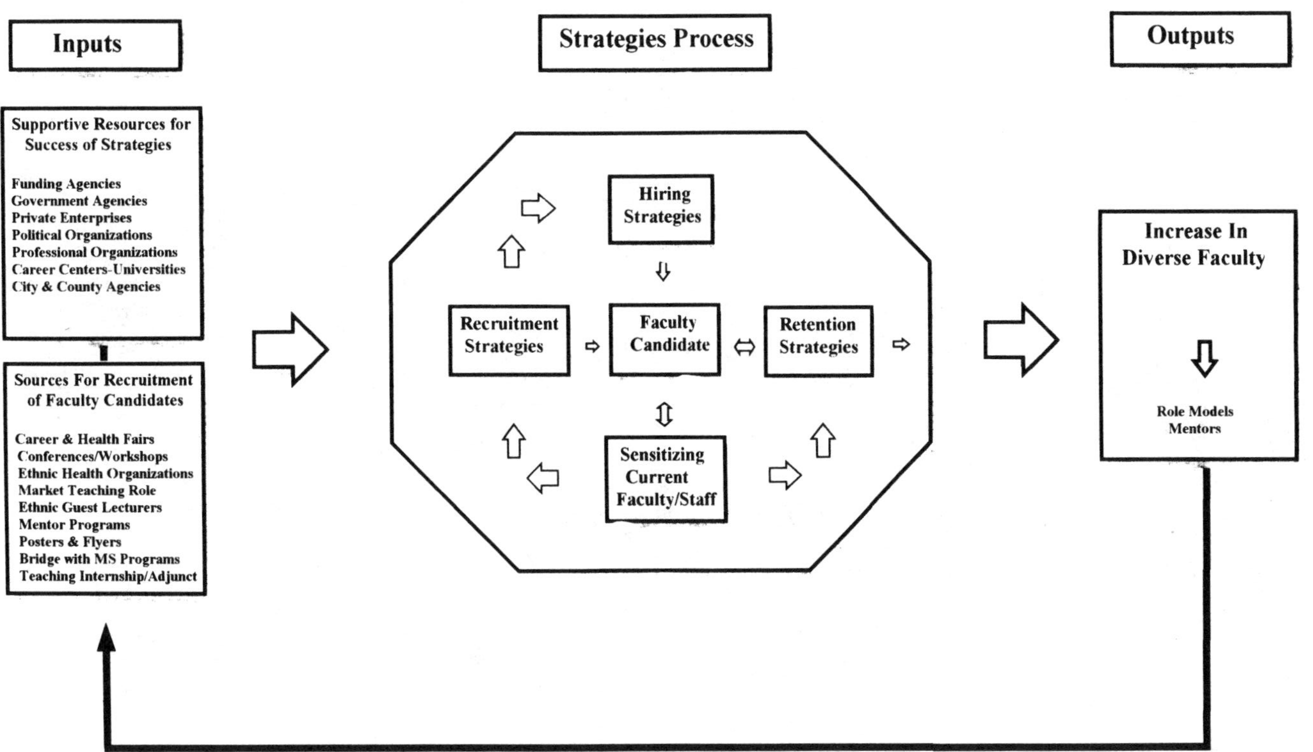

Figure 13.1 Model for Recruiting Ethnically Diverse Faculty into Health Occupation Programs.

STRATEGIES FOR RECRUITMENT

The process or the series of strategies are put into action beginning with recruitment strategies. Most of the strategies were identified by the workshop participants and some were identified by review of documents from previous proceedings or studies addressing the issues of ethnically diverse faculty. The strategies are as follows:

1. Respond immediately to letters of inquiry from potential candidates. Often candidates are discouraged by the slow response of many institutions. A good candidate may accept a position elsewhere if institutions respond slowly. A quick response increases the candidate's self-esteem and interest in a faculty position.
2. Provide a nonthreatening environment, such as inviting a candidate to campus for an informal lunch on a day different from the formal interview. Invite current ethnically diverse faculty to the informal lunch. It is not necessary to have faculty from the same ethnic group since often the number of diverse faculty on campus is small.
3. The composition of the search committee should be well planned and well thought out. Select ethnically diverse and gender-specific search committee members, including nontenured faculty. Include faculty that share the same expertise as the candidate. The size of the search committee should be small to decrease intimidation of the candidate. Include diverse faculty from other departments if there are no diverse faculty available in the recruiting department.
4. Preparation for the formal interview is an essential consideration. Provide guidelines and interview questions in advance. Mentor adjunct and part-time faculty in preparation for recruitment to full-time. Provide "coaching" assistance with curriculum vitas, mock interviews, and teaching demonstrations to ethnically diverse groups, during workshops such as for nursing organizations which provide access to a pool of potential faculty.
5. Feedback should be a step of the recruitment process. A candidate should be notified if the process is progressing favorably or if the candidate is not a viable choice as soon as possibly by formal and informal means. Often candidates are not given an indication or status of the process. For example, if someone's application is currently undergoing review or if the review process is on hold for some reason the candidate should be notified.

STRATEGIES FOR HIRING PROCEDURES

Hiring procedures sensitive to diverse faculty are designed for all candidates as well. Regardless of the candidate's ethnicity, hiring should be based on qualifications. To imply that "minorities cannot make it without affirmative action implies less intellectual, leadership, or administrative capability—and that certainly isn't true" (Steim, 1995, p. 5). However, inclusion of ethnicity as a hiring consideration is sensitive to diverse faculty candidates. Additionally, experiences other than scholarly activities should be counted as qualifications. For example, experiences of a nurse in a leadership role such as a manager or supervisor in a clinical setting may have prepared potential faculty well for supervising nursing students. Nursing departments or schools often use hiring criteria identified by other disciplines or human resource units in the college or university. It is essential that nursing faculty is hired using procedures specific to nursing or other health occupations. Just as important is the provision of salary negotiations in line with health occupation practice salaries. When salaries are not comparable, incentives can be provided to candidates to encourage the acceptance of faculty positions such as smaller teaching loads, flexible teaching schedules, or release time to pursue scholarly or research activities. Considering ethnicity as well as degree and experience to determine salary is such an incentive. However, more effective is the provision of a monetary bonus when the candidate is hired.

RETENTION STRATEGIES

The mentor concept provides the uniqueness to the retention strategies presented. Mentoring has been found to be effective in assisting students to succeed academically (De Mola, 1992; Dietz, 1992). Mentoring new faculty by senior faculty has been found useful as well (De Mola, 1992). Academia has it's own unique culture and politics and young or new instructors might need support. Assigning a full-time faculty mentor and staff to assist new faculty has been utilized by some institutions. The roles of full-time faculty and staff are determined to prevent overlap. Faculty mentors can be prepared for the role in retention by special programs developed for this purpose. Give monetary bonuses or release time to faculty mentors and staff assigned to orientation of diverse faculty or include in job descriptions which can be utilized to evaluate performance. As with other strategies, the following additional strategies for retention can be implemented for all new faculty regardless of ethnicity:

1. Develop written orientation programs sensitive to new faculty. Include deans and department heads in the development of orientation programs. Include a checklist to assure all elements of orientation are included. Provide a formal and structured 2–3 days of orientation.
2. Provide one-to-one orientation to procedures and policies for department and college, computers and other equipment, campus life and resources, and community resources. Include orientation of physical environment (i.e., bathrooms, kitchen, stairs).
3. Include ongoing orientation through first year for additional expectations. Implement a faculty development plan which includes guidance on tenure process, teaching effectiveness, grant writing, publications, and campus socialization.

STRATEGIES FOR SENSITIZING FACULTY/STAFF TO ADVANTAGES OF DIVERSE FACULTY

It is expected that current faculty and staff will be sensitized by the interaction with the individual faculty candidate as well as the strategies focused on increasing the knowledge about ethnic groups. Once the individual enters the subsystem of retention, sensitized faculty and staff will impact the retention process. In addition, it is expected that current faculty and staff will become effective participants of the recruitment process as sensitization occurs using the following strategies:

1. Increase culturally diverse media for faculty use in teaching. Implement a task force consisting of diverse faculty to review, critique, and choose culturally diverse media. Ask faculty to include articles and other references regarding ethnic beliefs and practices into course syllabi.
2. Promote faculty, staff, and student understanding of diversity through workshops and presentations by ethnic speakers, and faculty, staff, and student meetings. Include workshops which focus on ethnic beliefs and practices of diverse groups which may affect healthcare outcomes. Many ethnic nurses have firsthand knowledge of beliefs and practices currently utilized by patients they care for and often can provide insight into how mainstream nurses can intervene with health problems. Continuing Education Units should be provided for increased participation in workshops and other presentations.

3. Develop a retreat model package which can be used by other programs. Implement faculty retreats to increase faculty and staff knowledge about disparity in faculty representation and to identify advantages of having a diverse faculty and diverse student body. Retreats can be utilized as well to increase understanding and appreciation of diverse groups. Strategies may include sharing of family experiences with health issues to compare similarities and to identify contrasts. Case studies in which two faculty of different ethnicity are asked to solve a nursing problem involving patients from various ethnic groups which can be utilized later in teaching situations.
4. Develop questionnaires to obtain information regarding learning needs, barriers, and problems associated with teaching a diverse population. Often monetary incentives to participants in studies or surveys are useful in gathering large amounts of information. Workshops to identify teaching strategies sensitive to the diverse students can be developed from survey results. Focus groups as well as survey results can enrich faculty knowledge of diversity and help identify faculty perceptions about diverse students' learning needs.
5. Assign students to clinical preceptors from different ethnic groups to gain understanding of diverse nursing practice influenced by perceptions other than the mainstream population. Many nurses from different ethnic groups have been trained in their native country and nursing interventions may be different from what is currently taught in U.S. nursing schools.
6. Create alliances with ethnic professional health organizations which may lead to identification of role models, mentors, preceptors, and presenters for classes, seminars, or workshops. These groups often focus on mentoring students and awarding of scholarships.

SUMMARY

The rapid growth of a diverse student population in colleges and universities has tremendous implications for successful preparation of health care professionals. There is potential to increase the "pool" of Hispanic and other diverse faculty which can enhance the academic success of Hispanic students as more enter colleges and universities to become nurses. Matching a diverse student population with diverse ethnic faculty is one critical approach to addressing recruitment of Hispanics into academia.

It is expected that the final outcome of the strategies process will be the increase in diverse faculty. It is then expected that diverse faculty will participate in different activities to identify potential faculty candidates. The recruitment model is a complex system consisting of several subsystems, inputs, and outputs closely interrelated to increase diverse faculty. All the systems will require monitoring, evaluation, and possible changes.

Implementation of any model will put numerous demands on health occupations programs and on institutions of learning. The elements of the model still need to be developed further and operationalized. However, the strategies presented provide a broad formula on how a teaching institute can recruit diverse faculty. The first step in operationalizing the elements of the model is recognizing the significance of the development of recruitment strategies by ethnically diverse participants who have the expertise, experience, and insight into what will succeed.

The single most important concept in planning and developing recruitment strategies, and operationalizing the model is that of commitment. The efforts of the workshop participants verify the clear intention of carrying out the commitment. Now it is left to teaching institutions to determine how best to follow suggestions and recommendations. It may be that the same process can be implemented by different nursing programs or teaching institutions to develop a model that addresses issues unique to each, dependent on the cultural groups it is serving. It is hoped that teaching institutions will take this into consideration when identifying strategies to increase diverse faculty.

REFERENCES

American Council on Education. (1992). *Tenth annual status report on minorities in higher education.*

Banks, J. A. (1991, December). Multicultural literacy and curriculum reform. *The Education Digest,* 10–13.

Calvillo, E. R. (1994). *Workshop. Matching a diverse student population: Recruiting ethnically diverse faculty into health occupations programs.* Santa Barbara, CA: Regional Health Occupations Resource Center, Santa Barbara City College.

California Ethnic Minority Nurse Leadership Congress, (1993). *State action plan draft.* Unpublished manuscript.

De Mola, Y. (1992, June). Mentors and protégés: Making a difference. *The Hispanic Outlook in Higher Education, 2*(10), 3–4.

Dietz, R. (1992, June). A blueprint for Hispanic student success. *The Hispanic Outlook in Higher Education, 2*(10), 5–9.

Furata, B. (1992). Nursing faculty: Weavers of the dream. In Minority Nurse Leadership Congress, Division of Nursing, *Caring for the emerging majority: Creating a new diversity in nurse leadership,* pp. 61-75. Bethesda, MD: U.S. Department of Health and Human Services.

Higher Education Advocate. (1992, February). Minority faculty in higher education: Progress minimal. *National Education Association, 9*(5), 1.

Justz, M. J. (1995, July). Hispanics in higher education. *Hispanic,* 96.

Minority Nurse Leadership Congress, Division of Nursing. (1992). *Caring for the emerging majority: Creating a new diversity in nurse leadership.* Bethesda, MD: U.S. Department of Health and Human Services.

National Education Association. (1991, December). *Ethnic report: Focus on Hispanics.* Washington, DC: National Education Association.

National Institutes of Health. (1995, Spring). New program helps minority students by supporting academic collaboration. *NIH News & Features,* 24-25.

National League for Nursing, Division of Research. (1991). *Nursing data review.* New York: NLN Press.

National League for Nursing, Division of Research. (1992). Leaders in the making: Graduate education in nursing. *Nursing Datasource, 3.* New York: NLN Press.

National League for Nursing, Division of Research. (1993). *Nursing date review.* New York: NLN Press.

National League for Nursing, Division of Research. (1994). *Nursing data review.* New York: NLN Press.

Rhyno, R. (1992). *Creating success for students in the nursing program: Shifting the paradigm.* Napa Valley College, CA.

Steim, E. (1995, August). Are affirmative action programs still needed on campus? *Advocate, 22*(8), 5. Washington: National Education Association.

U.C.I. Health Sciences and Office of Nursing and Allied Health. (August, 1993). *Status of nursing in California.* Available from University of California, Irvine, CA.

U.S. Department of Education. (1991). *The condition of education: Postsecondary education.* National Center for Education Statistics. Washington, DC: U.S. Department of Education.

United Way Metropolitan Region. (1994). Los Angeles Census Tracts, CA.

Werning, S. C. (1992, October). The challenge to make a difference, Minorities in healthcare today. *Healthcare Trends & Transition, 4*(1), 33-47, 42-43.

CHAPTER FOURTEEN

Educational Opportunities for Hispanic Nursing: A Community-Based Model

Sally E. Ruybal, PhD, RN

This chapter presents the development of a community-based model for the recruitment, retention, and graduation of Hispanic Registered Nurses (RNs). This activity has been a continuing challenge for nurse educators for the last four decades.

During the last decade, there has been a concerted effort to recognize the plight of underrepresented populations in the health professions. There have been at least two national conferences to study these conditions in the nursing profession. The first conference, "The Emerging Majority," called for a national commitment from health professions to develop ways to increase the numbers of minority nurses into the nursing professions. The second conference, "Leadership and Partnerships," outlined the strategies by which networking and partnership building can augment efforts in the community for the recruitment, retention, and graduation of health care workers.

Although the nursing profession has representation from all minority groups, there is evidence that only 9% of the 2.3 million nurses are of underrepresented populations.

Educational preparation of nurses from underrepresented groups is concentrated at the associate degree level or lower. Ninety percent of these nurses are employed in nursing. The work setting is mainly in the hospital setting. This group provides and contributes a consistent work force for the U.S. health care industry. There is increasing need to prepare nurses with leadership capabilities and skills to move into developing and existing roles for nursing. The future preparation of a work force that

This project was made possible through the Award/Contract #HRSA240-90-0022, issued by the Health Resources & Services Administration, USPHS, 1990.

reflects the changing demographic patterns of the country warrants considerable attention. The Department of Commerce, U.S. Census Bureau, (1990) reports that by the year 2000 more than one-quarter of the U.S. population will consist of individuals from minority groups.

DEVELOPMENT OF A COMMUNITY-BASED MODEL

In order to address the problem of underrepresented Hispanic Nurses in the State of New Mexico, a community-based model for Hispanic career mobility was undertaken by the College of Nursing at the University of New Mexico.

A community-based model was defined as a multidimensional system that includes those aspects of community which lead to the description of the persons living in a community; a belief system which identifies the persons in the community, and a shared vision or a sense of belonging to a community. The structure in this model included (1) location, (2) education, (3) institutions, and (4) social support. Under these four dimensions, 16 subdimensions were identified for study and implementation.

FOUR DIMENSIONS

Within the dimension of location emphasis was placed on site location of each set of students within a set community, thus broadly defining the community at large. This included communities which had a large Hispanic representation, for example, with 71% of the population of Hispanic origin. Sites were then selected on the bases of large concentrations of Hispanic populations. The target populations were subdivided according to rural, urban, and suburban identifiers. According to these characteristics, three sites for the implementation of the community-based model were selected: Northern New Mexico was selected for two of the sites of the project; the third site of the implementation of the model was a large urban city where the main University is located and the primary site for the College of Nursing.

Education is the second dimension of the community-based model. This dimension includes the activities which were used in the recruitment/advising, retention, curriculum/instruction, and graduation of Hispanic Registered Nurses. Some utilized activities included the development of a Student Population *matrix*. This matrix was designed to identify every enrolled Hispanic Registered Nurse in the College of Nursing. This database was maintained at each site, as well as at the primary site by the Project

Director. A *student program profile* was designed and was utilized for advising and retention purposes, as well as projecting completion of a program of studies.

The curriculum/instruction dimension was one of the most challenging to implement. The current curriculum plan of the College of Nursing for educating RN to BSN/RN was used. As is common to most nursing educational programs, the curriculum is the most difficult to modify and adapt, but the most challenging if it is to work for the target population. The result was that there were many serendipitous discoveries while implementing this model. The use of community resources, the inclusion of community agencies in the educational process, and the wide use of community partnerships were rewarding in providing for the educational needs of the students. As a result of these efforts, many curricular changes took place within the educational system. The need for more intercultural communications courses, the apparent need or more use of electronic mail, and video-computer assisted instruction was identified through the process.

One concern addressed at the outset of the project was to assess the effect of language and acculturation on the successful completion of the program of studies for the enrolled Hispanic RNs. The phenomenon of acculturation is a powerful one in an educational setting. (Marin's *Short Acculturation Scale* was administered to each of the enrolled students.) There were no differentiating characteristics to indicate that the enrolled students were any different than any other student. Acculturation was defined as the smooth blending of many different traditions into one shared set of values and beliefs. This was fostered throughout the life of the implementation of the *community-based model.* One of the outstanding results of this project was the students' great sense of community. The students sought out opportunities in culture-related studies to enhance and enrich their knowledge base thus enhancing their cultural background. Ethnicity became a persistent organizing theme as opposed to the common assumption that it is basically an historical phenomenon. Community values were reinforced and acknowledged by the students and reflected in the community partnership building which was established in each of the sites of the model. Educational programs of study were categorized as enriching rather than remedial in nature.

Institution, as a major dimension of the *community-based model,* provided for the stabilization of the implementation of the model. In order to link and interface all the parts of the model there needed to be an infrastructure to promote the implementation of the model. Cooperative and collaborative efforts were launched between and among the various subdivisions of the larger University. The cooperative agreements made with each of the Community Colleges located in the selected sites became a strong link for the students participating in the project. The project site coordinators became the stakeholders, cultural brokers, and support systems for the Hispanic RNs going through the program of studies. Each of the participating Community Colleges was cooperative and committed to the implementation of the model. The focal point for the implementation of the model was at the community level, with the full participation of its member parts. The wider community at each of the sites was aware of the ongoing project and contributed accordingly. Collaborative arrangements were made and linkages were strengthened with the Nursing Educational programs of the participating community colleges. Articulation educational programming was done at each of the participating community colleges. The provision for clinical applications for students was carried out in the local communities with full cooperation from the existing clinical agencies. Several agencies and hospitals were given the opportunity to assist students in providing financial assistance and for providing for better working schedules so that the working nurses could take advantage of the classes provided by the community-based model.

Social Support is the fourth dimension of the community-based model, and perhaps the most integrating dimension of the four used in this model. Social support strongly influences the successful participation and outcome of educational attainment of the Hispanic RN. In the implementation of the community-based model, Barrera's definition and interpretation of social support was utilized. Barrera maintains that social support concepts can be organized into three broad categories, including social embeddedness, perceived social support, and enacted social support. Social embeddedness refers to the connections that individuals have to significant others in their social environments. Perceived social support characterizes social support as the cognitive appraisal of being reliably connected to others, and enacted social support can be conceptualized as actions that others perform when they render assistance to the focal person. Each of these categories is different but there are also important interrelationships among the three categories. Although the professional literature still indicates a number of discrepancies in how these concepts are defined, measured, and empirically verified, the concept of social support was one that became an integrating force in the implementation of the community-based model. Due to this complexity, the project staff focused on the categories of available and enacted social support. Within this dimension, four subdimensions were studied: family constellation of each of the enrolled Hispanic RNs; available support; enacted support; and institutional support.

The utilization of the Inventory of Socially Supportive Behaviors, developed by Barrera (1986) resulted in describing for the project staff the main characteristics of the student population. One of the important results was that location or site of the educational program of study was significant. When analyzing the Inventory of Socially Supportive Behaviors (ISSB), significant differences were found on the mean sources between the various locations for subjects who were identified as Hispanic. Social support strongly influences the successful participation and outcome of education attainment of the Hispanic Registered Nurse.

One of the most significant findings in the area of social support was the role of the *site coordinator*. The activities that were carried out by the site coordinators fully demonstrate how important this phenomenon can be. In addition to giving direct assistance, moral support, and encouragement, the site coordinators provided the motivating factors of success for the Hispanic student. The site coordinators were Hispanic and this had a major impact on the students. With the assistance and the training the two site coordinators received from the project director, the Hispanic students found a friend, an advocate, a stakeholder, a gatekeeper, and mentor in the site coordinator and project director. The site coordinators played a role in the integration of the community-based model. They served as ambassadors to the several publics (communities) they worked with. They built bridges where there were none; they interpreted the goals of the program where there was ignorance; and they promoted the Hispanic Educational program using the highest standards of communication and negotiation. The blending of values and beliefs among and between students was fostered by the project director. Cultural manifestations were interpreted according to the norms of the community. Subtle adjustments to recruitment, advisement, and retention activities were done to take into account the cultural characteristics of the Hispanic student. For example, at the outset of the program it was observed that the Hispanic students would rarely make repeated visits to the site coordinator, while the non-Hispanic students would bombard the site coordinator with questions regarding a multitude of problems, demonstrating more assertive behaviors than the Hispanic students. Adjustments were made by the site coordinators to be available in situations which were more culturally acceptable to the Hispanic students. These turned out to be in clusters, or dyads, and more intensive individual settings. Also, the Hispanic students responded to direct information strategies—they were given the name of a person whom they needed to talk to, the site coordinator would make the introductions, and then the Hispanic students would follow up on their own, thus demonstrating a need of independence or demonstrating their own way of being assertive.

Many myths and stereotypes about Hispanic students' characteristics were removed. The key phenomenon is to understand the cultural manifestations and adapt procedures so that the students are empowered to act, rather than being categorized as passive and inactive. The saying or attitude, "si, se puede," should be part of the vocabulary of nurse educators and students as well.

Lessons learned in implementing the Hispanic community-based model for educational opportunities are numerous. The large numbers of potential Hispanic RNs must be given the opportunity to participate in educational programs leading to higher levels of educational attainment. The provisions of educational programs from a community-base enhances the results of such endeavors. Providing for culturally sensitive curricular activities is essential. The use of mentors and creating a critical mass of leaders within Hispanic communities should be the focal point of nursing educational programs. Utilizing the strengths of community partnerships, thus maximizing resources, is a powerful tool to increase the numbers of prepared health professionals for their respective communities.

REFERENCES

Alemedo, E. L. (1979). Acculturation: A psychometric perspective. *American Psychologist, 34,* 1061-1070.

Barrera, M., Jr. (1981). Social support in the adjustment of pregnant adolescents: Assessment issues. In B. H. Gottlieb (Ed.), *Social networks and social support* (pp. 69-96). Beverly Hills, CA: Sage.

Barrera, M., Jr. (1983). The structure of social support: A conceptual and empirical analysis. *Journal of Community Psychology, 11,* 133-143.

Barrera, M., Jr. (1986). Distinctions between social support concepts, measures and models. *American Journal of Community Psychology, 14,* 413-445.

Barrera, M., Jr., Sandler, J. N., & Ramsey, T. B. (1981). Preliminary development of a scale of social support on college students. *American Journal of Community Psychology, 9,* 435-447.

Berry, J. W., Trimble, J. E., & Olmedo, E. L. (1986). Assessment of acculturation. In W. J. Lonner & J. W. Berry (Eds.), *Field methods in cross-cultural research* (pp. 291-324). Beverly Hills, CA: Sage.

Castro, F. G. (1976). Level of acculturation and related considerations in psychotherapy with Spanish-speaking surnamed clients. Los Angeles: Spanish Speaking Mental Health Research Center, University of California, Occasional Paper #3.

Cohen, L. H., McGowan, L., Jr., Fookas, S., & Rose, S. (1984). Positive life events and social support and the relationship between life stress and psychological disorder. *American Journal of Community Psychology, 12,* 564-587.

Cohen, S., Marmelstein, R., Kamarck, T., & Haberman, H. M. (1985). Measuring the functional components of social support. In I. G. Sarason & B. R. Sarason (Eds.), *Social support: Theory, research, and applications* (pp. 73-94). Dordrecht, Netherlands: Martinns Nijhoff.

Cuellar, I., Harris, L. C., & Jasso, R. (1980). An acculturation scale for Mexican American normal and clinical populations. *Hispanic Journal of Behavioral Science, 2*(3), 99-127.

Cyrs, T., & Smith, F. (1988). *Teleclass teaching: A resource guide,* 2nd ed. New Mexico State University, Center for Educational Development.

Deyo, R. A., Diehl, A. K., Hazuda, H., & Stern, M. P. (1985). A simple language-based acculturation scale for Mexican Americans: Valuation and application to health care research. *American Journal of Public Health, 75,* 51-55.

Dunkel-Schelter, C., Folkman, S., & Lazarus, R. (1987). Correlates of social support receipt. *Journal of Personality and Social Psychology, 53,* 71-80.

Ellner, C. L., Barnes, C. P., et al. (1983). *Studies of college teaching.* Lexington, MA: Lexington Books.

Frolan, C., Pancoast, D. L., Chapman, N. J., & Kimboko, P. (1983). Linking formal and informal support systems. In Gottlieb (Ed.), *Social networks and social support.* Beverly Hills, CA: Sage.

Fuszard, B. (1989). *Innovative teaching strategies in nursing.* Aspen Publishers Inc.

Gottlieb (Ed.). *Social network and social support.* Beverly Hills, CA: Sage.

Kahn, T. L., & Antonucci, T. C. (1980). Convoys over the life course: Attachment roles and social support. *Life Span Development and Behavior, 3,* 253-286.

Marin, G., & Sabogal, F. (1987). Development of a short acculturation scale for Hispanics. *Hispanic Journal of Behavioral Sciences, 9*(2), 183-205.

Padilla, A. M. (1980). The role of cultural awareness and ethnic loyalty in acculturation. In A. M. Padilla (Ed.), *Acculturation: Theory, models and some new findings.* Boulder, CO: Westview Press.

Sarason, B. R., Sarason, J. G., & Pierce, G. R. (Eds.). (1990). *Social support: An interactional view.* New York: Wiley.

Sarason, J. G., Levine, H. M., Basham, R. B., & Sarason, B. R. (1983). Assessing social support: The social support questionnaire. *Journal of Personality and Social Psychology, 44,* 127-130.

Wales, S., & Hageman, V. (1979, March). Guided design systems approach in nursing education. *Journal of Nursing Education, 18*(3), 38-45.

CHAPTER FIFTEEN

Spiritual Well-Being and Its Influence on the Holistic Health of Hispanic Women

Dahlia Zuñiga Rojas, PhD, CFNP, RN

This study came out of a desire to confirm what I had perceived as I grew up in a small town in south Texas along the Rio Grande River bordering the United States and Mexico. Both my parents had been born in the same area.

As I completed my doctoral courses in nursing, I began to think of how my research could contribute to the well-being (*bien-estar*) of my community. Because so much was needed, the answer seemed out of reach. As a family nurse practitioner, I wanted to promote the health of the women in my practice; as a Mexican-American, I wanted to help my people; and as a person with Spanish and Aztec roots, I had personally experienced throughout my life that body, mind, and spirit are three manifestations of one being.

As I read the literature, I found that previous studies had focused merely on common diseases, health belief practices, and illness behaviors. Further study was needed to paint "a picture of health." This study then began within a community of women who receive care in a neighborhood health center. As it progressed, I also found it important to clarify the relationships between perceived health status (mind), health habits (body), and spiritual well-being (spirit) in an Hispanic community. Using one term, *Hispanic,* exclusively to describe a people who are so diverse in culture and heritage diminishes their heterogeneity. However, the term will be used to denote a people who have Latin American or Spanish heritage or use the Spanish language in their homes. Hispanics will also be described as Mexican-Americans, Cuban, or Puerto Rican when information is specific for that group.

INTRODUCTION

A person is not just a body and a mind but also a spiritual being, and it is impossible to know the person if one disregards any aspect. The life a person lives in the body corresponds with that life lived in the mind and in the spirit. Each is distinct and relational.

Today, an individual's search for optimal health seems to be limited by the consequences of failing to view human beings in their entirety. Examination of the "whole" person is put aside for the study of one system or organ. Health maintenance as a whole is compromised.

HOLISTIC HEALTH

Begun in the 19th century, the holistic health movement in the United States has a long if marginalized history (Jones, Lepley, & Baker, 1984). As defined by the World Health Organization, health is "a state of complete physical, mental, and social well-being, not merely the absence of disease or infirmity" (WHO, 1947, in Whaley & Wong, 1993). The holistic health movement, which generally accepts this definition, also believes that the "body-mind-spirit-trinity" has the inherent capacity to *heal.* "Holism" or "wholism" thus refer to a basic belief that all parts of a living organism work together to determine the health of the entire person. With health as a harmonious balance of body, mind, and spirit, each person represents a complex but unique interaction of those elements. Disease here is a disturbance in the dynamic balance of this relationship, that is, *dis-ease.*

For many Hispanics, health and illness also include the spiritual nature of a person. Certainly, religious beliefs greatly influence attitudes toward life, health, illness, and death (Orque, Block, & Monrroy, 1983). In a recent survey of Hispanic diabetics who are not of Mexican-American descent, a majority believed that they had diabetes because it was God's will and 17% of the patients reported using herbs to treat their diabetes (Zaldivar & Smolowitz, 1994).

Many Hispanics commonly believe that health involves the body, mind, and spirit in harmony within oneself and the environment (Maduro, 1983). These beliefs may also be expressed in *curanderismo,* the art of Mexican folk healing.

Curanderismo is "a mixture of beliefs derived from Aztec, Spanish, spiritualistic, homeopathic, and modern medicine" (Maduro, 1983, p. 869). With origins in pre-Columbian times and influenced by 16th-century Spanish health care traditions, curanderismo uses herbs, ritual prayer, music, dance, and massage to cure people.

In curanderismo, the mind, body, and soul (spirit) are inseparable. A person's sense of *balance* and *harmony* are essential aspects of health and an imbalance or disequilibrium may produce disease or illness. *Bien-estar* (well-being) is thought to depend upon a balance in emotional, physical, and social arenas. Illness may be caused by a separation of body and soul (Maduro, 1983). An example of such an occurrence is due to "susto" (fright) when one experiences a "frightening" event such as a car accident, bad news of an unexpected death in the family, or a nightmare. Associated behaviors include restlessness during sleep, anorexia, depression, listlessness, and disinterest in personal appearance. In response, the curandero performs a ceremony, "a limpia" ("a clearing") using branches from a sweet pepper tree, and a bird's feather, which may be combined with a candle. Motions performed by the ill person and healer form a cross. Three Ave Marias (Hail Mary's) or credo (Apostles' Creed) are prayed.

In essence, too, the well-being and disease beliefs of many Hispanics are centered in and influenced by Christian-Catholic traditions of harmony of the body-mind-spirit triad.

ETHNICITY AND CULTURE

Health practitioners in the United States often erroneously assume that Caucasians constitute a single cultural group. Clinton's (1982) research indicated that Caucasian Americans are not homogeneous in their ethnic identity and patterns of health behavior. It also reveals that ethnic identity determines through the fifth generation much of what people of European descent in the United States believe and do about health. The term "ethnic" is derived from the Greek word *"ethnikos,"* which means "people" or "nation." Members of some ethnic groups or their ancestors coming from the same country are referred to as "nationalities." Mindel and Habenstein (1977) state that "an ethnic group consists of those who share a unique social and cultural heritage that is passed on from generation to generation" (p. 4).

Factors commonly used to determine an individual's ethnic identity are origins, sociocultural distinctiveness, subcultural social relations, territorials, kinship, and symbolic identification. Ethnicity distinguishes peoples on the bases of common origins, shared behaviors, and standards. In essence, the ethnic group is society's "culture-bearing unit" (Wright & Leahy, 1987).

Ethnicity colors perceptions of life and death, wellness and illness, and provides a framework for associated thoughts, feelings, and behaviors. Transmitted primarily through family emotional processes, ethnicity is also reinforced by the community at large (Giordano, cited in Wright & Leahy, 1987). But it is the family unit that provides a sense of community and history to its members.

Culture, on the other hand, includes such areas as "diet, language and communication processes, religion, art and history, family life processes, social groups' interactive patterns, value orientations, and healing beliefs and practices" (Orque, Block, & Monrroy, 1983, p. 8). Furthermore, culture is the "learned ways of acting and thinking that are transmitted by group members to others which provide for each individual ready-made and tested solutions for vital problems" (Walter, 1952, p. 17). For example, while Mexican-Americans represent one culture, those from Texas (Tejanos) are of a distinct ethnic group and differing from Mexican-Americans who live in other states such as Colorado, California, Illinois, or Florida.

Mexican-Americans constitute one of the most heterogeneous of all ethnic groups. There are four chief sources of Mexican-American culture: first, the initially overriding but subsequently attenuated influence of the "traditional" Mexican culture, the way of life brought from Mexico; second, the initially weak but subsequently growing influence of the surrounding majority North American culture; third, "class influence," also called socioeconomic status (SES), with the bulk of Mexican-Americans concentrated at the lower end of SES along with poor Appalachians and poor Blacks, for instance; and fourth, the consequences that result from sustaining the burden of "minority" status itself. Mexican-American culture is a multidimensional phenomenon to be studied within these four influences.

Clearly, ethnicity and culture influence an individual's perceptions and provide a framework for thoughts, feelings, and behaviors regarding holistic health.

HISPANIC HEALTH

The rapidly growing number of Hispanic people in the United States represents a heterogeneous population that health care providers increasingly encounter. As such, providers who interact in a multicultural, multiracial, and multilingual society must be prepared to meet the health care needs of populations other than of their own origin. So, to become increasingly responsive, a groundwork of current knowledge from which to form diagnoses and design holistic interventions is essential.

Nonetheless, and as Porter and Villarruel (1993, p. 59) point out, "Dramatically shorter life spans, higher illness rates and the inaccessibility to health care pose real and constant threats to members of ethnically and racially diverse groups." The disparity in health outcomes between White and ethnic/racial diverse groups has been well documented (U.S. Department of Health & Human Services [DHHS], 1985, 1990). In early 1984, the Secretary's Task Force on Black and Minority Health of the Department of Health and Human Services (DHHS) analyzed this disparity. The Task Force identified six health problems that account for more than 80% of excess deaths among U.S. Blacks, Hispanics, Native Americans, and Chinese Americans. These health problems are cancer, diabetes, heart disease/stroke, infant death, homicide/suicide/unintentional injury, and chemical dependency. Closely associated with substance abuse is the dramatic rise in the incidence of HIV among Hispanics. Nationwide, AIDS cases among Hispanics are occurring at triple the rate for non-Hispanics; tragically, this rate increase affects primarily women and children exposed to HIV (Caudle, 1993).

As the nation's fastest growing ethnic population, Hispanics face major barriers to accessing health care. Here, lack of financial resources represents the most important deterrent to the use of health care services. Data from the Hispanic Health and Nutrition Examination Survey (1982–1984) and the 1989 Current Population Survey demonstrated that about one-third of Mexican-Americans, one-fifth of Puerto Ricans, and one-fourth of Cuban-Americans have no health insurance. Among uninsured Hispanics, 53% of Mexican-Americans, 60% of Cubans, and 46% of Puerto Ricans work. These statistics reflect low salaries and employment without insurance such as is common in the service industry. Consequently, many working Hispanics either pay high prices for medical care, receive charity care, or go without care when it is needed.

Hispanics face cultural and language barriers in addition to socioeconomic barriers. Differences in culture and language from that of most health care workers does contribute to a lack of use of preventive care by Hispanics. When researchers minimized cultural and language obstacles by providing Hispanic Spanish-speaking health care providers, the use of health services increased. Also, researchers have found that Hispanics tend to visit the doctor less often than non-Hispanic Whites and Blacks because they are poor and lack health insurance (Caudle, 1993; Thompson, 1991). Populations of ethnic, culture, and racial diversity continue to be a population at risk for disproportionate illness like diabetes and AIDS plus premature death (Council on Scientific Affairs, 1991).

SPIRITUAL WELL-BEING

A concept found most frequently in the literature is "spirituality." This concept splits into four main terms: "spirit or spirituality," "spiritual dimension," "spiritual well-being," and "spiritual needs."

"Spirit or spirituality" is multifaceted, including a process and sacred journey; the essence of life principle of a person; the experience of the radical truth of things; a belief that relates a person to the world and gives meaning to existence; any personal transcendence beyond the present reality; a personal quest to find meaning and purpose in life; and a relationship or sense of connection with mystery, higher power, God, or universe (Burkhardt, 1989).

"Spiritual dimension," a unifying force within individuals integrating and transcending all other dimensions, provides meaning in life, and acts as a common bond between individuals, and individuals' perceptions and faiths (Banks, 1980). Banks, a health educator, surveyed 56 other health educators and found that a majority believed that there was a spiritual dimension of health and that this should be included in preparation programs of health educators.

"Spiritual needs" have also been described as representing the deepest requirement of self and any lack of any factor necessary to be in a dynamic relationship with God or universe (Burkhardt, 1989).

"Spiritual well-being" is understood as a manifestation of a positive relationship with God or universe and a satisfaction with life-meaning and its purpose. The higher the spiritual well-being is, the higher the sense of purposeful life and the less loneliness occurs (Paloutzian & Ellison, 1982).

Spiritual well-being and its association with psychological well-being has also been a topic of some interest. Miller (1985) compared loneliness and spiritual well-being among 64 chronically ill adults and 64 healthy adults, with the ill group having higher spiritual well-being and less loneliness. Chronic illness appeared to be a factor in stimulating the person's valuing religion, having faith in and a relationship with God or universe. Also, two studies among 170 college students showed that depression in response to life change is in some way intermediated by the individual's sense of spiritual well-being. For these college students, this mediation was reflected in a found purpose and in greater satisfaction in life. These results also support the existence of some relationship between stress responses and spiritual phenomena (Fehring, Brennan, & Keller, 1987).

Furthermore, spirituality has been shown as a potentially meaningful ingredient in the dying process. Reed (1987) found that terminally ill hospitalized adults indicated a greater "spiritual perspective" than nonhospitalized adults, and well-being increased as "spiritual perspective" increased. "Spiritual perspective" was defined as "a way of defining one's conceptual boundaries such that concepts like prayer and a higher being are meaningful in the present life situation" (Reed, 1987, p. 336).

O'Brien (1982) examined religious faith as associated with adjustment to end-stage kidney failure and its treatment over a period of 3 years. Religion was found by both tangible measurements and perceptions to be of notable positive influence for long-term adjustment to end-stage kidney failure and its treatment.

Adult burn patients also frequently mention religious thoughts, ideas, and questions as they struggle to come to terms with their injuries (Sherrill & Larson, 1988).

Further, positive therapeutic effects of prayer has found some validation (Byrd, 1988). Over 10 months, about half of a total 393 patients admitted to a coronary care unit received prayer by Christians outside the hospital, while the other half did not receive prayer. Byrd found that the patients who received prayer recovered with less complications during their hospital stay. Those receiving routine ordinary care without prayer needed more mechanical ventilator assistance, more antibiotics and diuretics.

Benefits of religion also occur in situations outside hospitals. Men who went to church more often and saw religion as highly important to them have lower systolic blood pressure readings (lower blood pressure at rest) than those who went to church less often and reported religion as less important. These differences persisted after controlling for differences in age, socioeconomic status, smoking, and weight/height ratios. Thus, there seems to exist a positive relationship between church attendance, religion, and physical health (Larson, Koening, Kaplan, Greenberg, & Tyroler, 1989).

In summary, spiritual well-being and its association with mental and physical well-being has been shown in healthy college students, those chronically ill, and terminally ill adults. However, the relationship between spirit and mind and body in a healthy adult population has not yet been examined. The following study was designed to investigate the relationship between perceived health practices, health status, and spiritual well being in Hispanic women.

CONCEPTUAL FRAMEWORK

Roy's Adaptation Model (1980), which provides a holistic view of health, was used to frame the present study. More specifically, the person is seen as a holistic adaptive system receiving output (stimuli), processing this as input, and producing output (response) which is then followed by a feedback loop to the system.

Adaptation suggests a capacity to adjust effectively to changes in the surroundings and, in turn, to affect the surroundings via physiological, self-concept, role function, and interdependence factors.

Self-concept concerns the "composite of beliefs and feelings that one holds about oneself at a given time" (Andrews & Roy, 1986, p. 124). This focuses on the need to know who one is so that one can be or exist with a sense of unity. The self-concept one has encompasses the physical self and the personal self, including the moral-ethical-spiritual self upon which this research focuses.

In summary, the person's self-concept directs one's behaviors in adaptation and acts as a feedback loop to the system. Practices such as health habits are behaviors in response (output) of adaptation to the environment. Thus, the exploration of a relationship, if any, is applied to perception of health (perceived health status), spiritual self (spiritual well-being), and its effect on adaptation, the health state.

Setting

A neighborhood health clinic providing pediatric, maternity, medical, and dental services was the setting for this study. This private, not-for-profit community health center, located on the south side of San Antonio, Texas, serves as a comprehensive primary health care center for medically indigent and working class families.

Population and Sample

The clients were predominantly poor, most often with an annual income of $5,000–$10,000; and all but two were of Mexican-American descent. The population included 100 women between the ages of 18 to 60 years who had an appointment at the clinic, who were initially identified with a Spanish surname, and who were able to read English or Spanish.

Questionnaire

A voluntary, self-administered questionnaire composed of three measurements was made available in English and Spanish. In addition, information describing age, birthplace, marital status, last grade completed in school, family size, and income were obtained. This author added a question on how often the women attended church to determine if there was a connection between church attendance and spiritual well-being. Finally, a dietary recall of all foods and drinks consumed in the last 24 to 48 hours was collected to describe eating habits and nutrition.

The Self-Rated Health (SRH) Scale measures perceived health status by asking for a rating of health quality (Lawton et al., 1982). Individual responses to four statements range from (1) to (4) where higher scores indicate better health perceptions. This tool was translated into Spanish and pilot tested by the author.

The Spiritual Well-Being (SWB) Scale measures religious well-being (RWB) and existential well-being (EWB) (Ellison, 1983). The participant responds to statements on a scale from one (1) strongly agree to (6) strongly disagree. This scale yielded three scores: a total score (20–120 points), a subscore (10–60) for the 10 religious well-being statements, and a subscore (10–60) for the 10 existential well-being statements. This tool was translated into Spanish by the author and tested.

RESULTS

Description of the Women

According to demographic data from a sample of 100 Hispanics, the majority of the women are 18–39 years old, with an average age of 32 years. Most women are married and not pregnant. Half of the women report low incomes from < $5,000–$10,000 with an average annual income of $9,281. About half of the women live in a household of five people which means that a family of five is living on a mere annual income of $9,281! In 1990, the national median family income of Mexican-Americans was $23,200 (USDC, Bureau of the Census, 1991).

The women on average had a 10th grade education. The largest group of women fell in the senior high level (10–12 years). About three-fourths of the women were Catholics and 4 out of 10 women attended church once a week or more often. The preferred language was English. Most report the United States as their birthplace. Of the women born in the United States, most chose the English questionnaire; and, of those born in Mexico, most chose the Spanish questionnaire as did the two Central American women.

Dietary Habits

Each woman's dietary recall was combined with age, height, weight, and pregnancy status estimates to describe nutritional habits. The average height of the women was 5 feet 2 inches. The average weight of the women was 154 pounds. The Ideal Body Weight for women ages 29–59 who are 5 feet 2 inches tall and small frame is 108–121 pounds. Thus, the women were heavier than expected for height and frame.

This dietary recall reports showed that the majority consumed *less* than the recommended daily caloric and protein requirements by height, weight and pregnancy status. For example, the average recommended daily caloric allowance for the 85 non-pregnant women was 1,655 kcal; 80% ate less while 20% exceeded that amount. The average number of calories consumed by these women was 1,235 kcal. The carbohydrate and fat requirements were met; however, one-third of the non-pregnant women were obese defined as 25% above Ideal Body Weight (American Dietetic Association, 1988). The pregnant women reported the same amount of caloric intake (1,244 kcal) while their requirements were actually doubled (2,559 kcal)! Thus, these women were meeting only *half* of their caloric needs for pregnancy.

The carbohydrate (starch) sources of food were moderately low in fiber with the best fiber sources reported as pinto beans and apples. Of the fat eaten, the saturated fat (SAT) *exceeded* the polyunsaturated fatty acids (PUFA). The recommended ratio of fat is 2 (PUFA): 1 (SAT) (DHHS, 1987). This ratio varied from 1:1 to 1:15 for these women. All the pregnant women consumed high saturated fats at an average ratio of PUFA: SAT 1:4 and ranging from 1:1 to 1:7. What effect, if any, a high saturated fat diet has on the health of Mexican American women would be a fruitful quest.

Exercising Activities

The women were asked to respond by checking "active things that people do in their free time." The most common physical activity reported was "taking long walks" which occurred on average "once a month." Dancing, gardening, and exercise were the next most commonly reported. Swimming and active sports were least popular. All activities were reported as happening on an average of "once a month." When asked, "Is there something else you do in your free time?" the women described things such as taking the family out to have a good day, sewing, crocheting/embroidering, lifting weights, reading and studying, caring for other children, bicycling, volunteer work, housework, and running 2 miles daily (stated a college student).

One additional question added to canvass perceptions of activities that promote and maintain health was "Describe what other things you do to keep or have better health." The responses included balanced nutrition (13%), exercise (9%), child-rearing activities (6%), walking (5%), housework activities (4%), spiritual activities (4%), recreational activities (4%), sleeping well (3%), avoiding junk, fatty, or sugar foods (3%), taking vitamins (3%), and keeping "hot/cold balance" (the 2 women from Central America).

Perception of Health

In general, the women rated their overall health as "good" ($x = 9.23$, maximum score = 12). They perceived their health "about the same" as it was 3 years ago. They believed that their health problems stood in their way "a little" or "not at all." They perceived their health to be about the "same" as others their age.

Associations between the mind, body, and spirit were found. Perceived health status was negatively associated with weight—the Self-Rated Health score increased, weight decreased. Also, as the Self-Rated Health score increased, so did physical activity ($r = 0.32$, $p = .001$) and the weight/height ratio decreased ($r = -0.323$, $p = .002$). These findings were a positive association for this group of women since one-third (34%) of the women were obese. Although the women's perceived health status increased as their physical activity increased, exercising habits were infrequent (Table 15.1).

Spiritual Well-Being

The women, on an average, scored high on the Spiritual Well-being Scale ($M = 91$, $SD = 13.83$). When a multiple regression and correlation analysis was applied to the variables of church attendance, spiritual well-being score, and perceived health status score, a linear relationship was found. This direct linear relationship existed between the spiritual well-being, (church attendance) and perceived health status. That is, the frequency of church attendance and spiritual well-being scores (independent variables) predicted perceived health status scores (dependent variable).

Table 15.1 Correlations between Perceived Health Status (SRH), Spiritual Well-Being (SWB), and Health Habits (HPI) among 100 Hispanic Women

Variable	Weight	Physical Activity	Quetelet Index (Weight & Height Ratio)
SRH Score	−0.334**	+0.334**	−0.323*
SWB Score	−0.031	+0.129	−0.055

*$p < .01$ (significant level)

**$p < .001$ (highly significant level)

Summary

Data analyses of the women's eating habits indicated an adequate carbohydrate intake, but an inadequate caloric and protein intake, plus a high saturated fat intake. The majority of women abstained from drinking alcohol and smoking cigarettes; however, women born in the United States were more likely to drink and smoke than foreign-born women. Those who preferred the English language were more likely to drink and smoke than those who preferred Spanish. Frequency of church attendance and spiritual well-being predicted participants' perceived health status. Perceived health status was also associated with decreased weight, decreased height/weight ratio, and with an increase in physical activity. Spiritual well-being was, in general, "high" and their health habits were also generally "good."

DISCUSSION

This study illustrates that spiritual well-being influences health—health has a mental-physical-spiritual essence. The frequency of church attendance and spiritual well-being affected the perceived health status which influenced the physical health of the women. A positive relationship between perception and health (weight, height/weight ratio, physical activity) was demonstrated. The degree to which spirituality is part of wholeness was reflected in the women's frequent church attendance and in their high spiritual well-being scores. This relationship may explain how these low-income women cope with the stresses of poverty and are essentially healthy.

Implications for Practice

In this increasing fast-lane, disposable society driven by information, the healer is challenged on just what methods to use in meeting the needs of the whole person within the time constraints set by those outside the provider level. After practicing nursing for 20 years, I am continually challenged by the demands of a disjointed institutional method of delivering care to people who live fragmented lives—disintegration vs. integration.

The patients I see yearn to tell their story, *historía,* and they are hurting to be heard, aching to be listened to. They are often frustrated by being treated, or should I say mistreated, as parts. One patient told me, "I have a list of things I'm concerned about but I dare not mention it to my gynecologist. They'll send me here and there, but I want one person to care for me. Can I get all of my care with you?"

After listening to her story for at about 20 minutes, I asked her, "What do you want to get out of this visit today?" Then she prioritized her needs and decided which one she wanted to address for our first encounter. As the visit progressed, she also told me about her hysterectomy and began to share other worries about her estrogen pill, "Why am I on the green pill when I was on the yellow one?" She was also worried about being on estrogen because of a "shadow" on her breasts seen on a mammogram which "they" were watching every 6 months. She said, "I've read that the estrogen makes the cancer worse." No biopsy had been done. She also shared that she "hadn't been with her husband, but it was uncomfortable." She would tell him that she didn't feel well, but she said to me, "I'm his wife and I want to be a good wife but I just don't feel like it." She had been experiencing marital discord due to her physical discomfort during sex because she didn't have enough vaginal lubrication.

Another woman that same morning came to me with her left knee wrapped in an ace bandage and a bag full of prescription medicines. She said, "I've exhausted all my resources, I haven't been able to work since my surgery. I have bills everywhere. I can no longer afford private doctors. I want to get my care here. Can you give me something for my diarrhea?" This woman went on to tell her story of how she had been having persistent pain but was given pain pills by her private physician and was otherwise ignored until she demanded a referral to an orthopedic surgeon. This surgeon ordered x-rays and, upon reading them, told the patient that her knees "were bone on bone—no more cartilage left." The woman was so "furious" at her physician that she reported him to the medical society. She went on to tell me about her feelings of anger at him. Then, she told me of her long history of stomach problems—"I suffer from irritable bowel syndrome and reflux." She was on several medications: Darvocet, a strong pain killer, for her knee pain after a "total knee replacement," "Lotensin for high blood pressure," "Zantac for reflux," "Nodine for degenerative osteoarthritis," and over-the-counter Immodium for diarrhea. She actually had formed stools for several days prior to our visit.

I listened to her as she vividly relived her painful experiences—the anger at her physician who had turned a deaf ear to her, her surgery, her lack of money, and her lack of work. She said, "God is the only person that's kept me going." We then prayed to God—a God of Healing, a God of Wholesomeness, a God of Wholeness. Then I asked her to forgive her doctor and let go. Her eyes became teary and glassy but I believe that she did let go of her anger. She was able to accept that one more drug for her diarrhea wasn't going to solve her problems. She also agreed to defer the "arthritis" pain drug. She looked calm, peaceful, and agreed to return for a complete physical exam. So, both women were frustrated over their care—one coped by being angry, the other coped by withholding and repressing her feelings. If I had cut them off without hearing them completely and thoroughly, then I would have also added to their hurt and their pain.

Further Clinical Research

The writer supports the use of guidelines for the design, conduct, and critique of research with Black and Hispanic subjects asserted by Porter and Villarruel (1993). Further testing of Rojas' application of Roy's model should continue the development of the concept of "spirituality" and its relationship with other health variables, especially in Hispanic populations such as Mexican-Americans. Further studies are also needed to define being "healthy," and to develop concepts of health promotion and well-being (*nuestro bienestar*) in Mexican-Americans and other ethnic populations using a culturally based methodology.

Mental health studies, including clarification of any relationship between church attendance and spiritual well-being, would be beneficial particularly for the healing of families under the stress of poverty, migration or immigration, and other on-going strain. The effects of immigration—changes in culture, in sex roles, and in family structure (Hayes-Bautista et al., 1988)—should be examined here as well.

Finally, the identification and development of instruments that are culturally sensitive, valid, and reliable in Spanish-speaking populations is needed.

Replicating this study is needed in other major cities and in the Southwestern, Midwestern, and Northeastern states to explore regional similarities and differences among Hispanic women such as in urban, rural, and border areas. A culturally based model, or further adaptation of Roy's model, for assessment, diagnosis, and treatment is also warranted for other ethnic and cultural groups.

As nursing continues to describe vistas of "human responses," it will be better able to design interventions that incorporate the three dimensions of health—body, mind, and spirit—in the context of the client's race, ethnicity, and culture. In conclusion, conducting cross-cultural and multicultural clinical research with racially, ethnically, and culturally diverse populations is necessary in a world that is getting smaller. As healers helping others to become whole again, we grapple with the fundamental question, "Am I my brother's keeper?" "Yes, here I am."

REFERENCES

Andrews, H. A., & Roy, C. (1986). *Essentials of the Roy adaptation model.* Norwalk, CT: Appleton-Century-Crofts.

American Dietetic Association (ADA). (1988). *Manual of clinical dietetics.* Chicago: Author.

Banks, R. (1980). Health and the spiritual dimension: Relationships and implications for professional preparation programs. *Journal of School Health, 50*(4), 195-202.

Belloc, N. B. (1973). Relationship of health practices and mortality. *Preventive Medicine, 2,* 67-81.

Burkhardt, M. A. (1989). Spirituality: An analysis of the concept. *Holistic Nursing Practice, 3* (3), 69-77.

Byrd, R. C. (1988). Positive therapeutic effects of intercessory prayer in a coronary care unit population. *Southern Medical Journal, 81,* 826-830.

Castro, F., Furth, P., & Karlow, H. (1985). The health beliefs of Mexican, Mexican-American, and Anglo women. *Hispanic Journal of Behavioral Sciences, 6,* 365-383.

Caudle, P. (1993). Providing culturally sensitive health care to Hispanic clients. *Nurse Practitioner,* (12) 40-51.

Clark, Martire, & Bartolomeo, I. (1985). *A study of Hispanics' attitudes concerning cancer prevention* (Research Report, May, pp. 1-28). New York: American Cancer Society.

Clinton, J. (1982). Ethnicity: The development of an empirical construct for cross-cultural health research. *Western Journal of Nursing Research, 4,* 281-300.

Council of Scientific Affairs (CSA). (1991). Hispanic health in the United States. *Journal of the American Medical Association, 265,* 248-252.

Diehl, A. K., & Stern, M. P. (1989). Special health problems of Mexican-Americans: Obesity, gallbladder disease, diabetes mellitus, and cardiovascular disease. *Advances in Internal Medicine, 34,* 73-96.

Duffy, M. E. (1988). Determinants of health promotion in midlife women. *Nursing Research, 37,* 358-362.

Ellison, C. W. (1983). Spiritual well-being: Conceptualization and measurement. *Journal of Psychology and Theology, 11,* 330-340.

Fehring, R. J., Brennan, P. F., & Keller, M. L. (1987). Psychological and spiritual well-being in college students. *Research in Nursing and Health, 10,* 391-398.

Hallal, J. C. (1982). The relationship of health beliefs, health locus of control, and self-concept to the practice of breast self-examination in adult women. *Nursing Research, 31* (3), 37-142.

Hayes-Bautista, D., Schink, W. O., & Chapa, J. (1988). *The burden of support—young Latinos in an aging society.* Stanford, CA: Stanford University Press.

Health Resources and Services Administration (HRSA). Bureau of Health Professions. (1990). *Seventh report to the President and Congress on the status of health personnel in the United States* (DHHS Publication No. HRS-p-OD-90-1). Washington, DC: U.S. Government Printing Office.

Jones, D. A., Lepley, M. K., & Baker, B. A. (1984). *Health assessment across the life span.* New York: McGraw-Hill.

Larson, D. B., Koening, H. G., Kaplan, R. S., Greenberg, E. L., & Tyroler, H. A. (1989, Winter). The impact of religion on men's blood pressure. *Journal of Religion and Health, 28,* 4.

Lawton, M. P., Moss, M., Fulcomer, M., & Kleban, M. H. (1982). A research and service oriented multilevel assessment instrument. *Journal for the Scientific Study of Religion, 25,* (1), 31–40.

Lopez, C. (1990). Curanderismo: a healing art. *Intercambios,* Vol. 5, No. 1.

Maduro, R. (1983). Curanderismo and Latino views of disease and curing. *Western Journal of Medicine, 139,* 868–874.

Marks, G., Garcia, M., & Solis, J. M. (1990). Health risk behaviors of Hispanics in the United States: Findings from HHANES, *AJPH, 80,* Dec. Suppl., 20–26.

Miller, J. F. (1985). Assessment of loneliness and spiritual well-being in chronically ill and healthy adults. *Journal of Professional Nursing, 1*(2), 79–85.

Mindel, C. H., & Habenstein, R. W. (Eds.). (1977). *Ethnic families in America.* New York: Elsevier.

Morris, D. L. B., Lusero, G. T., Joyce, E. V., Hannigan, E. V., & Tucker, E. R. (1989). Cervical cancer, a major killer of Hispanic women: Implications for health education. *Health Education, 20,* (5), 23–28.

O'Brien, M. E. (1982). Religious faith and adjustment to long-term hemodialysis. *Journal of Religion and Health, 21*(1) 68–80.

Orque, M. S., Block, B., & Monrroy, L. S. (1983). *Ethnic Nursing Care,* St. Louis: C. V. Mosby.

Paloutzian, R., & Ellison, C. W. (1982). Loneliness, spiritual well-being and the quality of life. In L. A. Peplau & D. Perlman (Eds.), *Loneliness: A sourcebook of current theory, research and therapy.* New York: Wiley.

Pender, N. J., & Pender, A. (1986). Attitudes, subjective norms, and intentions to engage in health behaviors. *Nursing Research, 35,* 15–18.

Porter, C. P., & Villarruel, A. M. (1993). Nursing research with African American and Hispanic people: Guidelines for action. *Nursing Outlook, 14,* (6), 286–288.

Reed, P. (1987). Spirituality and well-being in terminally ill hospitalized adults. *Research in Nursing and Health, 10,* 335–344.

Rodriquez, L. (1992). Census: Hispanics will be largest minority group. *Laredo Morning Times,* December 5.

Rojas, D. Z. (1992). Perceived health status, spiritual well-being, and selected health practices of Mexican-American women. (Doctoral dissertation: Texas Women's University, 1991). *Dissertation Abstracts International,* (University Microfilms No. 92-03, 077).

Roy, C. (1984). *Introduction to nursing: An adaptation model.* Englewood Cliffs, N.J.: Prentice-Hall.

Salmon, M. E., & Vanderbush, P. (1990). Leadership and change in public and community health nursing today—the essential intervention. In J. McCloskey & H. K. Grace (Eds.), *Current issues in nursing,* (pp. 187-193). St. Louis: C. V. Mosby.

Sherrill, K. A., & Larson, D. B. (1988). Adult burn patients: The role of religion in recovery. *Southern Medical Journal, 81,* 821-826.

Thompson, L. (1991, January 15). Examining the health status of Hispanics. *Washington Post,* p. 7.

Trotter, R. T. (1985). Folk medicine in the southwest: Myths and medical facts. *Postgraduate Medicine, 78,* (8), 167-179.

U.S. Department of Commerce (USDC), Bureau of the Census (1989). *Hispanic Americans press releases.* Washington, DC: Author.

U.S. Department of Commerce (USDC), Bureau of the Census (1991). Total money income of all Hispanic households up by 67% since 1982. Washington, DC: Author.

U.S. Department of Health & Human Services (DHHS), National Institute of Health. (1987). *Facts about blood cholesterol.* Bethesda, MD: National Heart, Lung, and Blood Institute.

U.S. Department of Health & Human Services (1985). Report of the secretary's task force on black and minority health. Vol. 1: Executive summary. Washington, DC: U.S. Department of Health and Human Services.

U.S. Department of Health & Human Services (1990). Healthy people 2000: National health promotion and disease prevention objectives. Superintendent of documents. Washington, DC: U.S. Government Printing Office.

Walker, S. N., Sechrist, K. R., & Pender, N. J. (1987). The health-promoting lifestyle profile: Development and psychometric characteristics. *Nursing Research, 36* (2), 76-81.

Walter, P. A. (1952). *Race and culture relations.* New York: McGraw-Hill.

Weitzel, M. H. (1989). A test of the health promotion model with blue collar workers. *Nursing Research, 38,* (2), 99-104.

Whaley, L. F., & Wong, D. L. (1993). *Nursing care of infants and children.* St. Louis, MO: C. V. Mosby.

Wiley, J. A., & Camacho, T. C. (1980). Life-style and future health: Evidence from the Alameda County study. *Preventive Medicine, 9,* 1-21.

Zalidivar, A., & Smolowitz, J. (1994). Perceptions of the importance placed on religion and folk medicine by non-Mexican-American Hispanic adults with diabetes. *The Diabetes Educator,* (4), 303-306.

Index